"Readers often have nebulous childhood memories of the story of Esther as the beautiful teenage girl who is chosen to be the queen of Persia and gets to save the Jewish people. Altrock rescues the story of Esther from its fairytale status. He takes it off the children's shelf and places it squarely in the adult section. Along the way, Altrock eloquently and convincingly unpacks the core theological theme of Esther: God is always at work in the world, bringing about his good purposes in ancient Persia and in ordinary lives today."

> —**Holly Catterton Allen,** Professor of Family Studies and Christian Ministries, Lipscomb University, and editor of *InterGenerate: Transforming Churches through Intergenerational Ministry*

"We live in an age when God is summarily dismissed, banished from the public arena. The crosscurrents of this secular age have pushed against those who have faith in Christ, leaving them confused, weary, and sometimes despairing. *Behind Esther* is a bold response in the opposite direction—to see God everywhere and in everything. Altrock's prescription for re-enchanting your life will leave you energized and filled with hope."

> —**Bill Delvaux,** Director of Landmark Journey Ministries and author of *Heroic: The Surprising Path to True Manhood*

"Despite the position evil has on the center stage of history, the righteous God of Esther writes and directs the human tragedy. Though unseen in the depressing play of godless injustice, Esther's invisible God still determines when the curtain falls upon the grand finale of agony. *Behind Esther* provides realistic hope and longed-for inspiration that enlivens our endurance against the masked characters of prejudice, politics, and pride."

> —**Jerry Taylor,** Associate Professor of Bible and Ministry, Abilene Christian University

"The Torah is filled with incredible stories that speak to the deep mysteries of the human heart. Altrock's careful reading of the Esther narrative will enrich your life as you think about what it means to be human in our time and place. Faith is not for the faint of the heart. It is tested, forged by the fire of suffering and waiting on God. In that spirit, *Behind Esther* shows us how Esther can serve as our spiritual guide."

—**Josh Graves,** lead minister, Otter Creek Church, Nashville, TN

"What a fresh and creative reading of the Esther story! In our time—somewhat like Esther's time—God is more hidden. In *Behind Esther*, Altrock highlights twelve spiritual disciplines Esther practiced to engage with God in the ancient Persian culture, disciplines he recommends for us in our time as well. Engaging and beautifully done!"

—**Leonard Allen,** Dean of the College of Bible and Ministry, Lipscomb University, and author of *Poured Out: The Spirit of God Empowering the Mission of God*

"All of us long to be more than ordinary. Altrock's fresh and insightful investigation into the life of an ill-equipped, ordinary woman shows us how powerful ordinary can be. The same God who transformed the Jewish orphan Esther into a world-changing queen is willing and able to transform us."

—**Lynne Gentry,** author of *The Carthage Chronicles*

"Who would have thought that tucked away in the little book of Esther was such a timely word for the post-Christian, Western world that many of us are living in today? Every chapter of *Behind Esther* is filled with fresh insights that bring this action-packed Bible story into conversation with our twenty-first century lives. Altrock does a phenomenal job of revealing through Esther how God is always working, even when we can't sense it—or maybe, especially when we can't sense it."

—**Jonathan Storment,** preaching minister, Pleasant Valley Church of Christ, Little Rock, AR

BEHIND ESTHER

BEHIND ESTHER

THRIVING WHEN GOD SEEMS DISTANT

CHRIS ALTROCK

LEAFWOOD
PUBLISHERS

an imprint of Abilene Christian University Press

BEHIND ESTHER
Thriving When God Seems Distant

LEAFWOOD
PUBLISHERS
an imprint of Abilene Christian University Press

Copyright © 2019 by Chris Altrock

ISBN 978-1-68426-190-1 | LCCN 2019007641

Printed in the United States of America

Library of Congress Cataloging-in-Publication Data
Names: Altrock, Chris, 1968- author.
Title: Behind Esther : thriving when God seems distant / Chris Altrock.
Description: Abilene, Texas : Leafwood Publishers, 2019.
Identifiers: LCCN 2019007641 | ISBN 9781684261901 (pbk.)
Subjects: LCSH: Disappointment—Religious aspects—Christianity—Biblical
    teaching. | Consolation in the Bible. | Bible. Esther—Criticism,
    interpretation, etc.
Classification: LCC BS1375.6.P9 A48 2019 | DDC 222/.906—dc23

LC record available at https://lccn.loc.gov/2019007641

Cover design by ThinkPen Design
Interior text design by Sandy Armstrong, Strong Design

Leafwood Publishers is an imprint of Abilene Christian University Press
ACU Box 29138
Abilene, Texas 79699

1-877-816-4455
www.leafwoodpublishers.com

19 20 21 22 23 24 / 7 6 5 4 3 2 1

CONTENTS

FOREWORD

A favorite C. S. Lewis quote came to mind while I was reading an early copy of Chris's book. In *Mere Christianity*, Lewis observes, "It may be hard for an egg to turn into a bird: it would be a jolly sight harder for a bird to learn to fly while remaining an egg. We are like eggs at present. And you cannot go on indefinitely being just an ordinary, decent egg. We must be hatched or go bad."

If you've ever watched birds nest in a tree outside your window, or lived on a farm with a chicken coup, or incubated eggs as a science class project, you've seen for yourself that hatching is an exhausting, messy, difficult process involving what, at times, seems like an impossible struggle. Why shouldn't it be? After all, it's preparing a tiny, naked, flightless creature for an existence that's as big, and bold, and broad as an endless blue sky. But first, the little warrior must break free of a world that's small, protected, safely encapsulated. It's a fascinating yet agonizing transition to watch.

I can only imagine what it must seem like from the bird's point of view. Inside the egg, does that bald-headed baby have any idea what awaits? That it's teetering on the precipice of a completely new life?

I mean, think about that for a minute. Let it sink in. *Flight* lies at the end of the struggle. The bird that gives up, that says to itself, "Forget it. This is too hard. The odds are stacked against me. The shell is too thick. The world is too unkind. The task is too difficult. I'm stuck. It's hopeless. God is nowhere in this. There is no divine plan here. I quit," stops just inches short of a miracle. It loses flight and chooses death.

Each of us is that bird sooner or later. Quite likely, we are that bird over and over and over again throughout our lives. We're faced with disasters, unforeseen circumstances, heartbreak, illness, job losses, betrayal, disappointment in the world, in our church families, in our own families. Even when we've tried to do everything right, bad things happen. Life spirals out of control. We end up asking *why*. We're left wondering how a benevolent, loving God could possibly be anywhere in such a messed-up, seemingly hopeless situation.

If you've been there, if those questions seem familiar, if you've traveled through the lonely, dark night of the soul, either on your own or with a friend or loved one, then this book is for you. If the state of life or the world has ever caused you to question until your mind was numb, or to cry until your eyes were raw. If you've ever wondered: Is God on vacation? Has he just given up on us? Why doesn't he do something? Then, read this book. Esther's tale is a story for our times. Her world is our world. Let Chris take you deep into it and through it. You'll come out on the other side a better person, a stronger Christian, and, most importantly, closer to the place God is trying to move you to.

Don't quit. Don't surrender. Don't die inside.

Stay in the fight. It's worth the struggle.

Something miraculous is in the making.

—**Lisa Wingate**
New York Times best-selling author of *Before We Were Yours*

THE LAND OF DISENCHANTMENT

My friend Abigail grew up in a Christian home, attended a small private Christian high school, and graduated from a private Christian university—all in two southern U.S. cities, havens of Christian culture. Then she moved to Wuhan, China, to teach English. In that massive metropolis of tens of millions, nearly 80 percent of city dwellers had no formal religion. Only about 3 percent were Christian.[1]

Upon her return, Abigail told our mission committee, "For my whole life, I'd been surrounded by Christian people and a Christian culture. I could just sit back and God would appear in amazing ways. But in Wuhan, for the first time in my life, I was surrounded by non-Christian people and a non-Christian culture. I found myself pouting, wondering why God wasn't showing up like he used to. Then I realized that I needed to take action. I needed to start actively looking for God. Once I did that,

I realized God was present and at work in people and places I'd never before imagined."

In a nutshell, this is the story of Esther. Before the book opens, she comes from a people whose history is the land of Israel and the city of Jerusalem—Jewish homes, private Jewish high schools, and private Jewish universities. People like her could just sit back and God would appear in amazing ways. But when we turn to page one in the book of Esther, we find her and her people in Persia. They are surrounded by a pagan culture and pagan citizens. God seems far away. In Esther's entire story, the Hebrew words for God are not found once. Esther lives in a place that's been called "disenchanted"—a world in which God is hard to hear and difficult to discern. It's not the enchanted world of Exodus and Acts, filled with obvious miracles and movements of God. It's a space where the daily news so often seems proof that God is on vacation. Yet, once Esther begins to actively investigate, she finds God present and active in all kinds of surprising ways.

This is our story as well, culturally and personally. Culturally, we find ourselves in a spot more like Persia and less like Israel; more like Wuhan and less like Abigail's southern cities. Though there are havens of enchantment still remaining, where God's presence is as easy to see as the sunrise, as a whole, according to thinkers like Charles Taylor, our Western culture has shifted. It used to be almost impossible to *not* believe in God. These days, belief is just one option among many, especially in certain places in the Western world, including the United States. "Belief in God," Taylor writes, "is no longer axiomatic."[2] It's no longer self-evident that God is at hand.

While this is true culturally, depending on where we live, it's also true personally. Suffering, loss, and disappointment often leave us blind to the presence and activity of God. "Will you forget me forever?" David cries out in Psalm 13, having suffered some terrible wrong. Adversity often leaves us feeling as if God has left us in the dust. Crisis makes sure we don't have time to just sit back and watch God appear in amazing ways. Difficulties lead us into times of disenchantment. I'm reminded of the widower who told me of the painful year of grieving he endured after his wife's death: "I've been praying to God, but I just don't think he's there."

Esther's story is written to help us deal with these cultural and personal realities. Through her story, we learn how to thrive even when it seems God is hiding. The book beckons us to look *behind* Esther, beyond the easily evident bigotry and butchery that are front and center in its pages. We are invited to find the God in the background, the One striving in the midst of Esther's and her people's suffering, the One present in the midst of all their mess. We learn from Esther what C. S. Lewis also learned. As he contemplated the cruelty and chaos caused by World War II, he urged listeners and readers to believe that in the background of this chaotic foreground was "Something Behind."[3] By reflecting on Esther, we learn to discern the God backstage, to bring God back into focus. We do this by adopting different disciplines or habits that enable us to reenchant our world. These practices empower us to rediscover God, to see him around corners, to encounter him in spots where we've failed or forgotten to look.

Each chapter takes up one of these practices. The book also includes practical ways for you to experiment with each discipline in your own life through a forty-day experience ("Forty-Day Study Guide for the Disenchanted"). The practices begin in Chapter One with what is the most critical habit in a disenchanted world—*examen*, or refocusing. As Abigail did, as Esther did, we must take an active stance and look for God in ways and in places we have never imagined. He may not be front and center as we wish, but he is, nonetheless, still here—still present and active. Disenchantment provides the opportunity to refocus, finding God not in the foreground but in the background.

The full list of habits and practices we find revealed in Esther's story are as follows, reflected in the twelve chapters of this book:

1. *Examen*
2. Waiting
3. Engaging
4. Humility
5. Radical prayer
6. Valuing others
7. Empathy
8. Generosity
9. Mercy
10. Purpose
11. Celebration
12. Service

Join me in an extended exploration of one of the Bible's most neglected stories. A story that, on the surface, appears to be Godless but, upon further examination, is God-full. It's the perfect story for today's world and, perhaps, for your life. A story that teaches us afresh how to discover God in the darkness, how to find God in the fog, how to share with God in his slow work in the world—a work unnoticed by some yet a work so powerful that, by the end of the story, an entire nation is saved and a party to end all parties is being thrown. Join me in making Esther's story your story. No matter where you find yourself today, I think you'll find that God is with you, and by the end of this, you'll be throwing a party as well.

REFOCUS

I was three years into my first full-time preaching ministry in the 1990s when I saw the movie *Jerry Maguire*. More importantly, I was only a decade into my Christian faith. I had spent my entire youth in an unchurched household.

The movie *Jerry Maguire* was inspired by the real-life experiences of sports agents like the legendary Leigh Steinberg. Most of the athletes and agents portrayed in the movie have relationships we might characterize as "professional." The players and reps are icy and distant with one another. Firm handshakes. Tight smiles. Brief conversations.

But sports agent Jerry Maguire and his client, a pro football player named Rod Tidwell, endure such an emotional journey together that their relationship transforms into something "unprofessional." Brief conversations morph into deep and lasting talks. Tight smiles evolve into wide-eyed laughter. And in a closing scene, in front of a mob of reporters after an NFL game, Jerry and Rod hug tightly, their tears a testimony of heartfelt respect and love.

Another athlete, standing nearby with his agent, sees this friendship. He aches for more from his rep than just the ability to secure the best salary or benefits. He turns to his agent and asks a question. It is the question to which the entire film points: "Why don't *we* have *that* kind of relationship?"

There I was—three years into my ministry, ten years into my Christianity—and I realized that was a question *I'd* been asking.

Not of a sports agent.

But of God.

Why don't *we* have *that* kind of relationship?

At seminary, before entering full-time ministry, I rubbed shoulders with missionaries and ministers whose God almost always seemed to answer mighty prayers in mighty ways. Meanwhile, my God seemed to respond to many of my solicitations with silence.

I wondered: Why don't *we* have *that* kind of relationship?

In my own congregation, where that pulpit of three years still felt like a pair of dress shoes I hadn't quite broken in, I pastored congregants like a woman who often shared that she heard God speaking to her and a man who frequently mentioned how the Holy Spirit had provided an answer to this question or that concern. Meanwhile, God's voice and the Holy Spirit's guidance were often hidden from me.

I wondered: Why don't *we* have *that* kind of relationship?

I recall a night during this time when I stood on the hill at Pepperdine University in Malibu, California. I'd flown out from my New Mexico congregation to attend a conference on Pepperdine's campus. The presentations were finished for the evening, and I'd found a spot on a grassy slope under the bright stars, facing the ocean—a vast void that commingled with the night sky, erasing the horizon, leaving me a Lilliputian before a boundless sea that poured seamlessly into a limitless sky. The glow of ships below and the glimmer of stars above were like interchangeable golden pegs in the Lite Brite before me. The measureless nature of it all became a mirror in which I saw some of the measureless features of God, and I ached for more of him. I cried out to God:

"Fill me with your Holy Spirit!"

"Talk to me!"

"Make this more real for me! Make *us* more real!"

But there was no voice from heaven in response. No bright light with an angelic messenger. There was only the sound of the waves slapping the sand. The sound of the breeze tickling the leaves of the trees.

And I wondered: Why don't *we* have *that* kind of relationship?

Center Stage versus Backstage

Many of us long for a God who is center stage, while experiencing a God who is backstage.

When I read Acts or Exodus, the curtain is raised on a God who performs center stage. He is in the spotlight. His voice rises above all others. He's the most visible actor on the stage. His action is indisputable:

He parts the sea.

He pours out the Spirit.

He sends plagues.

He heals flesh.

He speaks from bushes.

He appears in dreams.

Center stage is God's home in Acts and Exodus. That's the God for whom I was hungering in that Pepperdine plea. That's the relationship I was missing in those early days of ministry and during my first decade of faith.

Since those days, I've been blessed to enjoy times with a God more like the one I see in Acts or Exodus. I've seen God cure diseases for the helpless. I've watched him grant employment for the jobless. I've witnessed God stitch broken hearts back together for the hopeless.

- While visiting Christians worshipping in underground house churches in China, I've experienced an undeniable sense of God's providential work and presence.
- Watching a school in the Philippines blossom from a handful of kids in the living room of close friends to hundreds in a three-story educational facility, I've been able to easily detect God's handiwork.
- Recently, I was praying about an old relationship that still filled me with bitterness and anger. At lunch, that very person walked into the barbeque joint where I was eating. I hadn't seen him in years. I attributed the "chance" meeting to God's clear action.

I've had moments in my life when God has been center stage.

In spite of this, if I'm honest, God's still been backstage a lot more than he's been center stage. This confession doesn't come easily. I feel pressured by the lyrics of some of the songs on the Christian radio station in my car to say the opposite. I feel tempted by the chapter titles of some of the Christian books in my library to say the opposite. But the truth is that, early in the morning when I conduct my *examen* and I review my previous day to try to discern what God is up to in my life, I don't usually find my day reading like Acts or Exodus. Instead, God's voice is lost among the cacophony of other voices. His action seems difficult to track.

I often hear this same confession among those who are suffering. Friends in my congregation in Memphis have voiced this concern with various "why" questions:

- Why did my sophomore daughter die in a car wreck on the way to start her new school year at her Christian university?

- Why did my nine-year-old die of cancer in spite of the best treatment in the world and the prayers of thousands?
- Why haven't I found a job after months of intense searching, even though I'm highly qualified?
- Why did my husband, a preacher, walk out of the church and the Christian faith?
- Why won't God heal my cancer?

These are the kinds of questions that arise when our experience of God is more backstage than center stage—when his power or his presence isn't as front and center as we'd hoped.

Enchanted versus Disenchanted

Charles Taylor, a professor of philosophy at McGill University in Canada, doesn't use the words *center stage* and *backstage* to describe this tension. He uses the words "enchanted" and "disenchanted."

Sometimes, life feels "enchanted"—filled with a God who is visibly present and very active. At other times, life feels "disenchanted"—filled with a God who is hidden and whose actions are harder to discern. Many of us long for a life that is enchanted (filled with a visible God), while experiencing a life that is disenchanted (filled with a hidden God).

In fact, Taylor argues that our entire contemporary culture, when compared to the culture of the 1500s, experiences life as far more disenchanted.[1] Those living in the 1500s experienced life as enchanted. First, they believed things happening in the natural world (e.g., storms, plagues, flourishing crops) were the result of divine blessings or curses. Second, they believed that the rise and fall of human kingdoms and societies were rooted ultimately in the will and work of God. Finally, they believed in a world filled with spirits, angels, and demons.

Today, however, most in the Western world experience life as disenchanted. First, most use science rather than theology to explain events in the natural world. Second, most attribute happenings in human kingdoms to human choice rather than divine will. Third, the notion that angels, spirits, and demons are alive and active, while playing well in novels and movies, doesn't play well in response to the question, "Hi, honey, what happened today?"

Some of us, when we compare our relationship with God with the relationship others have (today or in another era), we are left to wonder: Why don't *we* have *that* kind of relationship? Sometimes, God feels distant. God appears to be working far behind the scenes. God seems to work in ways that are indirect and covert. Our culture seems disenchanted. And our seasons of suffering leave us feeling disenchanted.

How Do We Thrive in Disenchantment?

All of this raises a critical question: How do we thrive spiritually in a disenchanted world? How do we flourish when God is hard to hear and difficult to discern?

What we need is a book written in disenchanted times. What we need is a tale that equips us to thrive and flourish even when it seems that God is acting backstage. What we need is a resource that enables us to know it's OK when our experience of God is not miraculous.

What we need is the book of Esther. In Esther, God is so invisible that his name never appears. Yet in Esther, God is more present and more powerful than we might have ever imagined.

Secular Not Sacred

The story of Esther opens in a city called Susa—one of four capitals of the ancient kingdom of Persia. Susa was the winter palace of King Ahasuerus, who ruled from India to Ethiopia (Esther 1:1–2).[2]

The kingdom of Persia displaced the kingdom of Babylon. And the kingdom of Babylon, as Esther chapter 2 reveals, is where God exiled his people from Jerusalem after centuries of disobedience. Esther's family was included in those sent away in exile to Babylon. Babylon had now become Persia.

Jerusalem was sacred. It's where God once filled his temple with his presence. It's where God would visit us through his son. It's where God seemed near. Jerusalem was the land of enchantment—a place where heaven kissed the earth.

But Susa, the capital city of the kingdom of Persia, once the kingdom of Babylon, was secular. It was the land of disenchantment—a place where heaven and earth sat distrustfully apart like two lone riders in a subway car late at night. Old Testament scholar Adele Berlin writes, "Esther is the most secular of biblical books."[3] It is secular because it takes place in a secular land, a land where God seems absent. It's a time when God seems distant. In fact, there's hardly anything of God in the land or the story. This is an era of disenchantment.

God seemed so absent the Jews couldn't even sing their worship songs there. The Psalmist laments:

By the waters of Babylon,
    there we sat down and wept,
    when we remembered Zion.
On the willows there
    we hung up our lyres.
For there our captors
    required of us songs,
and our tormentors, mirth, saying,
    "Sing us one of the songs of Zion!"
How shall we sing the LORD's song
    in a foreign land? (Ps. 137:1–4)

In Babylon, succeeded by Persia (where Esther lived), Jews like Esther could hardly even hum their hymns ("songs of Zion"). That's how secular it felt.

Mercifully, the Persians allowed the Jews to leave this pagan place and return home to Jerusalem. In the years before the book of Esther opens, many of the Jews have done just that. They have gone back to those enchanted spaces, back to the places where God felt present. Where God could be seen and heard. Where praise songs flowed from the lips as easily as breath from the lungs.

But not everyone has returned from Persia. Some have remained—like Esther. Stuck in this town whose parks contain no statues with names like Abraham or Moses or David and no schools with names like Ruth or Deborah or Hannah. Surprisingly, here in Susa, we do not even find the word "God." The Hebrew words *Yahweh* and *Elohim* never appear in the book of Esther.

That's what makes this book strikingly different from a book written in a similar time and place—the book of Daniel. Daniel, like the book of Esther, tells of a Jew who serves in the court of a pagan king during the time of the Jewish exile. But in the book of Daniel, unlike the book of Esther, we witness miracles (e.g., Daniel and the lion's den). God is front and center. His signature appears on every page. Daniel portrays an enchanted world. Esther portrays a disenchanted world.[4]

Esther is written to help us learn to thrive in those seasons of life when God is hard to find. Esther is God's gift to us to carry us through those valleys when we're forced to live in Susa rather than Jerusalem.

My Kingdom Come

Esther reveals how, when God plays behind the scenes, others will try to steal the scene. Chapter 1 opens with two of the ten feasts featured in the book. The first gala lasts six months. It is thrown by the king of Persia, Ahasuerus:

> In the third year of his reign he gave a feast for all his officials and servants. The army of Persia and Media and the nobles and governors of the provinces were before him, while he showed the riches of his royal glory and the splendor and pomp of his greatness for many days, 180 days. (Esther 1:3–4)

The Greek historian Herodotus gives us insight regarding this feast. During this time period, the Persian king was rallying support within his kingdom to go to war against Greece.[5] This feast was part of his scheme to persuade his fighters and financiers to support the plan to take Greece. In other words, Ahasuerus was wining and dining them. That's why he gets so upset when his wife, Queen Vashti, refuses to display herself before his guests:

> On the seventh day, when the heart of the king was merry with wine, he commanded Mehuman, Biztha, Harbona, Bigtha and Abagtha, Zethar and Carkas, the seven eunuchs who served in the presence of King Ahasuerus, to bring Queen Vashti before the king with her royal crown, in order to show the peoples and the princes her beauty, for she was lovely to look at. But Queen Vashti refused to come at the king's command delivered by the eunuchs. At this the king became enraged, and his anger burned within him. (Esther 1:10–12)

This isn't the frustration of a seething spouse. This is the fury of a despairing despot. Queen Vashti was meant to be the culmination of the display of this king's wealth, the Santa at the end of the Macy's Thanksgiving Day Parade. If any fighter or financier was still on the fence about supporting the king's quest to take Greece, one look at the queen should have persuaded him that this king was worth backing.[6]

Susa is so secular that the king throws a party for six months to influence his fighters and financiers to support his bid to rule over one more piece of the world. Where Christians have been taught to pray, "Your kingdom come, your will be done on earth," Esther's world is ruled by a king who wants *his* kingdom to come, *his* will to be done. In Esther, the entire world is this king's kingdom. And if God won't act front and center, the king will. He will take the place of God.

Hallowed Be My Name

The first kingdom-wide feast culminates in a second feast, which is held solely for those in the capital of Susa. It lasts seven days:

> And when these days were completed, the king gave
> for all the people present in Susa the citadel, both great
> and small, a feast lasting for seven days in the court of
> the garden of the king's palace. There were white cotton
> curtains and violet hangings fastened with cords of fine
> linen and purple to silver rods and marble pillars, and
> also couches of gold and silver on a mosaic pavement of
> porphyry, marble, mother-of-pearl, and precious stones.
> (Esther 1:5–6)

Karen Jobes notes the language used here sounds very much like the language used in two other places in the Bible: the description of the tabernacle in the wilderness and the temple in Jerusalem.[7] Susa is so secular that the palace of this king is described in terms that make it sound like the temple of God. Why? Because in the book of Esther, a king is attempting to supplant God. "Ashasuerus is God," Old Testament scholars Samuel Wells and George Summer write.

That is how the book of Esther begins. There is much speculation over the presence or absence of God in this book of Esther. But the book begins with the one who is in charge of all the events and circumstances and arrangements and threats that affect the Jews. He holds the whole world in his hands.[8]

Christians are taught to pray, "Our Father in heaven, hallowed be your name." Sadly, in Esther's world, the only name being hallowed is the king's name. In the book of Esther, the king is God.

Give Me This Day My Daily Bread

This king now moves from kingdom building to homemaking. Chapter 1 opens with a roundup of all the influential men so the king can make war. Chapter 2 opens with a roundup of all the beautiful women so the king can take a new queen:

> After these things, when the anger of King Ahasuerus had abated, he remembered Vashti and what she had done and what had been decreed against her. Then the king's young men who attended him said, "Let beautiful young virgins be sought out for the king. And let the king appoint officers in all the provinces of his kingdom to gather all the beautiful young virgins to the harem in Susa the citadel, under custody of Hegai, the king's eunuch, who is in charge of the women. Let their cosmetics be given them. And let the young woman who pleases the king be queen instead of Vashti." This pleased the king, and he did so. (Esther 2:1–4)

Esther is caught up in this dragnet of young virgins. She and countless other women are forced by the king into a contest to see which of them will become his new queen.

There are two criteria for the new queen. The first is beauty. The virgins are given a full year to meet this requirement. Six months are devoted to one type of beauty treatment and six months to another. In Esther's world, no woman is beautiful enough on her own. She is reduced to a blank canvas that requires a year's worth of professional painting before she can even be considered worthy.

This is preparation for the second criterion: sex. The virgins are given one night to meet this requirement. They are given one night to please the king and gain the crown.

Just as Queen Vashti was a possession used by the king to try to impress his subjects, so these young women like Esther were merely property. In fact, the text bears linguistic similarities to the story in Genesis 41 of Pharaoh appointing commissioners to gather grain, suggesting the young women are no more than grain for the king.[9] That's how disenchanted Susa was.

Christians are taught to turn to God and ask God to supply what is needed for their basic hunger. Esther's world is ruled by a king who turns to his own people and uses them in order to satisfy his hunger. Here, people like Esther are treated as goods by a king who sees himself as God. We will see this theme played out in even more tragic ways throughout the book.

Esther is written to empower us in those times when God's hiddenness brings the ungodly out of hiding. The book dares us to believe that life may still be enchanted, filled with God's divine presence, even when it seems at its most disenchanted and filled with the profane plans of others.

Celebrating a Backstage God

The story of Esther takes place during a darkly disenchanted season of life. Those times when God labors in obscurity rather than notoriety. Those periods when God's presence is hard to perceive and his schemes are difficult to spot. Yet it was nonetheless a time when an orphaned Jewish girl became the queen of a god-less nation, *the* superpower of the ancient world (Esther 2:16–17). There was only one explanation for such an unlikely vocation elevation—God: "Then Mordecai told them to reply to Esther, '. . . And who knows whether you have not come to the kingdom for such a time as this?'" (Esther 4:13–14).

From this lofty locale, as we'll see in upcoming chapters, Esther saves the Jewish race from genocide. She, along with Mordecai, rescues their people from extinction at the hands of the Persians. In the long run, Esther, as much as anyone in the Bible, makes Jesus's birth possible. Without Esther, Jesus's lineage would have been snuffed out long before Mary and Joseph showed up, long before Jesus was conceived in Mary's womb by the Holy Spirit. Esther saves the Jewish people and thus all who came from the Jewish people, including Jesus himself.

And how did this nobody gain the throne of Persia and thus the power to save the Jews and secure the path for the birth of Christ? A careful reading of this book—a book that never uses the word "God"—reveals that, all along, God was intimately involved in all that was happening. Even when godless people were campaigning for God's role, even when the smoke of suffering suffocated the flame of hope, even when no divine fingerprints could be found with the strongest magnifying glass, God was in play and at hand. God performed without visions and voices from heaven. He engaged without miracles and mystical appearances. God did it all in the midst of the most secular people and through the most secular means possible.

Here is the fundamental claim of Esther: Even when God seems awfully absent, he is profoundly present; and even when God seems decidedly dormant, he is astonishingly active. Even from the hiddenness of the backstage, God accomplishes more than we can ever imagine. Even from the remoteness of the valleys, God can be more intimate than we can ever fathom. The disenchanted seasons of life are periods when we learn new ways of seeing God's work and experiencing God's presence. Esther reveals that spells of disenchantment are not meant for depression but for celebration. For in them, we discover the adventure of disclosing the clandestine movements of God.

As we'll see in future chapters, Esther's people celebrated the hidden work of God in a feast called *Purim*. Purim was the antithesis of Passover. Passover lauded those times when God worked in extraordinary ways few could deny. Purim memorialized those times when God worked in ordinary ways most could easily miss. Yet even those were worthy of a party.

This is why in the worst days of World War II, Jewish inmates of Auschwitz, Dachau, and other camps could write the entire book of Esther from memory. This is why they would read it in secret and celebrate Purim covertly in concentration camps.[10] They wanted to testify to their conviction that even there, where God seemed awfully absent, he was profoundly present. Where God seemed decidedly dormant, he was astonishingly active. And his secluded steps were still worthy of celebration.

For those of you going through a dark valley, a tough crisis, a painful time, Esther's story is your story. Even in the very worst of times, when some oaf of an overlord was taking over the world and had overtaken her life, Esther lived a story that said God was powerfully at work. And no matter what seems to have overtaken your life, God is still at work. No matter how absent he seems, God is still present. No matter how dormant he appears, God is still active.

Consider this summary of Esther by Karen Jobes:

The book of Esther is perhaps the most striking biblical statement of what systematic theologians call the providence of God. When we speak of God's providence, we mean that God, in some invisible and inscrutable way, governs all creatures, actions, and circumstances through the normal and the ordinary course of human life, without the intervention of the miraculous. The book of Esther is the most true-to-life biblical example of God's providence precisely because God seems absent.[11]

I won't speak for you, but the life I live is one in which I rarely see miraculous things happening. God usually works through the normal and ordinary course of human life for me. God's movement in my life is more often invisible and inscrutable than stunning and surprising. But this is still reason for thanks and for celebration.

There is a tendency within contemporary Christianity to think that if we're not living out the book of Acts in our churches, if we're not experiencing the stories of Exodus in our lives, something must be wrong. "Why don't *we* have *that* kind of relationship?" we may wonder. But what Esther shows is that those stories aren't the only norms for life with God. Esther is another norm. God is at work just as powerfully in an Esther life as he is in an Acts life or an Exodus life.

If you find yourself living in a season or a space when it's hard to find God because things are secular or routine or filled with suffering, trust that just as he was in Esther's life, God is present and active in your life. Give thanks to God. Don't pine away wishing you had a different story—one more like Acts or Exodus. Give thanks for your Esther story. Because even when God seems awfully absent, he is profoundly present, and even when God seems decidedly dormant, he is astonishingly active.

It may require you to do some hard investigative work. You may not be able to passively sit back and just wait for God to act and appear. You may need to get up, get out, and sift through the events of each hour, day, and week as you've never done before. Never fear. The evidence is there. The proof confirming God's habitation lies all around, if we know how to look.

The Cadaver King and Country Dentist is the true story of some of the defendants in Mississippi courts who were wrongly convicted and imprisoned because of the testimony of two "expert" witnesses. For years, doctors Steven Hayne and Michael West testified in about 80 percent of the court's criminal cases. Tragically, they often misled jurors, fabricating evidence and offering false testimony in order to secure guilty verdicts against those whom officials most desired to see punished for the crime. This was before processes like DNA testing had been perfected. Thus the evidence proving the innocence of some of the victims of Hayne and West simply couldn't be seen, even though it was present. Thankfully, DNA testing progressed and the evidence documenting the innocence of some of those wrongly convicted was revealed. The book focuses on how this now-visible proof enabled Kennedy Brewer and Levon Brooks to gain their longed-for freedom after years behind bars.[12]

In much the same way, sometimes the evidence for God's presence and activity is difficult to see. Times of disenchantment call for a closer look, another examination, another set of tools. The evidence is there. And it will set you free.

This practice of refocusing is called the *examen* in classical Christianity. Five hundred years ago, St. Ignatius of Loyola used this ancient practice as a way of exploring and experiencing God, a means of attuning to his presence and leadership. Fundamentally, it was designed to enable Christians to find God in their daily lives. So important was this refocusing that Ignatius urged it on his fellow Jesuits twice a day, at noon and before sleep. He stressed that even when one was too busy for other spiritual practices, the habit of *examen* must remain.[13] There are many things we miss during a typical day because our focus is elsewhere. Mark Thibodeaux writes of more than thirty of these that can be recovered through the *examen*.[14] But, at its core, the *examen* enables us to find God in all things.[15]

Each morning, in my study, I pull out my journal and replay the previous day in my mind and through my pen. As yesterday spills onto the page, I find it possible to look past all the loud and urgent things that took up the foreground of my day and see anew the quiet and important things God was doing in the background. This morning routine slowly builds in me a capacity for ongoing refocusing, an ability to look at days, weeks, and even years and view what had once been invisible—a God laboring lovingly from backstage. This is the first and most important habit we need in a disenchanted world. It lays the foundation for flourishing even when we feel forsaken.

2

SIT TIGHT

During the summer of 2016, my children, Jordan and Jacob, completed their first half marathon. I ran with them. The race, the inaugural "Great American River Run," was held in downtown Memphis, Tennessee. It featured views of one of the greatest rivers, the Mighty Mississippi.

The run also featured one supreme challenge—the finish line was hidden from view. We couldn't see it until we were nearly upon it. It's hard to not see the very thing you've been waiting thirteen miles to see! In its final four hundred yards, the course wound back and forth around trees and large banners, among which the finish line played hide-and-seek. The three of us were exhausted by this point. Jordan wheezed out, "I can't see the finish line!" Her run slowed to a jog. "I can't see the finish line!" Her jog became a walk. "I can't see the finish line!" She nearly couldn't finish because she could not see the finish line.

I'd experienced something similar the first time I ran the Saint Jude half marathon in Memphis. Those last four to five miles were deceptive. They covered rolling hill after rolling hill. At the top of each asphalt dune, you'd catch a glimpse of Autozone Park downtown where the race concluded. But due to fatigue and perspective, the end never seemed any closer, no matter how many hills we topped. I felt ready to quit because I was certain I'd never be able to close the gap between my current mound and that finish line. The frustration of that seemingly unobtainable finish line nearly caused me to fail in finishing the race.

It's finish lines and our frustration with them that often cause us to falter as we move through life's miles. When we peer ahead down the course of a day or a decade, and the ending we're hoping for is still hiding, or the finish we're dreaming of is still distant, it's easy to give up and drop out.

John is a longtime member of my congregation. The finish line he hoped for was obvious for years, and then, one day, it was obscured. As a high school student, he was an exceptionally skilled athlete. During his senior year, he received scholarships to play both football and basketball in college. He raced toward a finish line of collegiate athletics and, who knows, perhaps professional athletics afterward. But two years into his college athletic career, a knee injury sidelined him. His athletic career was over. That finish line, so visible for so long, was suddenly veiled. Where was the finish line now?

David's finish line remained so remote it seemed it would never become reality. In his work for AT&T, David connected people with one another. His real passion, however, was connecting people with God. I walked with him as he discerned a call to set aside media and home communication and enter ministry and home transformation. On weekdays, David continued as a serviceman. On weeknights, he became a student and earned a bachelor's in biblical studies. On weekends, he apprenticed with me in ministry at Highland.

Finally, with degree and experience in hand, David applied for preaching positions in a few congregations and was hired. We rejoiced together on that day! The finish line, it seemed, was crossed.

Only it wasn't.

Months later, for reasons outside of his control, David was without a pulpit. For months, he searched. He inquired at three dozen churches. He interviewed at nineteen. All nineteen said, "No, thank you. You're not what we're looking for. You're not what we need."

David was ready to call AT&T. Ready to put the uniform back on. Ready to quit the race.

Finish Lines and Feasts

The book of Esther is a book about finish lines. From its opening lines to its closing credits, Esther is about endings. It's a story that forces us to reexamine the way things wind up, especially when that finish we hoped for is in hiding or that conclusion we dreamed of remains distant. Esther calls us to cultivate one of the hardest habits: waiting.

In disenchanted periods of our lives, it seems God is not on the job in the present—much less laboring for something we'd like to see in the future. Yet, surprisingly, Esther reveals that even in the most disenchanted seasons, even when God is not dishing out the miracles or the mighty works, even when he's silent and absent, he is definitely working on finish lines. If we will faithfully wait, even when it feels God is doing nothing to better our today, Esther reveals God is doing everything to brighten our tomorrow.

The book discloses God's finish line work in two ways. First, the book of Esther uses feasts to demonstrate the way in which the unseen God labors for a cheerful conclusion.[1] There are ten feasts in Esther. If you swaggered through the front door into one of them, you'd probably just see the headliners and higher-ups managing the bands and buffets. But if you slunk through the back door into one of the ten feasts in Esther, you'd catch sight of God in the kitchen reworking that feast's happily-never-after into a happily-ever-after. Five times, a feast or a set of feasts in Esther seems to spell a sad end for one group. Five times, God uses another feast or set of feasts to reveal his new and improved ending for that same group.

Five Sad Feasts and Five Glad Feasts		
1. A feast for all the *Gentile nobility* in Persia (1:2–4)	→	A feast for all the *Jews* in Persia (9:10)
2. A feast for all the *men* in Susa (1:5–8)	→	A feast for all the *women* in Susa (1:9)
3. Five feasts thrown by *Gentiles* (1:2–4, 5–8, 9; 2:18; 3:15)	→	Five feasts thrown by *Jews* (5:5–8; 7:1–9; 8:17; 9:17, 19)
4. The *villain* (Haman) celebrates his supposed victory with a feast (3:15)	→	The *victims* (Jews) celebrate their real victory with feasts (9:17–18)
5. A feast *leaves Susa in dismay and confusion* (3:15)	→	A feast *leaves Susa rejoicing and merry* (8:15)

You might attend one feast in Esther and think, *Well, I guess that's it. That's life in this world of Esther.* But just wait. Wait in anticipation. Eventually, another feast comes along and God turns that upside-down life right-side-up.

A feast is thrown for the Gentile nobility, and five feasts are thrown by Gentiles. The primary conclusion is that only a certain class or a certain race gets the happily-ever-after (Gentiles and/ or nobles). It's a conclusion reached by the poor and by minorities in numerous countries in many eras of our world. But hang on. Eventually, God ensures that a feast is also thrown *for* all the Jews and that five feasts are thrown *by* Jews. The poor and the minorities are given that ending once denied them. If the one set of feasts left us feeling God was doing nothing to better our today, the second set disclosed he was doing everything to brighten our tomorrow.

A feast is thrown for all the men. The logical conclusion is that only one gender gets the happily-ever-after. It's a conclusion reached by women of all ages in many countries throughout history. But don't give up. In response, God ensures that a feast is also thrown for all the women. They are given the ending once denied them. If the first feast left us feeling God was doing nothing to better our today, the second disclosed he was doing everything to brighten our tomorrow.

A villain (Haman) throws a feast to celebrate his injustice. One can only assume by this that only the powerful and influential get the happily-ever-after. Those with no voice, with no seat at the table, are robbed of any cheerful conclusion. But don't quit. God ensures that Esther ends with feasts thrown for/by the victims of this injustice (Jews), celebrating justice once denied now delivered. If the first feast left us feeling God was doing nothing to better our today, the final feasts reveal he was doing everything to brighten our tomorrow.

A feast pitches the entire city of Susa into dismay and confusion. One conclusion seems to be that sometimes there's just no hope for a city. Things can get so dark that an entire city is lost. But don't conclude that this is the end. God labors to add one more feast to the list—a feast that leaves this same city rejoicing and merry. Where hope and dismay were once the final chapters for the city, now joy and celebration close the book on that city. Just when we were certain God was up to nothing with respect to today in the city, it turned out he was up to everything with respect to tomorrow in the city.

Don't make hasty conclusions about God simply because your finish line has gone into hiding or seems too distant to reach. You're just in column number one on the table above. You're attending one party in a story filled with plenty more parties. If you'll wait long enough, another will arrive. This isn't the end. The feasts in Esther reveal that, slowly and secretly, God is tenaciously transforming today's table of frustration into tomorrow's table of fulfillment. The bitter mess that may be in front of you isn't your final meal. Keep checking the mailbox. A divine invitation to another feast is on its way. In Esther's day, God knew how to rewrite the endings of racism, classism, gender roles, injustice, and urban decay. He can also rewrite whatever ending you feel like you're facing today.

Finish Lines and Reversals

The second way Esther reveals God's finish line work is through reversals. Think of the book of Esther as two narratives racing in opposite directions. One narrative consists of steps and stories leading toward one inevitable conclusion—the death and annihilation of the Jews. Each stride takes us closer to the finish line of the destruction of the Jewish people by the Persian Empire. This path is characterized by mourning and sadness.

The alternate narrative consists of steps and stories leading toward the opposite conclusion—the salvation and exaltation of the Jews. Each stride moves us miles closer to the finish line of the rescue of the Jewish people from the Persian Empire. This path is characterized by celebration and joy.

These two accounts race side by side throughout Esther. We'll call one the "Sadness Path" and the other the "Gladness Path." Each step on the Sadness Path is countered by a reversal, a corrective step down the Gladness Path. Notice how each of these seven strides along the Sadness Path is reversed by an opposite stride on the Gladness Path.

Sadness Path	Reversal	Gladness Path
1. The king gives his signet ring to *Haman*, who writes a decree to *kill* the Jews. (3:10)	→	The king gives his signet right to *Mordecai*, who writes a decree to *save* the Jews. (8:2)
2. The king sets *Haman* over all the *Jews* and all their property. (3:11)	→	The king sets *Mordecai* over *Haman* and all his property. (8:2)
3. Letters are sent decreeing that the *people* should attack the *Jews*. (3:13)	→	Letters are sent decreeing that the *Jews* should attack their *enemies*. (8:11)
4. A *humbled* Mordecai dresses in *sackcloth and ashes*. (4:1)	→	An *honored* Mordecai dresses in *royal clothing*. (8:15)
5. Haman's wife urges him to build a *stake and impale Mordecai on it*. (5:14)	→	The king has *Haman impaled on the stake* intended for Mordecai. (7:10)
6. *Haman urges the king to honor him* with royal garments and a public display. (6:7)	→	*The king honors Mordecai* with royal garments and a public display. (6:11)
7. "And in every province, wherever the king's command and his decree reached, there was great mourning among the Jews, with fasting and weeping and lamenting, and many of them lay in sackcloth and ashes." (4:3)	→	"And in every province and in every city, wherever the king's command and his edict reached, there was gladness and joy among the Jews, a feast and a holiday." (8:17)

As you dart down the path on the left, the Sadness Path, the finish line is visible and close at hand. It's a finish line of death and destruction. It leads to weeping and lamenting. By the time you reach the end, you are wearing sackcloth and ashes.

The clandestine God refuses to allow that course to stand alone. He quietly lays the groundwork for a complete turnaround. He makes possible a path with a different conclusion. Its finish line is life and renewal. It leads to celebration. By the time you reach it, you are wearing your very best party clothes.

This theme of reversal is summarized with these words:

> Now in the twelfth month, which is the month of Adar, on the thirteenth day of the same, when the king's command and edict were about to be carried out, on the very day when the enemies of the Jews hoped to gain the mastery over them, the reverse occurred: the Jews gained mastery over those who hated them. (Esther 9:1)

When it seems your course will conclude in sadness, the book of Esther reveals a reverse—God can flip sadness into gladness. The finish you fear may happen in life is not a foregone conclusion. The completion you crave but don't believe can come about still can. Esther reveals a God who drives in reverse. He stealthily replaces sadness with gladness. Our role is to wait in faithfulness.

Gregory Boyles, author of *Tattoos on the Heart*, is the founder and Executive Director of Homeboy Industries in Los Angeles. Every year, fifteen thousand gang members pound on the doors of Homeboy Industries seeking help to escape gang life. Speaking in Memphis a few years ago, Boyles shared that when a gang member infiltrates an enemy gang member's territory, many times it's not because he wants to go kill someone. It's because he wants to be killed by someone. He's infiltrated enemy territory because he wants to die. Boyles says people often join gangs because they've lost hope. They look down their life's path, and they see nothing but pain and futility. They want to die. The only cure for that, Boyles says, is hope—hope that there might be another path besides the path of sadness. This is what Boyles and Homeboy

Industries try to do. They strive to show that the sadness path is not the only path.[2]

This, the story of Esther declares, is the primary work of God. The Good News, the gospel of God, is that there is another road. God is a God of reversals. He's provided a Gladness Path onto which a U-turn can be made from the Sadness Path.

For far too many people, life appears to be a one-way street destined for despair. Existence is a path that, as people peer forward, only seems to end in pain. What so many seek is an alternative avenue. A highway that might end in hope. A trail that might lead to triumph. Esther's story promises that even though it may be difficult to discern, this is what God is up to in the world. God is constantly carving new roads, blazing new byways. He knows how to turn a sadness path into a gladness path.

I saw this in a stunning way in Mildred's life. A few weeks ago, Mildred shared with our congregation her story of God's reversal at work in her life. She was born to a crack-addicted mother in Memphis. The state handed her over to her grandmother, although her grandmother's health was ailing. One day, Mildred's mother dropped by with two gifts for Mildred—twin babies! The grandmother was physically unable to raise these abandoned infants, so Mildred raised her twin siblings by herself, dropping out of school to do so. She never completed more than the seventh grade. Several years later, now raising three children, she was taking out the trash from her low-end, two-bedroom apartment when a man attacked and raped her. Mildred became pregnant and contracted HIV.

It seemed like her life was headed down the Sadness Path at a hundred miles per hour. She was racing toward a finish line of futility and failure. It all seemed irreversible.

But then God showed up—and threw everything into reverse.

Mildred came into contact with a Christian nonprofit agency in Memphis called HopeWorks. My friend Ron is the executive director. HopeWorks helped her gain the spiritual, emotional, educational, and social resources she needed to get back on her feet. She went from dying to thriving. Within a few years, Mildred actually met with President Bush and then President Obama as part of a delegation seeking funding for HIV patients. Today, she is a vibrant, joyful, and productive woman. She is filled with hope and laughter. She's got both feet on a Gladness Path. Mildred is a living testimony of a God who drives in reverse.

Remember my friend David, the former AT&T representative and aspiring pastor? Interview after interview, he endured nineteen churches rejecting him. Yet he and those of us close to him stubbornly believed that God had an alternative path charted for him. In the end, a wonderful church in upper New York State hired David. What seemed certain to be a finish line of sadness was not. God called David to put his trust in reverse. David did. And sadness turned to gladness.

This is what ultimately kept my friend John going. When his athletic career came to an end in college, he believed that God had another path carved out for him. He put his faith in reverse. At first, he thought that alternative path was teaching and coaching. But he soon realized that was not it. Then he discerned it was in water filters and pumps—a business he's been in successfully for more than fifty years. What could have felt like the end all those years ago when an injury sidelined him was not. God blazed a new trail for John. One that ended in gladness.

In another instance of faith in God's great reversals, for several years, the Highland Church of Christ where I preach has partnered with Timothy Hill Children's Ranch to begin a new ministry for young adults aging out of the foster care system. Our hope was to launch accommodations and training for them on two hundred acres of rolling hills east of our church building. But one by one, obstacles arose. Neighbors questioned the project. Commissioners rejected the plan. And on one evening in 2019, after another setback, it seemed the end had come. All plans were paused. But as we comforted one another in our disappointment, Thaddaeus Hill, executive director of Timothy Hill, reminded us that it was not the end. Our God delights in creating continuances where there only seem to be conclusions. Even though we couldn't see it at the time, we could trust that God just might one day turn all this sadness into gladness. And so, for now, we are waiting. In full faith, we are waiting.

This is the story of the gospel. Jesus seems set on a path that leads only to death, mourning, and sadness. A path that leads to the cross. Friday ends with his tortuous crucifixion. But all along, God has set an alternative path in place. A path that leads to resurrection. A path that leads to joy and happiness and celebration. If we will hang on, eventually that stone sealing the tomb will roll away.

A king named David understood this. He had his fair share of heartache. But he also knew how God could bring joy even in the midst of pain. He often put his faith in the great ability of God to reverse mourning and turn it into dancing. In fact, he wrote a song about it. In a way, this is Esther's song. It can be your song as well. No matter what you're going through today, a reverse is possible. This tune can be yours:

> I will extol you, O LORD, for you have drawn me up
>> and have not let my foes rejoice over me.
> O LORD my God, I cried to you for help,
>> and you have healed me.
> O LORD, you have brought up my soul from Sheol;
>> you restored me to life from among those who go
>>> down to the pit. . . .
> *You have turned for me my mourning into dancing;*

> *you have loosed my sackcloth*
> *and clothed me with gladness.* (Ps. 30:1–3, 11—
> emphasis mine)

This is what God is up to in the world. It may not be fast acting. It may not seem miraculous. The world may still appear disenchanted. But be patient. Give him time. Be quiet and still. And look. All around you, great reversals are in process. *The* great reversal is in process—the one that stretches from Genesis to Revelation. Trust that God *is* at work in the world. And, as we're about to hear, believe that he wants you to be part of that work.

This is why that same David could command us, "Wait for the Lord; be strong, and let your heart take courage; wait for the Lord!" (Ps. 27:14). And this is why David wrote of himself, "For God alone my soul waits in silence; from him comes my salvation," and "For God alone, O my soul, wait in silence, for my hope is from him." (Ps. 62:1,5). Waiting for and trusting in God's presence and God's great work is the second discipline that enables us to thrive when it seems God is in hiding. Henri Nouwen reminds us that, in fact, "the largest part of our existence is waiting," and that, therefore, we must develop what he calls "a spirituality of waiting."[3] "Waiting," Mark Batterson writes, "is necessary for faith in the same way a chrysalis is necessary for a caterpillar, to change it from a grub that crawls the earth to a butterfly that dances in the air."[4] Waiting is a fundamental part of our spiritual transformation. Sue Monk Kidd tells of a monk who took her by the shoulders and said, "I hope you'll hear what I'm about to tell you. I hope you'll hear it all the way down to your toes. When you're waiting, you're not doing nothing. You're doing the most important something there is. You're allowing your soul to grow up. If you can't be still and wait, you can't become what God created you to be."[5] So, sit tight. It's how to abound when God doesn't seem to be around.

Jump In

A few years ago, a series of books by Suzanne Collins called *The Hunger Games* dominated bookshelves and movie screens. They painted a portrait of a postapocalyptic earth when children from districts were chosen to fight to the death in "hunger games."

Soon after their release, these novels, along with millions of others, became available in electronic editions. In 2014, the retailer Amazon released statistics for the all-time most highlighted passages in e-books. The most highlighted passage came from *The Hunger Games*: "Because sometimes things happen to people and they're not equipped to deal with them."[1] Something about that line forced a recess in reading. When readers' eyes hit that sentence, it so aligned with their experience that they highlighted it—more than seventeen thousand times. Why did so many readers mark it? It's not particularly well crafted in terms of its language. It's not unusually insightful in terms of its content.

It is noteworthy, however, because it elicits a nearly universal, "Yes!" Nearly all of us have experienced what it expresses. Rarely does a sun set without us having had at least one hour when we weren't equipped to deal with a conversation, concern, or crisis that came our way.

A friend of mine recently asked me to share a few things I learned in ministry that I wasn't taught in seminary. Were there some things, he wondered, for which I wasn't equipped while I was in school? As good as my professors were, there was a limit to what they could teach.

I thought back to my first few weeks in full-time ministry. One day, a man named Brian lurched into my office. He asked if he could talk with me. After plopping on my couch, he looked around nervously, greasy hair hiding his eyes, and said, "The mob's placed a listening device inside my chest, and I want to get it out. Can you help me?"

I can say with clarity that no class in seminary equipped me to deal with Brian's request. It turns out Brian had some mental health challenges. Thankfully, we were able to connect him with some people in the mental health field, but there wasn't a lot I could do for him.

There are many times in life when we are ill-prepared for things that happen.

I think of my friend Doug who went out one afternoon to survey several acres of property for a children's home. In a split second, all four tires of the all-terrain vehicle he was driving left the earth as the road veered sharply and unexpectedly downward at an embankment. He and the vehicle soared and somersaulted, metal and bone snapped, and Doug was instantly paralyzed. Nothing in his life had adequately prepared him for that.

I think of my friends David and Jenny. They stood in the shade of the oaks and maples in the driveway of their Memphis home, praying with their daughter Liz. They waved goodbye as Liz headed down the driveway and began the three-hour drive on Interstate

40 to Nashville to start another year at Lipscomb University. Later, they picked up the phone and listened incredulously as a stranger regretfully, apologetically, and apprehensively told them that Liz had died in an accident on the interstate. Nothing in their lives had adequately prepared them for that.

So often, we are caught completely off guard by the things that come our way.

This is especially true in moments when our world feels as if God is long gone. (We call that kind of world "disenchanted.") The less present God seems to be in our world, the less prepared we seem to be for what's happening in our world. This is the challenge—the more disenchanted the world appears, the more despondent we become.

That's why the book of Esther is so helpful. It's a story focused on what it's like when it seems God has left us unaccompanied and unequipped to face the unrelenting stuff of life. Sometimes what makes the days dark is a freak accident. But more often, it's a person. The wall we smash into is a human who is mean or insensitive or hostile or simply inhumane. Esther's person has a name. He is Haman.

Haman

It is one thing be forced to face an adversary. It's quite another when that adversary holds a position with nearly unlimited power and resources. Haman is that adversary. He's just been promoted to second in command in Persia:

> After these things King Ahasuerus promoted Haman
> the Agagite, the son of Hammedatha, and advanced him
> and set his throne above all the officials who were with
> him. And all the king's servants who were at the king's
> gate bowed down and paid homage to Haman, for the

king had so commanded concerning him. But Mordecai
did not bow down or pay homage. (Esther 3:1–2)

No one but the king is higher than Haman. As a visual symbol of
his supremacy, all the servants of the king bow before him. The
one whom the entire empire fears is Esther's foe.

There is one, however, in all the land who refuses to bow.
Esther's adopted father, Mordecai, will not take a knee when
Haman struts past. This infuriates Haman (Esther 3:5). His rage
compels Haman not only to "lay hands on Mordecai," but also
to "destroy all the Jews, the people of Mordecai, throughout the
whole kingdom." (Esther 3:6). Hatred and hubris grow in Haman's
heart like tumbleweeds in West Texas. Mordecai's refusal to bow
and Haman's intense contempt are at least partly explained by a
long-standing racial conflict.[2] Centuries earlier, the Amalekites
had acted brutally against the Jews as the Jews escaped across the
desert from slavery in Egypt. Before they entered the Promised
Land, Moses reminded his people of the abuse they had suffered
at the hands of the Amalekites: "Remember what Amalek did to
you on the way as you came out of Egypt, how he attacked you
on the way when you were faint and weary, and cut off your tail,
those who were lagging behind you, and he did not fear God"
(Deut. 25:17–18).

Years later, the Jewish king Saul was commanded by God
to completely destroy the Amalekites and their king, Agag, in
response to the Amalekite's malevolence (1 Sam. 15). Here, in
Esther, Haman is revealed to be an Agagite—a descendent of the
Amalekite king Agag. While there may be more practical and ego-
tistical motives at play (as we'll see in a later chapter), Haman's
violence against Mordecai and all those who share Mordecai's
ethnicity, and Mordecai's defiance of Haman, are rooted in this
abiding racial conflict.

One of Haman's first official acts after his promotion is therefore to determine a date on which to murder Mordecai and his people. To do this, Haman casts lots (Heb. *pur*) until he believes they indicate he should slaughter the Jews in the twelfth month (Esther 3:7). These were clay cubes inscribed with characters or dots. They were cast like dice.[3]

Haman then visits the palace to sell his violent plan to the king, presenting his majesty a truth, a half-truth, and a lie.[4]

Truth: A Certain People

"There is a certain people scattered abroad and dispersed among the peoples in all the provinces of your kingdom" (Esther 3:8a). The Jews *were* exiled and scattered among the Persian kingdom. This is fact. They were not, however, the only people dispersed throughout Persia. There were other exiles. Haman's message is true and misleading. He intends for the king to hear something like this: "These Jews—they are everywhere!"

Half-Truth: Their Laws

"Their laws are different from those of every other people . . ." (Esther 3:8b). This is true in that the Jews have some religious laws that are different from Persian laws. However, they have some laws that are consistent with Persian laws. When Jewish religious laws and Persian civic laws do not conflict, the Jews keep the Persian laws.

Lie: They Do Not Obey

". . . and they do not keep the king's laws" (Esther 3:8c). It may be true to say that one Jew, Mordecai, does not keep one of the king's laws—the one commanding reverence to Haman. But it is a lie to say that Jews, in general, do not keep the king's laws.

Haman parades around in a world he believes has no Redeemer to reign in his ambition. The king rules in a world that appears to have no God to guide his decisions. So, he takes this horrible Haman's word at face value. He believes every sentence—the truth, the half-truth, and the lie. In the end, the king gives Haman complete freedom: "Do with them as it seems good to you" (Esther 3:11).

A decree was broadcast immediately announcing the annihilation of the Jews on the date Haman believed the *pur* indicated—the thirteenth day of the first month of the year (Esther 3:12). Haman's news regarding the portending purge of Jews from the Persian Empire broke on the eve of Passover. As the children of Moses gathered to celebrate God's greatest act of deliverance, they must have staggered at what felt like God's greatest act of desertion.

Just as Moses felt ill-equipped to engage in the monumental mission that would lead to the first Passover, so Esther must have felt inadequately outfitted to assault Haman's annihilation of Passover. On the eve of Passover, as news of Haman's scheme to slaughter the Jews like lambs reached the ears of Jews, they lamented, cried aloud, wore sackcloth and ashes, tore their clothes, fasted, and wept.[5] The very event they had gathered to remember was dismembered before their very eyes. Esther's is the story for all of us who have ever felt unequipped and unaccompanied in facing the hard stuff of life.

Disengaged

We needn't wonder just how unequipped Esther felt. After all, Esther's first step in this world, against this foe, was to make excuses and to disengage. Esther's adopted father, Mordecai—sending word through a common friend, Hathach—implores Esther to march into the king's presence and beg for royal assistance in stopping Haman's plan. All Esther can see, however, are all the reasons why she can do no such thing. In response to the great emergency facing her people and the great evil prompting it, Esther sends word back to Mordecai that there is nothing she can do. One of the most inviolable laws of the land is that no person, not even Queen Esther, may approach the king with a request without first being invited. And it's been a month since Esther's been summoned to the sovereign's side (Esther 4:10–14).

To undo the unthinkable now unfolding in her world, Esther must engage. She alone stands in a position to terminate this evil plot. But Esther's first instinct when faced with God's invitation to join his intervention against the dreadful things in her disenchanted world is also our first instinct—disengagement. She, just as we do, makes excuses about why it's too dangerous or too disagreeable to get involved in the danger of the surrounding world.

Esther's excuse comes with a degree of truth. In her culture, she can't just demand an appointment with the king to talk about this plan proposed by Haman and authorized by the king. There were only a handful in the court allowed in the king's presence unannounced and uninvited, and all of those were men. Esther, though the queen, was "only a woman." She faced death for plunging through the closed doors of the palace to press for an audience with the king.[6] Her predecessor, Queen Vashti, discovered that her crown could not compensate for her gender. She was a woman in a man's world, and when she refused to parade her beauty before the king's guests like a show horse, she was deposed. The same was true for Esther. Not even the queen could seek an audience with the king because of her gender.

But Mordecai helped her to hear God's call: "Do not think to yourself that in the king's palace you will escape any more than all the other Jews. For if you keep silent at this time, relief and deliverance will rise for the Jews from another place, but you and your father's house will perish" (Esther 4:13–14). If Esther chose to lock herself up behind the walls of the palace, she would not remain untouched by the evil about to be unleashed in the world around her. The plague of Haman's plot would eventually infect even Esther. No person of God can expect to find refuge behind the walls of any hall, home, or even house of God, hoping to remain untouched by the harshness of the outside world. What's outside always finds a way inside.

Yet Esther's first instinct is disengagement. It's ours as well.

When we accept a dogma that says God is distant from our hurting world, many of us will adopt a demeanor of distance toward that same hurting world.[7] If God's not getting involved, why should we?

Disengagement takes many forms. Sometimes it starts with excuses. Good excuses. Like Esther's.

When our daughter Jordan moved from Memphis to attend college in Nashville, people asked strange questions when they learned she was from Memphis.

"Did you have a gun growing up?"

"Were you ever robbed?"

"Aren't you scared to live there?"

Memphis has a reputation of being a tough town. With its high poverty and river-town heritage, some outsiders look at it as crime-ridden and violent. The reputation is undeserved. But there are challenges in the metro area, more than in some cities in the United States. As a result, some who live here leave. They move to places like Nashville. And some who hang in hole up. I know Memphians who hardly ever venture downtown. They rarely leave a three-mile radius from their manicured neighborhoods and sun-kissed shopping areas. They sojourn only where it feels secure. They disengage.

I have to admit: felt the same temptation to disengage as we spent six years studying and surveying China in preparation for the launch of new mission work there. As we spoke to missionaries and then made visits to cities and interviewed house churches and Christians who told us stories of pollution and of loved ones who'd been imprisoned for their faith, my own faith began to falter. As we identified a young couple with a newborn to send to this most challenging field, I wondered, more than once, if we were doing the right thing. Moving to China was something I'm not sure I could muster the courage to do. There was a part of me that felt like disengaging.

God's Engagement

While Esther is in a state of disengagement, Mordecai steps in to help her understand that God is calling her to engage the daunting needs of the disenchanted world around her. He begins by persuading Esther of a surprising truth: the God who our worst days incline us to imagine is more isolated from our world than we could have ever feared is, in fact, more intimately involved in our world than we could ever fathom. Mordecai gives fuel to Esther's imagination with this line: "And who knows whether you have not come to the kingdom for such a time as this?" (Esther 4:14b).

Consider what Mordecai is claiming. How did Esther "come to the kingdom"? If we survey her journey into the Persian kingdom, to the throne she now occupies, it is filled with milestones that she and we might consider mostly painful or pointless:

- Her family was snatched from their ancestral home in Israel by Babylon and transplanted as exiles to Babylon.
- Her parents died, and she was taken in by Mordecai.
- After the Persians displaced the Babylonians, Esther was seized from her home by officials of the Persian king because the king was seeking a new queen among these young women.

- And now she and her people faced slaughter by the
  Persian second-in-command, Haman.

Who would blame Esther for tossing each of these, and more, away as worthless markers in a worthless life? It would be difficult for Esther to look back on her life and see divine providence or purpose.

Yet, without ever speaking the name of God, Mordecai hints to Esther that God is using all her pain for his purpose, transforming her mess into greater meaning. Mordecai is proposing that the God who seemed more isolated than Esther could have ever feared is more intimately involved than she could have ever imagined.

God used the forced exile of Esther's family to Babylon; God used the Persian king's ambition for world domination, which led the king to banish his first queen after she wouldn't support his cause; God used the degrading roundup of young virgins to find a new queen, which included Esther; God knew what was happening with Haman. God redeemed all of these and used them to place Esther on the throne for this exact purpose—to save his people from Haman. Just when Esther was tempted to disengage from the world, Mordecai wanted her to know God was fully engaged in the world and was inviting Esther to join him.

And just look at the person to whom the invitation to engage has been extended. God is calling a heroine, not a hero. In this man's world, God is summoning a woman. This stands in stark contrast to the way women are treated in Esther's story. In chapter 1, Queen Vashti is objectified and dehumanized by the king when she is ordered to display her beauty before his guests. In chapter 3, Esther and countless young virgins are enslaved, abused, and raped when they are forced to participate in the kingdom's obscene competition to find the next queen after the king removes Vashti. The people of Esther's world only seem interested in exploiting women.

But the God of Esther's world is passionate about employing this woman. God believed a woman would be the hero of this story.

Esther was not the only woman God petitioned for partnership. Five women in the Old Testament were called "prophetess": Miriam (Exod. 15:20), Huldah (2 Kings 22:14), Isaiah's wife (Isa. 8:3), Noadiah (Neh. 6:14), and Deborah (Judg. 4:4). Deborah also functioned as one of the "judges," a civil leader (Judg. 4:6–10; 5:7) and one who decided cases (4:4–5)—a role often reserved for men. The Old Testament also carries stories of women like Ruth, Hannah, Jael, and others who lived courageously and faithfully in cooperation with God.

We find the same in the Gospels. When God decided to enter the human race in the form of Jesus, his first steps were with a woman, Mary (Luke 1:27). Women were among Jesus's disciples at a time when women were not allowed to study under rabbis, following him and funding his ministry out of their own resources (Luke 8:1–3). Women were the ones who remained with Jesus at his death (Luke 23:49). When Jesus was resurrected, his first appearance was to women. And his first commission for proclaiming the resurrection was to women (Matt. 28:9).

Acts records that Priscilla and Aquila taught Apollos about Christ. The original text records Priscilla's name first—which is unusual—and thus draws attention to her (Acts 18:26). Acts mentions other women who played an important role in the early church, such as Lydia, who became a disciple and hosted the church in her home (Acts 16:14–15), and four prophetesses (Acts 21:9).

Paul describes women as ministers of the church (Rom. 16:1–7), such as Phoebe, who was possibly a deacon (Rom. 16:1). He refers to Andronicus and Junia possibly as apostles (Rom. 16:7)—Junia being a female name in Greek. Paul refers to Euodia and Syntyche as "women who have labored side by side with me in the gospel" (Phil. 4:3).

Esther stands in a long line of women whom God called upon to engage the world and its needs. Though Esther may not have sensed God at work in her world or in her own life, God was truly laboring in both. And God wanted her to join him in his hidden work in the world.

The same is true for us.

In this life where Hamans oftentimes pulverize people, where God is sometimes concealed in the clouds, and where we perceive ourselves powerless to face it all, Esther's story challenges us to believe that God is calling us—yes, even us—equipped and accompanied by him in hidden ways, to engage the daunting needs of the disenchanted world around us.

This line from Mordecai—"And who knows whether you have not come to the kingdom for such a time as this?"—compels us to pick up every little and large detail of our lives for the purpose of reexamination. The pieces of our timeline that we've tossed as trash turn out to be veins of gold. We go dumpster diving into our past expecting only garbage, and we discover the mother lode. For those who think our past precludes us from a powerful partnership with God in the present and future, Esther's story begs us to reconsider. God has been at work in our past where we never expected, preparing us to go to work with him in the world around us. God has chosen us, though others have rejected us, written us off, rebuffed us. Through the pain of what has passed by, God has been preparing us to be part of his rescue and redemption of the world.

Mordecai's single sentence, spoken to Esther on her darkest day, sparks hope that our disenchanted world is actually enchanted; that we've been divinely shadowed since day one; that in some mysterious way, God has been weaving each of our happy and hard circumstances into a divine design so that even we can be part of what he's doing in our world. In short, Mordecai reminds

Esther and us that God's invitation is always for us to engage. No matter what we may not see, God is at work in the world. And he is inviting us to join him. He's urging us to engage—no matter who we are. No matter what others think of us.

The novel *Silence* by Shusaku Endo wrestles with the issue of suffering. In the seventeenth century, two Jesuit priests secretly enter Japan while Christians are being persecuted and martyred. One of the priests, Rodrigues, is eventually betrayed by a Japanese Christian named Kichijiro into the hands of Japanese officials. Just as Judas turned Jesus over to his persecutors, Kichijiro turns Rodrigues over to his persecutors. In prison, he is mentally, physically, and spiritually tortured. He is forced to watch another Christian be killed by the sword. Later, Rodrigues is compelled to watch three Christians wrapped in straw mats be thrown into the ocean to drown. Finally, he is required to watch a group of Christians hung upside down in a pit and tortured. In each case, their lives will be spared if Rodrigues will just renounce his faith in Christ. Through it all, Rodrigues prays and prays. Yet God remains silent. Christ remains silent. Rodrigues wrestles with this silence. Months pass. Rodrigues has never experienced such suffering and such silence. Finally, he has a vision of Christ. Christ says to him, "I understand your pain and your suffering. It is for that reason I am here." Rodrigues responds, "Lord, I resented your silence." Christ answers, "I was not silent. I suffered beside you."[8]

Jesus was more present in this painful world than Rodrigues had first fathomed. And as Rodrigues continued to suffer, that knowledge was transformative. Knowing that Jesus was present in his world, though hidden, gave Rodrigues courage and faith.

Stan Granberg leads a church planting organization called Kairos. He spoke at our congregation a few years ago. Stan told of one of the church plants he started in the northeast United States, where he met a non-Christian woman named Susan. When Stan first met Susan, she said to him, "I don't see God anywhere." As far as she could tell, God was completely uninvolved in her life and in her world. But not long ago, Stan returned to that church plant. Susan was there. She's now a Christian. During the worship service, her hands were lifted in praise. She leaned over to Stan and whispered over the music, "I see God everywhere now!"

Where others might look at the landscape of Esther's life and see only rock and sand, Mordecai saw streams and grass and flowers. He could see God everywhere. A God who had led Esther to this very moment. A God who had prepared her to make a difference. A God who was inviting her to engage.

This same God is present, sometimes in unseen ways, in our world. He is weaving the tapestry of our lives into the Grand Purpose of his Grand Story.[9] And he is urging us to trust in his presence, to desire his partnership, and to get out there and make a difference.

Our Engagement

The moment Esther clarified her conviction that God was entangled in her messy world, she confirmed a course to entangle herself as well. Once you believe God is at work in the world and capable of compelling kings, navigating nations, and making meaning from messes, you'll walk out from behind your watchful walls and get to work in the world—even at the risk of losing your life. Esther responds to Mordecai's line with one of her own: "Then I will go to the king, though it is against the law, and if I perish, I perish" (Esther 4:16).

Mere seconds pass between Mordecai telling of God's engagement in Esther's world and of God's invitation to Esther in verse 14, and Esther sharing her courageous commitment to enlist in God's grand plan in verse 16. But it seems like a lifetime has passed. Esther seems like an entirely different woman in verse

16 than she was before verse 14. In those few seconds, a switch has been flipped. A light has come on. A heart has been renewed. A mind has been transformed. Once Esther perceived that God had been quietly at work in this wounded world to place her in a position to partner with him to alleviate people's pain, she dove into the deep end, signed on the dotted line, raised her hand, and stepped forward—come what may. Once Esther realized that God had selected her while most in her world had spurned her, she accepted God's assignment, even if it meant death. Esther would rather die trying to make a difference with a God to whom she and her world mattered than live making no difference at all.

So must we.

Leo Tolstoy's parable *Two Old Men* tells the tale of two men, Efim and Elisha, who decide that before they die, they must make a pilgrimage to Jerusalem. Their lifelong dream has been to travel to that holy city. One day, they leave together to turn their dream into reality. Along the way, they come to a village filled with sick people. Efim wants to press on to Jerusalem. Elisha wants to stay and help the villagers. Unable to agree with one another, Efim leaves, but Elisha stays.

Elisha nurses the entire village back to health. He depletes the few resources he brought with him, has nothing left to continue his journey to Jerusalem, and thus returns home.

Efim makes it to Jerusalem, sees all the holy sites, does all the holy things, and returns home.

The end.[10]

This story tells of two men with the same dream of journeying to Jerusalem and enjoying its sights. On the way, they encounter a village filled with sick people. One man neglects the hurting and clutches to his dream. The other helps the hurting, using all his resources, and surrenders his dream.

Tolstoy and Esther are telling the same story. There's a God who has placed us on the road at just the right time in just the right place so we can partner with him in helping a hurting world.

But engagement exacts a price.

Plans can perish.

Dreams can die.

In the end, however, the price is worth our participation. Fulfilling our divine purpose, rather than our personal plans, is why we are here in the first place. As Brené Brown writes, "It's not the critic who counts. Not the man who points out how the strong man stumbles, or where the doer of deeds could have done them better. The credit belongs to the man who is actually in the arena, whose face is marred by sweat and dust and blood; who strives valiantly; . . . who at the best knows in the end the triumph of high achievement, and who at the worst, if he fails, at least fails while daring greatly."[11] Brené Brown, like Esther, urges us to get out of the stands and into the area.

So, jump in. Engage. Like Esther, once we understand how mysteriously and meticulously God has worked to bring about our unique purpose and place in his world, we'll exchange our desires for his dreams, our own security for the salvation of others. We'll want nothing more than to partner with God for the rest of our lives, even if it costs us our lives.

Lie Low

A few years ago, over the course of a few months, I experienced several disturbing physical ailments. They felt completely independent from one another—disconnected dots. I soon learned, however, that they all shared a common cause. First, my ears started ringing. Day and night, an unending roar sounded in my ears, sometimes even drowning out conversations. Second, bright lights began to bother me. Whether it was the headlights of an oncoming car or the lights that brightened the stage from which I preached, I grew painfully sensitive to intense illumination. Third, three to five times every week, my head ached so miserably I could not function. I couldn't write sermons. I couldn't hold meetings. All I wanted to do was find a dark room and pull a blanket over myself.

I visited my primary care physician. I saw an ear, nose, and throat specialist. I called upon a neurologist. Finally, they pieced it all together. These multiple symptoms had one source: migraine headaches. Migraines were causing the ringing in my ears, the sensitivity to light, and the intense headaches. Once we discovered an effective treatment for the migraines, the three separate symptoms subsided.

The book of Esther presents two maddening maladies infecting Esther's world: sexual exploitation and racial extermination. They appear to be independent from one another—disconnected dots. But they actually share a common root. Treatment of that cause not only resolves each of these illnesses; it also better enables Esther to partner with God in reenchanting her disenchanted world.

The book of Esther reveals that these deadly disorders ravaging her disenchanted world were multiple manifestations of just one malady: haughtiness. Esther also discloses the one cure for the conditions caused by haughtiness: humility. In Esther, we find that Evil uses the haughty to dismantle the world. God uses the humble to deliver the world.

Here, then, are the two disorders affecting Esther's world—both stemming from the illness of pride or ego.

Malady #1

The world in the book of Esther begins to crumble in chapter 1. We watch in disbelief as the king sexually exploits the women of his kingdom, starting with the queen. After many days of massive feasts, King Ahasuerus commands his queen, Vashti, to place herself on exhibition before his guests—the powerful and propertied of Persia. Just as he has been using rich foods, savory drinks, and luxurious seats and settings to incline the hearts and wallets of Persia's elite toward him and his causes, so now Ahasuerus treats the most well-known woman in the kingdom, Queen Vashti, as another possession—a decoration to be displayed in order to compel his guests to laud and adore him. She is valued only for her external beauty, and that is valued only as a means toward another end—the king's own elevation. When Queen Vashti defends both her gender and her humanity, her own inherent worth, and refuses to be placed on exhibition, the king flies into a rage and banishes her (Esther 1:1–22).

The king is now without a queen. This simply will not do. Not only does it look bad in the eyes of the kingdom, but the king himself has needs only a queen can fulfill. Thus Ahasuerus launches a quest for a new queen. But this is no romantic *Snow White* or *Sleeping Beauty* tale of a royal man seeking true love. Instead, it is the mass abduction and sexual violation of countless young women. The king's advisors recommend that all the "beautiful young virgins" in the kingdom be brought to the king. These young women, Esther included, are caught up in a kingdom-wide kidnapping. They are seized from their homes and transported to the capital city. There, they are treated for twelve months with makeup in order to "make up" for any flaws that might keep them from being fully beautiful (because, heaven knows, a woman can't be beautiful just as she is). Finally, they are forced to spend a night in the king's bed. These young women are objects meant for the king's gratification—tried on like new clothes in a dressing room, picked over like food at a dinner buffet (Esther 2:1–14).

The book of Esther speaks loudly for the many who are victims of objectification and exploitation today. It pulls back the curtain and refuses to keep hidden this ancient and shameful practice of treating girls and women as things to be used for personal pleasure and selfish purpose. We cannot read Esther without the voices of today's countless victims of sex trafficking, domestic abuse, rape, and incest ringing in our ears. Sadly, Esther and all those like her had no #MeToo movement, which might have given them a voice against the powerful men who used their position to abuse and assault these women. They suffered in silence. Yet the narrative's trajectory reminds us that it wasn't absolute silence. An unseen God saw and was at work in this miserable mess, eventually raising

Esther to a place where she and he could partner together to fundamentally change the culture and the power structure.

But here, as it always is, sexual exploitation is driven by ego and self-centeredness: a man who believes himself and his needs to be at the center of his world treats all others, especially women, as a means to his end.

Malady #2

The second ruinous disease that plagues the narrative of Esther runs a course through most of the book.

> After these things King Ahasuerus promoted Haman the
> Agagite, the son of Hammedatha, and advanced him and
> set his throne above all the officials who were with him.
> And all the king's servants who were at the king's gate
> bowed down and paid homage to Haman, for the king
> had so commanded concerning him. But Mordecai did
> not bow down or pay homage. . . . And when Haman saw
> that Mordecai did not bow down or pay homage to him,
> Haman was filled with fury. But he disdained to lay hands
> on Mordecai alone. So, as they had made known to him
> the people of Mordecai, Haman sought to destroy all the
> Jews, the people of Mordecai, throughout the whole king-
> dom of Ahasuerus. (Esther 3:1–2, 5–6)

Haman is the second most powerful man in what is probably the most powerful kingdom on earth. The entire nation bows before him. Yet this is not enough. Haman the Gentile nurses a grudge toward Mordecai the Jew, because the Jew will not bow before the Gentile. Bigotry emboldens him to find a way to not just force this Jew into line, but to end his life—and to end the life of every Jew in Babylon.

Esther's narrative reveals how racism and hatred targeted toward one person can swiftly spiral into racism and hatred targeted toward an entire population. Within two sentences, Haman's bigotry toward Mordecai the Jew ballooned into bigotry toward all Jews. When we permit ourselves the sinful delight of self-centered supremacy over just one person due to their race, class, gender, or orientation, that single seed can grow into an unfathomable crop. And with the rising of the sun, we'll find our heart has poisoned against all who are just like that one. We'll find ourselves feeling superior to all who share that person's race, class, gender, or orientation—and willing to treat them all as inferior.

And, as we've seen in Chapter Three, Haman's rage toward Mordecai and toward all the Jews in Persia is likely rooted in a simmering disdain that Haman's people have nurtured toward the Jews from the time the Jews first fled across the desert to escape slavery in Egypt (Deut. 25). Haman, a descendent of the Amalekites who persecuted the Jews in the desert (Esther 3:1), seems to have carried his forefather's racial bias against the Jews, like a disease passed from one generation to another.

Rooted in Ego

Two tragic situations: the sexual exploitation of women and the viral spread of racism. They may appear to be disconnected. Yet in each case, the culprit causing the disease is the same: ego. Both dilemmas are caused by the same virus: ego. The belief that the world revolves around me. The conviction that I matter more than others. The position that says my plans, priorities, and perspectives are more valuable than everyone else's.

Ego leads to sexual exploitation. The king's sense of self-importance was so elevated that when Queen Vashti refused to take her place in the parade of possessions, he threw her out. He also refused to treat the young women of his kingdom as humans.

Instead, he skimmed the cream of the crop and raped them, leaving them unfit for marriages of their own. This, too, grew out of ego.

Ego leads to racial extermination. Haman's sense of self-importance was so elevated that when Mordecai wouldn't bow before him, he not only wanted to kill him; he wanted to kill anyone who shared his race. The plan for racial extermination was hatched out of Haman's unhealthy belief in his own importance. It grew out of ego.

Haman's hubris is further revealed when Mordecai terminates a plan to end the king's life. His heroics are noted in the royal records and then tragically forgotten. Early one morning, when insomnia plagues the king, he flips through the records and remembers Mordecai's good deed.

The king wants to honor Mordecai, so he seeks suggestions on how to honor such an outstanding person. Fortunately, Haman, has requested an audience with the king. He too wishes to discuss Mordecai. Ironically, Haman wants to talk about how to execute Mordecai. The king hopes to brainstorm about how to exalt Mordecai.

The king asks Haman a simple question: "What should be done to the man whom the king delights to honor?" (Esther 6:6). On the surface, the question is not even about Mordecai, and Haman has selective hearing. Because of his hubris, he makes assumptions. His personal agendas filter his interpretation. As a result, he endures a public humiliation—one of his own doing. One he will never forget:

> So Haman came in, and the king said to him, "What should be done to the man whom the king delights to honor?" And Haman said to himself, "Whom would the king delight to honor more than me?" And Haman

said to the king, "For the man whom the king delights
to honor, let royal robes be brought, which the king
has worn, and the horse that the king has ridden, and
on whose head a royal crown is set. And let the robes
and the horse be handed over to one of the king's most
noble officials. Let them dress the man whom the king
delights to honor, and let them lead him on the horse
through the square of the city, proclaiming before him:
'Thus shall it be done to the man whom the king delights
to honor.'" Then the king said to Haman, "Hurry; take
the robes and the horse, as you have said, and do so to
Mordecai the Jew, who sits at the king's gate. Leave out
nothing that you have mentioned." (Esther 6:6–10)

Haman is so distraught at this public shaming, brought about by
his own hand, that he runs home with his head covered (Esther
6:12). All of this is a window into Haman's pride and ego. It's what
births the story's racial extermination. It's the same quality found
in the king that gives rise to the story's sexual exploitation.

In the sixth century, Pope Gregory I proposed that pride was
the root cause of all other sins plaguing the human race. Pride,
he believed, even gave birth to the seven deadly sins.[1] If the seven
deadly sins were branches on a tree, pride was the root of the tree.
No sin was equal in its pernicious power. This conclusion was
reached in the book of Esther, long before Gregory I.

The world of Esther has been described as disenchanted, a
world in which it appears as if God is gone. It's a world where
women are sexually exploited, minorities and the marginal are
abused, and political power is used to gain popularity. The overwhelming cause for this disenchantment is one thing: ego, or
pride—the conviction that I mean more than the masses around
me. Esther reveals that the moment I begin believing I am to be

prized more than other people, the world begins to feel as if God is completely gone. It gives birth to a world filled with all kinds of vile vices—so much so that it may appear as if the Almighty is absent.

Ego Today

Ryan Holiday is the author of the book *Ego Is the Enemy*. He walks briefly through the lives of people like Steve Jobs, Malcolm X, Bill Belichick, Vince Lombardi, John Wooden, Howard Hughes, Lance Armstrong, Jackie Robinson, Benjamin Franklin, Angela Merkel, and others. He shows how, again and again, those who were motivated by ego experienced fallout and were driven to hatred and harmful goals. Those motivated by humility, ego's opposite, experienced fruitfulness and were driven to compassion and constructive goals.

Ego, Holiday proposes, is *the* underlying problem of the human race. It is the cause of every bad news story in the headlines. Holiday arrived at such a deep conviction about ego's danger that he had it inked in his skin. On his right forearm, he tattooed the words "Ego is the Enemy."[2]

In a series on the seven deadly sins, I recently spoke to my congregation on the seriousness of pride. A few weeks later, a mother approached me. "Thank you for your sermon on pride," she said. "As a parent, I've come to believe that pride is *the* primary sin most endangering my children. There's such a spirit of competition among children today and such a temptation to desire to be elevated above their peers. And it's the complete antithesis of the spirit of Christ." She went on to explain how she's dedicating all of her parenting skills to attacking pride and ego in her kids. She agrees with Ryan Holiday and Esther: ego is the enemy.

A few years ago, as part of her undergraduate program, my daughter Jordan studied abroad in Vienna, Austria. One week, she traveled with forty-three students to Poland. There, they spent time at Auschwitz. It was a heavy moment for these young hearts. They walked through the gate with its empty promise: "Work will make you free." They toured the gas chambers. They witnessed the place where the trains spewed out millions of Jews and others. They walked through the spaces where one and a half million victims were murdered.

That evening, they ate dinner with Lydia. Lydia was a young girl when she and her family were taken to Auschwitz. Thankfully, she lived to tell the story of all those who didn't survive. Lydia showed Jordan and her friends the ghostly blue ink on her skin. She still has her camp number inked into her body. It is as if someone had tattooed on Lydia, "Ego is the Enemy."

How does something like Auschwitz happen? Ego. The belief that one person or one group or one nation is better than another. It's the conviction that the world revolves around one nation or race or person. It's the disease that unraveled the world of Esther. It's the plague that ravaged the world of Lydia. It's the illness still infecting our world today. Slay it, and you just might save the world.

Hannah Arendt's controversial book *Eichmann in Jerusalem* explores this truth.[3] Adolf Eichmann, the Nazi lieutenant colonel responsible for transporting Jews to concentration camps, escaped Germany after World War II and made his way to Argentina. In 1960, Israeli intelligence operatives captured Eichmann and brought him to Jerusalem to face charges of crimes against the Jewish people. Arendt attended the trial and wrote about it in a series of articles, which eventually became a book. The heart of the controversy surrounding Arendt's writing was her assertion that Eichmann wasn't the monster everyone wanted him to be. He was, instead, remarkably normal. He was, she believed, not driven by some grand and epic vision of world victory. Instead, he was motivated by something far more personal:

> For when I speak of the banality of evil, I do so only
> on the strictly factual level, pointing to a phenomenon
> which stared one in the face at the trial. Eichmann
> was not Iago and not Macbeth, and nothing would
> have been farther from his mind than to determine
> with Richard III "to prove a villain." Except for an
> extraordinary diligence in looking out for his personal
> advancement, he had no motives at all.[4]

The advancement of self seems to have contributed greatly, at least from Arendt's perspective, to one of history's greatest atrocities. What he was doing was "looking out for his personal advancement." And it was this pride, this ego, that drove him to murderous ends.

Humility

The book of Esther reveals the one quality capable of rescuing humanity from bigots and braggarts. It is the only virtue with the capacity to overcome inequality and injustice. This trait alone topples the powers who use the marginal as a means to their end. It is humility.

In King Xerxes and Haman, we find what happens when life is lived "full of me." The end result is intolerance, scandals, hatred, and the attempt to destroy all who are different. In Esther, we find what happens when life is lived "free of me." The end result is love, courage, and the sacrifice of self to save all.

The book leaves us with one of the most crucial choices in life. Will we live "full of me" or "free of me"?[5] Will we chose vanity or humility? One will rip the world apart. The other will stitch it back together.

God uses Mordecai to lead Esther down the path of humility:

> And they told Mordecai what Esther had said. Then
> Mordecai told them to reply to Esther, "Do not think

to yourself that in the king's palace you will escape any
more than all the other Jews. For if you keep silent at
this time, relief and deliverance will rise for the Jews
from another place, but you and your father's house will
perish. And who knows whether you have not come to
the kingdom for such a time as this?" (Esther 4:12–14)

Mordecai is trying to make a case for Esther to get involved. She
wishes to remain behind the scenes. Mordecai presses for her to
get to the frontlines. After all, she's the only one in a position to
do so. Only she has a shot at influencing the king who can, in turn,
influence Haman.

The way Mordecai motivates Esther is fascinating. Negatively,
he reveals that if Esther stays on the sidelines, she and her family
will be consumed by the very evil she's trying to avoid: "For if you
keep silent at this time . . . you and your father's house will perish."
Through the mouth of Mordecai, the book of Esther reveals that
those who remain speechless or sluggish in the face of injustice
against others will be swept away by the torrent of the very terror
they are ignoring.

Positively, Mordecai reveals that God's been at work in the
background to get Esther to this position so that she has the
resources and opportunity to make a difference: "And who knows
whether you have not come to the kingdom for such a time as this?"
God's invested years in placing Esther in this exact spot at this
exact second she can leverage her influence to save her people.

But just as Mordecai is making a case for Esther's involve-
ment, notice what else he says: "For if you keep silent at this
time, relief and deliverance will rise for the Jews from another
place." Mordecai wants Esther to realize that as God seeks a way
to confront Haman's racism and intolerance, Esther is a *desired*
instrument, but she isn't *decisive*. Esther is God's *preference*. She is

not, however, God's *prerequisite*. God has the capacity and audacity to choose anyone else to rescue the Jews from the grip of Haman.

Mordecai understands that when it comes to any particular mission, we are *valuable* to God, but we are not *vital*. God wants to employ us. God labors diligently in history to arrange things so that he can use us in a chosen moment in time. But God is so supreme, he could just as easily utilize another in our place, in spite of our suitability for the task.

This sharp statement is intended to cultivate within Esther and us the one quality so absent in Esther's world and ours: humility. Mordecai has seen what happens when one human puts himself on the top rung of the ladder. He's witnessed the results of a nation embracing the ultimate "Persia First" policy. When the world is full of me, whoever "me" happens to be, the result is a nightmare. Mordecai seeks to end the nightmare by cultivating within just one person the antidote of humility. If even one person like Esther can be gripped by the force of lowliness, there just might be hope.

Thankfully, Mordecai's message finds an open heart. Esther spends the next three days in prayer and fasting. This is not the posture of one who believes the world revolves around her. It is not the stance of one who sees herself higher than all the rest. This is the posture of humility. Esther's desperation to be "free of me" is what God uses to save the world from those who are "full of me." Haman's pride and ego rip the world apart. Esther's humility stitches it back together again.

How Humility Saves the World

I recently visited the second largest faith-based primary care provider in the nation. I was shocked to learn they are based right here in Memphis. Christ Community Health Services has eight clinics situated in "health deserts"—low-income neighborhoods of metro Memphis where health care is nearly nonexistent. In these eight clinics, they serve more than sixty thousand patients a year. From primary care to dentistry, HIV treatment to cancer screening, behavior health to women's health to spiritual health and beyond, Christ Community Health Services seeks to mend body and soul in the name of Christ. It's a massive operation. They are literally saving lives. Tens of thousands every year.

How? One word: humility.

My friend and his wife turned down a tenure-track position in a world-class Christian university and a senior pastorate in a Chicago neighborhood whose average income was $120,000 so they could both work for CCHS in neighborhoods where the average income is often far less than $20,000.

Humility.

He told me about a lead doctor in one of the CCHS clinics. A patient came in one morning suffering from incontinence. As the patient made his way down the hallway to the patient room to see the doctor, he urinated, wetting his clothes and the floor. The doctor cleaned the embarrassed patient, took his clothes, and gave him a dry gown. Then the doctor went the extra mile. Or two. Or three. The doctor went home, grabbed an extra set of his own clothes, returned to the clinic and dressed the patient in his own clothes.

Humility.

Ego may destroy the world. Humility may save it. It's what we see in Esther. It's what we see in Jesus:

> Do nothing from selfish ambition or conceit, but in
> humility count others more significant than yourselves.
> Let each of you look not only to his own interests, but
> also to the interests of others. Have this mind among
> yourselves, which is yours in Christ Jesus, who, though
> he was in the form of God, did not count equality with

God a thing to be grasped, but emptied himself, by
taking the form of a servant, being born in the likeness
of men. And being found in human form, he humbled
himself by becoming obedient to the point of death,
even death on a cross. (Phil. 2:3–8)

Jesus emptied himself. There was no trace of ego. Not a crumb
of self-promotion or self-interest. All that remained by the time
Jesus got to the cross was humility. Jesus's humility saved the world.
Esther's humility that saved a nation. What could be saved through
your humility?

Contrary to some misconceptions about humility, it is not
about beating ourselves up or belittling ourselves. Humility is
a discipline rooted in a renewed view of self. "Humility," John
Ortberg proposes, "has to do with a submitted willingness. It
involves a healthy self-forgetfulness . . . the realization that the
universe does not revolve around us."[6] Self-forgetfulness, not self-
hatred, is the starting point for humility. David Benner writes
that "Christian spirituality involves a transformation of the self
that occurs only when God and self are both deeply known. Both,
therefore, have an important place in Christian spirituality. There
is no deep knowing of God without a deep knowing of self, and no
deep knowing of self without a deep knowing of God."[7] Therefore,
we must come to a true understanding of just who we truly are if
we desire to know just who God truly is. Benner also writes that
many misunderstand this point of humility. Many Christians see
themselves primarily as sinners. This is only half the truth: "You
are not only a sinner; you are a deeply loved sinner. And there is all
the difference in the world between the two."[8] Esther's story doesn't
call us to think of ourselves as useless or expendable. Rather,
her narrative invites us to consider ourselves appropriately—as
people bent toward ourselves yet nonetheless deeply loved by this

backstage God and called to live for his purposes and passions rather than our own.

Learn to lie low. Think more of others than of yourself. Center on them, not on self. Do this, and your world will become a lot more enchanted.

5

PRAY BRAVE

The lives of Jim and Cheryl White were featured in the 2015 Disney movie *McFarland, USA*. Jim taught for forty years in the economically challenged farming town of McFarland, California. For twenty of those years, he coached, building a cross-country team from scratch that won nine state championships. His athletes were mostly the children of poor, immigrant fieldworkers who had never run competitively. The cross-country team enabled many of them to escape poverty by gaining athletic scholarships to attend college. Some of them even returned to the McFarland area to work.

The movie depicts a moment when Jim and Cheryl are tempted to leave McFarland. The pay is low. The neighborhood, in decline, is feeling dangerous. It would be nice to find a school in a city with a higher salary and more safety. Cheryl leaves the decision in Jim's hands, but with this caveat: "It's your decision, OK? And I know it's hard. But, please don't just let this be about our safety."[1]

The movie portrays the Whites caught in a tension between the profitable and the perilous, between the comfortable and the chancy, between doing what is safe and doing what is substantial. In the end, the Whites stayed. The lives of many young people in an impoverished community were enriched because the Whites endured discomfort. Their decision in the film hinged on Cheryl's statement: "But, please don't just let this be about our safety."

No individual or institution can make a difference and also play it safe. We can never sincerely serve others while also seeking to save ourselves. It's like wanting to swim to the rescue of those drowning at sea while also wishing to cling to the dock. At some point, we've got to plunge from the pier and brave the waves. If we covet a life full of significance, we must choose one free from security. The kingdom doesn't come through those who crave comfort. The world is changed by people willing to be wounded. No one models this better than Esther.

A Dangerous Decision

Esther portrays a safety-last posture. It's a stance that is surprising, given the fact that, for most of her life, decisions were made for her. Her entire life seems determined by the commands of others. This would make it especially difficult to then turn around and make a risky decision for herself.

- Esther has no voice in who raises her once she is orphaned. That determination is made for her.
- Esther has no vote in where she lives. Like countless other Jews, she's been forcibly exiled to Persia. This ruling was made without her assent.
- Esther has no say in whether or not she participates in the king's search for a new queen among the beautiful young women of Persia. She is taken from her home

in Persia and placed in the king's harem. If she doesn't please the king, she will be sent back to the harem. She cannot return to her family. She cannot marry.[2]

- Esther has no choice when the king crowns her queen. Though the royal position may be better than the alternative, it carries its own risks.

Then one day, Esther is finally faced with a ruling that is all hers to make. It is a selection that has everything to do with her safety and security. Having made few decisions during the course of her life, she now must make one of the most dangerous decisions a person can make.

Esther learns that the king's right-hand man, Haman, has manipulated the king into signing a royal order to exterminate the Jews. On one specific day, the Jewish people of Persia will be purged—all because of the egotism and racism of one man. It will be one of the most egregious moments of genocide in history.

There's only one person who can stop the slaughter—the king. And there's only one person who can stop the king—Esther. But in order to do so, in order to engage, Esther must risk her own life. She must let go of the dock and brave the waves. Esther's only move is to plead her case before the king. But unless she's summoned first, she'll be put to death for making this move (Esther 4:11). In Esther's world, she cannot simply march up to the king and demand he halt Haman's plan. Anyone, even the queen, who approaches the king without first being invited by him risks their own execution. It's been thirty days since the king has called for Esther. To barge into his presence now is to put her life in his hands—and thus far in the drama, the king's hands are not faithful, compassionate, or trustworthy. Yet Esther is the only person who even has a shot. If the Jews are to be rescued, Esther has to take a risk.

For the first time in her life, Esther has a compelling choice to make entirely on her own. It's a decision that can make the difference between life and death. But to engage in her disenchanted world will be dangerous.

We have every reason to believe Esther will stumble with this staggering choice. She hardly has the life experience or the mentoring and coaching that would lead her to successfully navigate one of life's major "firsts." It seems that fear would win the day, or uncertainty might gain the upper hand.

But they don't. Esther boldly steps into the gap. The first verse of chapter 5 calls Ahasuerus "king" three times. Three times, the word "royal" or "royalty" is used. Esther is stepping into another world when she steps into this verse—the royal world of the king.[3] Undaunted, she steps into this world and walks until she is in the king's sightline, directly across from, but not inside, the throne room where he is seated (Esther 5:1). By placing herself squarely in the king's field of vision, she has essentially violated the law. She is not eye-to-eye with a devoted husband delighted to see his beloved wife. She is eye-to-eye with a dicey despot who, given his behavior toward his last queen, is likely to sign her death warrant.

Thankfully, Esther catches the king on a good day. She wins his favor and is able to make her case (Esther 5:2). The first time up to bat in life's decision-making game, Esther hits a homerun. She chooses courage over convenience. She chooses to risk her life in arguing the king out of a royal order rather than safely sitting on the sidelines.

Living in a world from which it seemed a silent God retreated and over which spiteful people ruled, given the choice of serving others or saving herself, Esther demonstrated uncommon courage in choosing to engage her world, endanger herself, and make a difference.

The kind of courage Esther displayed was the "twenty seconds of insane courage" revealed in the 2011 film *We Bought a Zoo*. The film was based on the true story of a British man named Benjamin Mee. In 2006, Mee and his family purchased and moved into a thirty-acre zoo. In his book with the same title, Mee says that his new "neighbors" included five Siberian tigers, three African lions, nine wolves, three big brown European bears, four Asian short-clawed otters, two flamingos, and a Brazilian tapir called Ronnie.[4] The zoo was run-down and on the verge of being shut down. Mee faced a series of challenges to resurrect the zoo, including a rat infestation, fundraising, and a jaguar that escaped and endangered the neighborhood.

In the book, Mee and his family are shown around the zoo by a man named Nick, and Mee confesses that he knows nothing about zoos. Nick replies, "Oh, there's no reason for you to know about zoos in order to buy one. You'd have to be a bit mad, but I assume you've got that part covered."[5] In the film version, Mee continues, "Sometimes all you need is twenty seconds of insane courage. Just literally twenty seconds of embarrassing bravery. And I promise you, something great will come of it."[6] There is truth in this statement. If you really want to make a difference in a world that appears disenchanted, if you truly wish to engage your world rather than play it safe, all you need is about twenty seconds of insane courage. That's about all the time it would have taken Esther to break the traditions, enter the king's presence at risk of her life, and instigate a plan to topple Haman and rescue her people. It took weeks to work out that plan, but about twenty seconds of insane courage boosted that plan off the launch pad.

The Prayer for Courage

Where did Esther get this courage? How did an orphan exiled from her homeland, kidnapped from her bedroom, and sexually abused by the most powerful man in the kingdom gain the audacity to take on his right-hand man in a fight for her people's survival? In a story of personal perplexity and divine puzzlement, Esther's grit and pluck grew out of a surprising place—prayer:

> Then Esther told them to reply to Mordecai, "Go, gather all the Jews to be found in Susa, and hold a fast on my behalf, and do not eat or drink for three days, night or day. I and my young women will also fast as you do. Then I will go to the king, though it is against the law, and if I perish, I perish." (Esther 4:15–16)

It was only after Esther spent three days fasting and praying that she found the courage to risk her life and rescue her people (when the Old Testament mentions fasting, it always assumes praying). For Esther, twenty seconds of courage came from 259,000 seconds of prayer. The most courageous thing Esther did was not stepping into the throne room to talk to the Persian king. It was stepping into her bedroom to talk to the heavenly King. The reason Esther had bravery to confront one who could take her life was that she had spent three days praying to the one who had given her life. The courage to make costly yet compelling choices grows out of passionate prayer.

This is one of the key disciplines Esther models for living in a disenchanted world. Making a difference when you can't always tell if God is there and when you're not sure you can bear the cost requires insane courage. This courage grows from passionate prayer. If we want to be brave, we've got to first pray brave.

Jesus modeled this discipline. It took mere seconds for Jesus to let Judas kiss him and to say to Judas, "Friend, do what you came to do" (Matt. 26:50). Those words set into motion Jesus's eventual crucifixion—the most costly yet compelling choice Jesus would ever make. It took seconds of insane courage for Jesus to make this decision. From where did this courage arise? It's no coincidence that a time of significant prayer in the Garden of Gethsemane preceded this momentous movement to the cross. The courage to make costly yet compelling choices grows out of passionate prayer.

The book of Esther is designed to draw our attention to her pause for prayer.[7] The narrative is filled with feasting. Five feasts are held before Esther's three-day turning point. Five feasts are held after it. Esther's fasting (and prayer) flies in the face of her culture's feasting. Her three-day benediction is the sole break in an unending flow of banquets. It's impossible not to notice it. Esther's pluck grows from this time of prayer.

Those seeking the grit and the determination to make a difference in a disenchanted world will find it by first doing what seems most counterintuitive—doing nothing. Pausing. Stopping. Bowing down. And praying. Prayerfulness leads to an unimaginable fearlessness.

Beyond Courage

At Highland, we're becoming good friends with many people in China. We're also becoming good friends with people who are partnering with us to minister to those in China. One partner we are especially fond of is a man who lives in Singapore named Winston. Winston and his wife were once in Shanghai, China, meeting with a gathering of Chinese Christians in a house church. A young Chinese woman who was pregnant with her second child was at this gathering. That doesn't sound remarkable or unusual to many of us. But to her and those in that house church, it was a particularly painful and dangerous situation. The child growing within her was illegal. China had a one-child policy at that time. The life within her was child number two. The mother had come to this little house church desperate for help. She asked Winston and his wife what she should do with the forbidden child growing within her.

They regretfully walked through the only options they could think of or imagine. Option one was the only legal option according to the government. The mother should abort this child. But she could not fathom doing this. Option two was to find a large amount of money and use it to bribe several Chinese officials and to have the record of this child's birth falsified to indicate he was actually child number one. But there was no way the mother could secure this amount of money. In addition, she didn't feel right about doing this. Option number three was to simply have the child. There would be grave financial and cultural consequences for her, the child, and her family.

Winston told her, "We don't know what you should do." He said, "Let's pray about it." So they prayed and prayed. Weeks passed. The woman returned to her home. Winston and his wife returned to Singapore. And the praying continued.

Then one evening, Winston turned on his television and heard the reporter announcing news of a major change in Chinese policy: "The Chinese government announced that the one-child policy would now be abolished. Chinese families are allowed now to have two children."

Not long afterward, in Winston's inbox was an email from the woman in China. "Did you hear the good news?" she asked. They couldn't believe how God had answered not only their prayers, but also the prayers of thousands and perhaps millions of others who had been begging God for this very change.

Those are the kinds of things that happen when people pray courageously. You not only find twenty seconds of insane courage to change some little corner of the world; you also become part of God's unbelievable efforts to change the entire world.

It's the same spirit we see in the early church. Luke records for us in Acts 2 and the following chapters how the church grew by leaps and bounds with lives being changed day and night. This happened in the face of hostility and adversity. But Acts 2 grew out of Acts 1. Luke records in Acts 1 how a large number of followers of Jesus had gathered and "were devoting themselves to prayer" (Acts 1:14). Where did the courage and audacity of Acts 2 come from? It grew from the passionate prayers of Acts 1.

Esther and countless like her were victims of government-sanctioned sexual abuse. Her people were targets of unfathomable racism. Yet Esther's first move was not invasion. It was invocation. Esther's step one was not a call to punish those abusing power. Instead, it was a call for prayer. Esther knew that without submissive supplication, she would have neither the open doors nor the courageous heart needed to wage war against the evil in the land.

In a world where daily headlines continue to reveal heart-wrenching misogyny and bigotry, mind-blowing tragedy and tyranny, it's time for God's people to follow the lead of this bright star named Esther. It's time for the church to fall on our knees and fast and pray for God to put an end to these evils, and to use us if he will.

What Esther models is what Richard Foster calls the practice of "radical prayer": "Radical Prayer refuses to let us stay on the fringes of life's great issues. It dares us to believe that things can be different. Its aim is the total transformation of person, institutions, and societies."[8] Through a passionate practice of radical prayer, we take on the giants in our land, the walls standing in our way, and the mountains and valleys hemming us in. Prayer moves beyond our narrow concerns for personal success or safety into much broader concerns related to businesses, governments, justice, and the fate of those outside our circle.

One expression of this is "praying the news." After the 2016 U.S. presidential election, Sister Susan Francois gained significant attention when people learned she was tweeting a prayer every day to President Trump. When interviewed by NPR, she commented that it grew out of her discipline of "praying the news." For more than fifteen years, she's reviewed the day's headlines and lifted up all those local and global issues to God in prayer.[9] To "pray the news" is one aspect of "radical prayer." Radical prayer believes that behind the critics and conflicts looming so large in our world is a backstage God with even greater power. So pray brave. It's a sure defense against the disenchantment.

6

TREASURE

God's name appears nowhere in the book of Esther. Not once does the name above every name surface in the scroll. This book in the book about God is shockingly silent about God.

Many other names do appear. The names of ten men close the book like weathered headstones:

1. Parshandatha
2. Dalphon
3. Aspatha
4. Poratha
5. Adalia
6. Aridatha
7. Parmashta
8. Arisai
9. Aridai
10. Vaizatha

These ten perished in a massive battle that shook Susa, the citadel of the kingdom of Persia. In previous conflicts, Persia prevailed over countless peoples in the ancient world, including Queen Esther's Jewish brothers and sisters. But on this day in Susa, emboldened by Esther, the Jewish people prevailed against a Persian assault.

Five hundred were killed by the Jews in the clash. We are given the names of only ten of these casualties (Esther 9:7–9).

In the Hebrew text of Esther, these names are listed one by one, each name falling under the other. Our eyes are drawn to each name. We cannot just read quickly over them.[1] We are forced to linger.

The list reminds us of the rolls of names recorded in places like the Vietnam Veterans Memorial Wall or the 9/11 memorial. Catalogues of names like this remind us that the fallen are real people. They had faces mothers had memorized. They came from places filled with friends. They meant something to someone.

But these ten names meant nothing to the most important person in their lives, because God meant nothing to him.

As we've seen, the book of Esther describes a season of life we might call "disenchanted."[2] A disenchanted season is a time when God seems inactive and inattentive—a moment when his name appears nowhere on the list of credits in the movie of our lives.

At a micro level, this is often what we experience when suffering happens. When cancer hits, tornadoes roar through, or relationships rip apart, we enter disenchantment. We assume God is as far away as the normal life we once knew and loved.

At a macro level, our culture appears to be experiencing a form of disenchantment. In the Western world, large numbers feel as if God is not an active part of human life in general. Fifteen hundred years ago, our culture was more open to the possibility of a God who participated spiritedly in the happenings of the events of day-to-day life. Not anymore. We live in disenchanted times.

We live in a season like Esther. A moment when it's hard to hear God's voice. Difficult to discern his activity. No parting of the Red Sea. No falling of the walls of Jericho. Not even the name of God. Not once.

Something happens when we begin to think that God has checked out, that he's jumped in his car and we can no longer see his taillights. What happens is that we check out on others. We figure that if God has checked out on us, we'll just check out on everyone else.

It's the same thing that happened to the people in a parable Jesus told in Matthew 21. The master of a house retreated to another country. How did those who stayed behind react? They beat, stoned, and killed the master's servants so they could have more of the master's stuff (Matt. 21:33–41). Because the master retreated, they rationalized their mistreatment of others. This is the response of Haman in the book of Esther when it comes to these ten names.

In Esther, Haman represents all who believe God is uninvolved in human life and are therefore justified in devaluing human life. In Esther, we find "Haman's principle": the less involved we believe God to be in human life, the more justified we can be in devaluing human life.

For Haman, this leads to the cheapening of the life of his own sons—the ones standing behind these ten names. And it leads to the near slaughter of the Jewish people—those considered minorities, the marginal, and the "monsters" of his day.

Worth Nothing

The ten names near the end of the story of Esther are recorded not merely because they are casualties of conflict. They are casualties of conceit. These are Haman's sons, and they ultimately die because Haman believes he, not God, stands at the center of the world. Haman's self-centering, his decentering of God, leads to such a devaluing of life that even his sons lose all worth in his eyes.

Haman sees a world in which God plays no part and he plays the solo part. And even though he is number two in the Persian kingdom, he demands subservience from everyone in the kingdom. His wish is his command. The entire dynasty falls at his feet—except one. Mordecai will not bow. This sends Haman into a free fall:

> And Haman went out that day joyful and glad of heart. But when Haman saw Mordecai in the king's gate, that he neither rose nor trembled before him, he was filled with wrath against Mordecai. Nevertheless, Haman restrained himself and went home, and he sent and brought his friends and his wife Zeresh. And Haman recounted to them the splendor of his riches, the number of his sons, all the promotions with which the king had honored him, and how he had advanced him above the officials and the servants of the king. Then Haman said, "Even Queen Esther let no one but me come with the king to the feast she prepared. And tomorrow also I am invited by her together with the king. Yet all this is worth nothing to me, so long as I see Mordecai the Jew sitting at the king's gate." Then his wife Zeresh and all his friends said to him, "Let a gallows fifty cubits high be made, and in the morning tell the king to have Mordecai hanged upon it. Then go joyfully with the king to the feast." This idea pleased Haman, and he had the gallows made. (Esther 5:9–14)

Haman gathers his wife and his wise friends. In their presence, he "recounts." This word means to count, to add up, to list. Haman "adds up" two inventories. On the one hand, Haman recounts a list that includes numerous things:

- The splendor of his riches
- All the promotions with which the king had honored him

- How the king had advanced him above the officials and servants of the king
- The fact that Queen Esther had invited him and no other to the feast with the king
- The number of his sons

Your "What's right in my life?" list might look a lot different than Haman's. But if you lived in ancient Persia, and you were Haman, and this was your list, things couldn't look any better. Haman's wallet is fat. He's been promoted fast and far by the king. He's been noticed by the queen. Just as importantly, he's the father of ten sons. In the ancient Orient, it was considered a great gift to have many sons. This was especially true in Persia.[3] Haman's ten boys round out the first list Haman recounts.

But Haman's not done recounting. His accounting involves two lists. In his other hand is the second inventory. It is a list of one: Mordecai the Jew sitting at the king's gate. Haman has the reverence of 99.999 percent of those living within the empire. But he does not have the satisfaction of seeing this one person of another race submit himself to Haman's superiority. Haman has everything else. But because he does not have Mordecai's deference, he looks at the first list in light of the second list, makes a calculation, and reaches this shocking conclusion: "Yet all this is worth *nothing* to me, so long as I see Mordecai the Jew sitting at the king's gate" (Esther 5:13—emphasis mine).

As he undertakes this life accounting, Haman concludes that List One is worth nothing because of List Two. Forget for a moment the items on List One, such as the mountainous bank account and the corner office. Consider this item: "the number of his sons." When Haman says, "Yet all *this* is worth *nothing* to me," *this* includes ten living, breathing children who call him Dad.

This word "nothing" is no stranger to Haman's mouth. He's used it before to indicate just how little he values others. "Nothing" is the same word Haman tosses at the king when he says it is not to the king's "profit" to keep the Jewish people around:

> Then Haman said to King Ahasuerus, "There is a certain people scattered abroad and dispersed among the peoples in all the provinces of your kingdom. Their laws are different from those of every other people, and they do not keep the king's laws, so that it is not to the king's *profit* to tolerate them." (Esther 3:8—emphasis mine)

There is no *profit* to be found in people of Jewish heritage, argues Haman. These minorities, these marginal misfits, are worth *nothing*—especially when you can't even get one of them like Mordecai to acknowledge his mediocrity next to Haman.

Similarly, Haman sees no profit in his own sons. We might anticipate a white supremacist adoring his own children. We would expect a radical terrorist to embrace his own toddlers. Not Haman. Haman sees his ten sons as worthless. What profit comes from possessing them when they fail as a means to the only end that matters—Haman's unquestioned supremacy over every ethnicity in the empire? Haman thus plans the murder of Mordecai and the genocide of the Jews. He will massacre these monsters. His rage will unleash a conflict so heated it will, in the end, consume his own sons who are sent to fight and are killed in the conflict. But Haman couldn't care less, because they are, just like everyone else around him, worthless.

These sons weren't the only casualty of this attitude. Ancient Persia was a place where youth were diminished and demeaned for the policies and purposes of adults. King Xerxes used the young virgins of the country to satiate his ego and libido. One by one, they were dragged to his bedroom to please him. If he remained unsatisfied, the girl was banished to the royal harem, which was, in essence, a detention center. In addition, ancient historian Herodotus reports that five hundred young boys were packed to the Persian court each year, emasculated, and forced to serve as eunuchs for the king.[4] The king's second-in-command, Haman, counted his ten sons as nothing, causing them to lose their lives in his quest for greater control in the kingdom. Esther is the only child in the entire story ever treated with care and compassion. Because one person (Mordecai) spoke up for her when she was homeless and voiceless, an entire world was changed.

Haman represents all who believe God is uninvolved in human life and are therefore justified in devaluing human life. This is "Haman's principle": the less involved we believe God to be in human life, the more justified we can be in devaluing human life.

Instrumental versus Intrinsic

What we find in Haman is a way of viewing humans that sees them as possessing "instrumental" worth. This is contrasted by ethicists and philosophers who view humans as possessing "intrinsic" worth. *Intrinsic worth* means people possess value within themselves. People have inherent worth. Merit is carved into who they are. *Instrumental worth* means people have value only if they can lead to or produce something else valuable. Alone, they have little to no worth.

Kenneth Feinberg was forced to come to terms with this distinction. He was a New York attorney specializing in mediation and dispute resolution. He was best known for his role as special master of the Federal September 11 Victim Compensation Fund.

In calculating the amount of compensation due to each 9/11 victim's family, the law required Feinberg to award greater funds to the stockbroker, the bond trader, and the banker than to the waiter, the policeman, the fireman, or the soldier. According to the law, the settlement for death had to be directly related to the financial circumstances of each victim. The greater the net worth of the person who died, the greater the payment to the family. This is a view of humans based on instrumental worth.

While it may seem sensible, Feinberg began to question its premise. Families would respond with, "Mr. Feinberg, my husband was a fireman and died a hero at the World Trade Center. Why are you giving me less money than the banker who represented Enron?" He didn't have a reasonable explanation.[5]

Ultimately, Feinberg felt it would make more sense for Congress to provide the same amount of public compensation to each victim. This would be a view of humans based on intrinsic worth. Each life has equal value in and of itself, regardless of its contribution to the economy. Despite Feinberg's desire, the law remained. He was required to act by instrumental worth.

Later, in the wake of the Virginia Tech shootings, which caused the death of thirty-two people, Feinberg was again asked to design and administer a compensation system for surviving families. Because this one was privately funded, he was not required to follow the law governing 9/11 compensations. This time, all victims—students and faculty—received the same compensation. Feinberg explained the difference in these words:

> In the case of September 11, if there is a next time and
> Congress again decides to award public compensation,
> I hope the law will declare that all life should be treated
> the same. . . . I believe that public compensation should
> avoid financial distinctions which only fuel the hurt and
> grief of the survivors. I believe all lives should be treated
> the same.

This critical point is lost on Haman. When he stresses the worthlessness of Jews and his sons, it is based on an instrumental view of humanity. Just as people have done through the ages when it comes to other races, the handicapped, or immigrants, Haman only grants worth to others if they can produce something of profit. They have no value by themselves. Here, the Jews stand between him and a life of veneration. Not even his sons can contribute to this goal. Therefore, even they are worthless.

Believing that people's value is instrumental (based on what they can create as beings) rather than intrinsic (based on who they are as created beings) is easier when you also believe that there is no Creator involved in their lives. Haman lived in such a world.

We live in a similar world. Most of the violence we see playing out in our news stories today is rooted in Haman's view of humanity. Much of the racism we see still plaguing our society is still based in this view of humanity. Many of the stories we hear concerning the plight of children are rooted in this view of humanity. Life is treated as valuable as long as it can contribute to a profitable goal. But it's treated as vile when it can't.

Worth Everything

On the pages of the book of Esther, God's name may appear nowhere. But his fingerprints are everywhere. In the narrative of Esther, a cursory peek may lead us to think God is absent. But a careful probe will lead us to see that he is present.

Mordecai sees this. He is Haman's antithesis. Mordecai is the first in the narrative to acknowledge that God is the director behind the drama, the producer behind the plot. This becomes clear when he says, "And who knows whether you have not come to the kingdom for such a time as this?" (Esther 5:14). Mordecai proposes that the messy and unexpected path that has led to Esther's place in the palace has been paved by the providence of God. It is no coincidence, therefore, that Mordecai is also the person in the narrative who demonstrates a different value for human life. Notice how Mordecai is introduced to us. The first description given to us of Mordecai is that he too "had been carried away from Jerusalem" (Esther 2:6) and that he "was bringing up Hadassah, that is Esther" (Esther 2:7). Before Esther could create value, before she could contribute profit, Mordecai took her as his own daughter. We don't know how young Esther was when Mordecai assumed responsibility for her life, but she was young enough for Mordecai to have to "bring up" Esther (v. 7). The Talmud, an ancient Jewish commentary on the Hebrew Bible, maintains that Esther's father died when Esther's mother was still pregnant and her mother died when giving birth to Esther.[6] In this case, Esther would have been merely an infant, incapable of productivity or profit. Regardless of specific age, Mordecai cared for Esther not because she was diligent, or dynamic, or dazzling. Simply because she was.

Mordecai's perspective of Esther stands in stark contrast to Haman's perspective of his sons. She *who is not* Mordecai's daughter is deemed invaluable. They *who are* Haman's sons are dismissed as inconsequential.

This is Mordecai's principle: the more involved we believe God to be in human life, the more compelled we are to value that same life. When we realize that our seemingly disenchanted world is truly enchanted, that our story of a God not at work is in fact a story of God hard at work, we are compelled to treasure and cherish all his works, especially his most wondrous work—humanity. All humanity. The marginal. The minorities. The monsters.

Mordecai provided what so many orphans never have. I was reminded of this when reading Lisa Wingate's stirring historical novel *Before We Were Yours*. She tells the true story of the infamous Georgia Tann, who ran the Tennessee Children's Home out of Memphis. Tann and her employees stole infants and young children from single mothers and families living in poverty, placed them in her orphanage where they were often neglected and abused, and then sold them to the wealthy, making a healthy profit. Children were abducted from hospital maternity wards, welfare clinics, front porches, and dirt roads. They were advertised in newspapers as "Yours for the Asking" and "Perfect Christmas Presents." Some five thousand children were stolen by Tann. Some five hundred died in her care.

In Wingate's fictional retelling of the tragic, true tale, Rill is abducted from her parents' riverboat in Memphis and sold to the Seviers, a cinema music composer and his wife. They are the first of a very small handful of people in Rill's life to show her care and compassion in the midst of her trauma. Near the end of her life, reflecting on these graces, Rill simply concludes, "People don't come into our lives by accident."[7] There's a hidden divine hand at work striving to overcome the malady and mistreatment caused by so many. It was felt by Rill in the novel. It was felt by Esther in her story. Mordecai was the source of that providential philanthropy in Esther's life. He saw Esther the orphan as worthwhile in and of herself while living in a culture that viewed most as worthless unless they could earn their keep.

A Community for the Worthless

In Mordecai, we catch a glimpse of the way that God sees all human life. Mordecai reflects the vision of God painted by Jesus in his parable of the son who squanders his inheritance and then comes home empty-handed and shamefaced. He rehearses the speech he will give when he finally sees his father: "Father, I have sinned against heaven and before you. I am no longer worthy to be called your son. Treat me as one of your hired servants" (Luke 15:18–19). Did you hear the language of worth and profit? "I am no longer *worthy* to be called your son." The son means that his instrumental worth has plummeted. He's no longer behaving in a way that contributes to the family. He is of no profit to the family.

To a degree, he's correct. The son has brought debt to the family. As the older brother bemoans, the son has "devoured" the father's property (v. 30). The son has also brought dishonor to the family. In a shame-based culture, his behavior has resulted in shame to the household. This son has subtracted worth from his family, rather than contributing to their collective worth. From the story's beginning to its ending, his instrumental worth plummets.

Yet notice the Father's response. When the son's profit to the father is the lowest, the father's passion for the son is the highest. The father runs to him, embraces him, kisses him, and throws a party for him:

> But while he was still a long way off, his father saw him and felt compassion, and ran and embraced him and kissed him. . . . But the father said to his servants, "Bring quickly the best robe, and put it on him, and put a ring on his hand, and shoes on his feet. And bring the fattened calf and kill it, and let us eat and celebrate." (Luke 15:20, 22–23)

Why did the father do this? It's because, unlike Haman and like Mordecai, the father views his son through the lens of intrinsic worth, not instrumental worth.

Jesus is painting for us an image of God. When our profit to the Father is the lowest, the Father's passion for us is still at its highest. He loves us not for anything we do or do not do. He loves us simply because we are.

And he calls us to be a community who loves in the same way. Just prior to this story, Jesus is criticized because he has created a community where people are valued simply for being. Jesus loves people for their intrinsic worth, not their instrumental worth, because this is how his Father views humanity. He set out to build a community, a church, that will do the same.

It's a view of others seen in Paul Kalanithi. In 2013, Paul, a thirty-six-year-old neurosurgeon, was struck with lung cancer. A nonsmoker who enjoyed the outdoors, Paul was rising through the ranks at Stanford University School of Medicine. In school, he had dedicated himself to one question and two sources of answers.

Paul's question was this: What gives meaning to life? He sought answers to this question through two disciplines: literature and neuroscience. Literature, he believed, provided the themes that point toward meaning in life. Thus he earned a degree in literature. Neuroscience allows us to understand the brain. The brain is what interprets meaning and happiness. Thus he earned degrees in neuroscience.

Paul and was on the way to becoming one of the most gifted neurosurgeons in the country when weight loss and severe back pain sent him to the doctor. He knew what was coming even before the CT scan revealed it: multiple tumors. No longer the doctor, he was now the patient. No longer faced with the future he had long worked for—years of neurosurgery, followed by teaching, followed by writing—now he had years, perhaps months, left to live.

At first, he wrestled with how to spend these remaining months or years. He decided to return to the operating room. But as his health diminished, it became clear what his task should be. He gave himself to the writing of one book. This book, *When Breath Becomes Air*, would chronicle his death and the struggle to find meaning and happiness in the face of death. Paul brought his Christian faith, philosophy, and literature to bear on this task.

In one of the book's most poignant moments, he lies dying on a cot in a hospital room next to his wife. She is giving birth to their daughter, Cady. Paul dies eight months later. In the book's final chapter, written with the very last of his strength in those final eight months, the first eight months of Cady's life, Paul writes to his daughter:

> I hope I'll live long enough that she has some memory of me. Words have a longevity I do not. I had thought I could leave her a series of letters—but what would they say? I don't know what this girl will be like when she is fifteen; I don't even know if she'll take to the nickname we've given her. There is perhaps only one thing to say to this infant, who is all future, overlapping briefly with me, whose life, barring the improbable, is all but past. That message is simple: When you come to one of the many moments in life where you must give an account of yourself, provide a ledger of what you have been, and done, and meant to the world, do not, I pray, discount that you filled a dying man's days with a sated joy, a joy unknown to me in all my prior years, a joy that does not hunger for more and more but rests, satisfied. In this time, right now, that is an enormous thing.[8]

At eight months old, Cady had no instrumental value. She could produce nothing of value. But she was loaded with intrinsic value. Simply by existing, she brought joy to her father—a joy unknown to him in all his prior years.

The same is true for us. Our mere existence brings joy to our heavenly Father. This is the love of a father for a child. The love of our Father for his human race.

In her book *Gilead,* Marilynne Robinson writes the fictional story of Reverend John Ames. Ames pastors a small church in the small town of Gilead, Iowa, in the late 1950s. Dying of a heart condition, he writes a series of letters to his seven-year-old son. In one letter, Ames tries to help his son understand what a miracle he's been by merely existing:

I'd never have believed I'd see a wife of mine doting on a child of mine. It still amazes me every time I think of it. I'm writing this in part to tell you that if you ever wonder what you've done in your life, and everyone does wonder sooner or later, you have been God's grace to me, a miracle, something more than a miracle. You may not remember me very well at all, and it may seem to you to be no great thing to have been the good child of an old man in a shabby little town you will no doubt leave behind. If only I had the words to tell you . . . it's your existence I love you for, mainly. Existence seems to me now the most remarkable thing that could ever be imagined.[9]

There's great worth simply in being, simply in existing. This is the love our Father has for every human he's ever made.

The book of Esther points us toward a God whose love for people is not based on their instrumental worth. A love not contingent upon their capacity to contribute or based upon their benefit to any segment of society. A love, instead, formed and founded upon intrinsic worth. A love tender and fierce from day one, when all we can do is sleep and cry and eat. A love that beats like a drum even when we stagger home empty-handed and shamefaced from a season of selfish mutiny. A love that sees that underneath our indiscretions, we still bear God's image; behind the flaws, we still carry God's fingerprints. It's a love that endures simply because we exist.

It's the love that Jesus himself experienced:

And when Jesus was baptized, immediately he went up
from the water, and behold, the heavens were opened
to him, and he saw the Spirit of God descending like
a dove and coming to rest on him; and behold, a

voice from heaven said, "This is my beloved Son, with whom I am well pleased." Then Jesus was led up by the Spirit into the wilderness to be tempted by the devil. (Matt. 3:16–4:1)

Before he could "prove" his worth through life-changing ministry, Jesus's value was affirmed by the father. Before Jesus "proves" his "worth" or "value" by his obedience on the cross, the Father affirms his love for his son. Jesus is the beloved simply because he is.

Henri Nouwen once wrote that this same label of beloved is given to us as a reminder that God's love is granted to us before we do anything of worth for him. Just as there were voices surrounding Jesus and urging him to verify his value, these same voices victimize us. And just as Jesus attended to only one sound, so we too must give ear only to the voice of God, which says, "You are my beloved":

> If you keep that in mind, you can deal with an enormous amount of success as well as an enormous amount of failure without losing your identity, because your identity is that you are the beloved. Long before your father and mother, your brothers and sisters, your teachers, your church, or any people touched you in a loving as well as in a wounding way—long before you were rejected by some person or praised by somebody else—that voice has been there always.[10]

That voice has always been there. Before your first paycheck. Before your GPA. Before your first step or even your first breath. And it will always be there. In fact, that breath goes all the way back to Esther. It's a voice that even she heard through the kindness of Mordecai.

And Jesus is seeking to create a community where everyone can hear this voice—minorities, the marginal, even "monsters." Richard Beck writes about these "monsters." Monsters are often what we call the misfits, social outcasts, freaks, and weirdos. In high schools and middle schools, monsters are bullied. In neighborhoods, workplaces, and churches, monsters are isolated and victimized. One contemporary pop singer, Lady Gaga, became well-known for referring to her fan base as "little monsters." Many who felt unwelcome in society found acceptance and belonging in her community of fans. Beck argues that what Gaga has done is what the church is called to do: create a community for monsters. He writes, "Religious institutions—in Jesus's time and in our own—continue to scapegoat outsiders. . . . The 'little monsters' should feel affection from the church."[11]

Ultimately, the book of Esther enables us to see this. It calls us to be the community that believes in a God who is present and active in the world to benefit all humanity. And believing this, we too live to benefit all humanity. Not for what they may contribute. Not for how we may benefit. But simply because they are.

Esther calls us to be the one community on earth that can value people not for what they do but for who they are. A community that can see more than skin color, hear more than accent of speech, record more than every mistake that's caused someone's value in another community to plummet. A community that peers past political affiliation, education, citizenship status, or sexual orientation. A community whose first step toward every human, be they hero or heel, is not the hurtful step that Haman took toward those who were his sons, but the healing step that Mordecai took toward the one who was not his daughter. The step the heavenly Father takes toward each one of us—the move of enduring love simply because we exist.

Treasure everyone. This is a discipline critical for living in a world that so often feels disenchanted. This disenchantment creates people who are labeled lousy, treated as monsters, and pushed to the margins. And one of the most fundamental callings of the people of God in that world is a calling to discern the true worth in all, but especially in those who are so often treated as worthless.

7

ADVOCATE

For about fifteen years, a group of about twenty of us have gathered in early July on the rolling lawns between the middle school and the Performing Art Center in Bartlett, Tennessee, to eat chicken (fried, salad, or sandwiched), cold pasta salads, chocolate chip cookies, and brownies, and to witness the eruption of city-sponsored fireworks in the night sky. Each year, the soundtrack to the fireworks includes Lee Greenwood's "God Bless the USA," with its refrain, "I'm proud to be an American, where at least I know I'm free." One of the purposes of the song is to remind us that, despite our other identities, we are all Americans.

The Name We Wear

We may be fans of the Tigers or the Titans. Our houses may be in Millington or Memphis. We may be Church of Christ or Church of God in Christ. We may have family trees with roots in Poland or Peru. We may have grown up in the United States or moved here from another country. We may be Republicans or Democrats. But

Independence Day reminds us that there is something that supersedes those distinctions. We are, above all, Americans.

Despite what differences may divide, generation after generation has come together to fight for one another and to fight for the principles that undergird that shared name. On June 11, 1776, the American Colonies' Second Continental Congress met in Philadelphia to draft a document severing America's ties with Great Britain. They adopted the final version of the Declaration of Independence on July 4, 1776. One year later, Philadelphia marked Independence Day by celebrating with bonfires, bells, and ballistics. Congress established Independence Day as a holiday in 1870. For hundreds of years, we've marked this date and celebrated this common American name.

It's a name that's come at great cost. From the American Revolution to the Global War on Terror, more than forty million men and women have served in America's armed services. More than one million have died in that service.[1] Indeed, wearing the name American has cost us greatly.

The Name Others Wear for Us

Others have also worn that name for us. In the days after the 9/11 attacks in the United States, France demonstrated a touching degree of compassion for the United States. This was especially true in Paris. Many called the U.S. embassy in Paris, offering their beds to Americans stuck at the airport. At noon on the official day of mourning, pedestrians in Paris stopped in their path and cars pulled off the road to observe the three minutes of silence. Hundreds of Parisians gathered at Notre Dame to sing "The Star-Spangled Banner." A massive U.S. flag was unfurled before the Eiffel Tower. The Eiffel Tower itself was flanked by an eighty-two-foot-tall scaffolding replica of the World Trade Center, emblazoned with a slogan of solidarity, in French and English: *Les Français N'oublieront Jaimais.* "The French Will Never Forget."[2]

But perhaps most striking was something done by the French newspaper *Le Monde.* The headline on the top of the first page on the September 12 edition read: *Nous sommes tous américains*— "We Are All Americans." The editorial below the headline gave this explanation:

> In this tragic moment, when words seem so inadequate to express the shock people feel, the first thing that comes to mind is this: We are all Americans! We are all New Yorkers, just as surely as John F. Kennedy declared himself to be a Berliner in 1962 when he visited Berlin. Indeed, just as in the gravest moments of our own history, how can we not feel profound solidarity with those people, that country, the United States, to whom we are so close and to whom we owe our freedom, and therefore our solidarity?[3]

For a brief moment, people in Paris wore two names. They wore the name "French." But they also wore the name "American." It was their way of showing solidarity with us.

The Names We Wear for Others

In November 2015, terrorist attacks in Paris, France, killed more than one hundred people. U.S. Secretary of State John Kerry flew to Paris soon after the attacks. He spoke publicly outside the U.S. Embassy in France. The U.S. embassy was lit with blue, white, and red, the colors of the French Flag. Kerry said this: "These terrorists have declared war against all civilizations. This is a battle between civilization itself and barbarism, between civilization and medieval and modern fascism, both at the same time. Tonight, we are all Parisians."[4] For a brief period, we in America wore two names. We wore the name "American." But we also wore the name "Parisian." Just as others have worn the name "American" to show their solidarity with us, so at times we have worn the names of others to show our solidarity with them.

Seasons like these can make the wearing of another's name seem natural and effortless. There are other seasons, and other names, when the show of solidarity requires far greater intentionality and exertion. Langston Hughes once wrote a poem to illustrate this fact. It is called "Let America Be America Again." In it, he recognizes how grand is the American name and dream:

> Let America be the dream the dreamers dreamed—
> Let it be that great strong land of love
> Where never kings connive nor tyrants scheme
> That any man be crushed by one above.[5]

But as the poem progresses, another voice interrupts. It keeps saying things like this:

> America never was America to me . . .
> There's never been equality for me,
> Nor freedom in this "homeland of the free."

Hughes asks the voice to identify itself. The voice is coming from the mouths of several individuals. They include a struggling white farmer, a black man targeted by hate, a Native American, an immigrant, a young person drowning in debt, and a homeless person with no food. Each longs to wear the American name and fulfill the American dream. But each also laments how the name doesn't fit and the dream won't materialize.

Hughes finishes with a rousing call for others of us to come alongside these neglected and forgotten neighbors, to show solidarity, and to ensure that they get their chance to don the name and experience the dream.

In other words, we may all be Americans, but would we be willing to also wear the names of struggling white farmers, blacks targeted by hate, Native Americans, immigrants, the young straddled with debt, and the homeless? Would we dress in their names so they might know we stand with them while they struggle to realize their own dream to stand with us?

We wear the name American. In times of global crisis, we may effortlessly adorn ourselves with another nation's name. But what other names are we willing to wear because we see in them such value that we gladly take on their identity as our own?

Esther's Names

In some ways, this is *the* question of the book of Esther, because the main character of the book is the one person in the story with more than one name.[6] She is introduced to us in this way: "He was bringing up *Hadassah*, that is *Esther*, the daughter of his uncle, for she had neither father nor mother" (Esther 2:7—emphasis mine). This is a woman with a double alias: Esther and Hadassah.

1. "Esther" is a Persian or Babylonian name. It is the Persian word for "star." It is also the Babylonian name for the goddess of love and war, Ishtar.[7]
2. "Hadassah" is Esther's Hebrew/Jewish name. It means "myrtle."[8]

It was not uncommon for Hebrew people to have both a Hebrew name and a second name taken from the culture in which they lived. For example, Daniel and his three friends carried their Jewish names but were also given Babylonian names when they were taken into exile (Dan. 1:6–7). Thus Esther has one name representing her Hebrew heritage and one representing the Persian culture in which she resides. These two names signify that Esther moves between two worlds—the Persian world of the palace and the Jewish world of her own people.

For the first part of the story, Esther lives like she has one name—her Persian name, Esther. After all, Mordecai, her adopted father, has urged her to keep her Jewishness a secret. Twice, we're told that he commanded her not to make known "her people or her kindred" (Esther 2:10, 20). Esther lives primarily as a Persian. She behaves as if she has no connection to the rest of her people. When she wakes in the morning, she adorns herself with royal robes and her Persian name, Esther.

But in in the second part of the story, Esther begins to behave as if she has a secret identity. When she learns of Haman's plan to murder her people, something within her changes. This is evident by the way she stands in solidarity with "my people" as she explains Haman's plan to her husband, the king:

> Then Queen Esther answered, "If I have found favor in your sight, O king, and if it please the king, let my life be granted me for my wish, and *my people* for my request. For we have been sold, I and *my people*, to be destroyed, to be killed, and to be annihilated." (Esther 7:3–4—emphasis mine)

> Esther rose and stood before the king. And she said, "If it please the king, and if I have found favor in his sight, and if the thing seems right before the king, and I am pleasing in his eyes, let an order be written to revoke the letters devised by Haman the Agagite, the son of Hammedatha, which he wrote to destroy the Jews who are in all the provinces of the king. For how can I bear to see the calamity that is coming to *my people*? Or how can I bear to see the destruction of *my kindred*?" (Esther 8:4–6—emphasis mine)

Earlier, Esther disavowed the countless people surrounding her as her people or her kindred. Now, she discloses they *are* her people and her kindred. She's gone from protecting this part of her identity to proclaiming it. She's no longer merely Esther—a Persian woman. She's now also Hadassah—a Jewish woman. It's almost as if Esther now wears her other name in an act of solidarity with those who are endangered. It's as if, now, she finally wears the name of others to demonstrate solidarity with them. It's almost as if she's not content to simply call herself Esther. She now also sees herself as Hadassah. She identifies with those suffering and hurting and bonds with them. Their struggle is her struggle. Her resources are theirs. They are her people. She is their queen.

Esther's courageous and compassionate willingness to stand with those in need provokes us to consider how we might do the same. When have we coldly worn the name that suits only our needs? When might we choose another name that could benefit those who are alone in their adversity?

For several years, hundreds of us in Memphis have taken the name "Carson" as we've run one of the St. Jude races during the first week of December. We've donned pink or yellow shirts with "Team Carson" on them and run in honor of childhood cancer victim Carson Head. We've taken her name as our own name as an act of solidarity. We made her struggle our struggle. And though cancer took her life as a young child, we continue to run for her and with her name because the St. Jude races raise money to treat childhood cancers. Carson, and many like her, became our people, our kindred. We've decided to live as people who no longer have only one name.

That's one of the things the book of Esther prompts us to do. Esther prompts us to ask: What name is God calling me to wear next? With whom is God calling me to demonstrate solidarity?

Betty Cannon, a member at the Highland Church of Christ, saw the needs of those in Ukraine after the fall of communism and decided to take their name as her own. She moved from Memphis, Tennessee, to Bila Tserkva, Ukraine, and devoted herself to serving orphans, teaching the Bible, and doing all she could to bring light to the lives of others in Ukraine.

Mendy Breeden, another church member, saw the needs of children in downtown Memphis and decided to take their name as her own. For years, she's served week after week as a volunteer to enrich the lives of the students and their parents at LaRose Elementary. Principal after principal has come and gone at this critical urban school—often transferred out despite their objections when they prove successful in leading in this challenging environment. But Mendy has remained constant.

Barry Mitchell, an elder at Highland, saw the needs of the unemployed and the formerly incarcerated, and he decided to take as his own. He's served on the board of HopeWorks and as a Faith Encourager for HopeWorks for years in Memphis, investing in the lives of those seeking healing, hope, and jobs.

Jim Ward saw the needs of the many whose lives have been turned upside down by the corruption of a landlord managing several apartment complexes in Memphis. He's decided to take their name as his own. He's been doing all he can to try to find housing and resources for these families caught in homelessness because of this corruption.

Eric Gentry has seen the ugly face of racism in Memphis and those who have been hurt by it, and he's decided to take their name as his own. He's taken leadership of the Racial Unity Leadership Summit, teaching classes on racism, organizing local church leaders for conversations about racial reconciliation, and helping connect churches to resources for overcoming racism.

What about you? What name is God calling you to wear next? With whom is God calling you to show solidarity?

In a disenchanted world, treating others with value, as Esther did, is one of the most significant ways of life we can adopt. The more invisible God seems, the more inconsequential people may feel. If it seems to people they are dwelling in a world God cares little about, we must be the living reminders that they are living in a world God cares about very much. When we who are God's people treat those who feel worthless as though they are priceless, they will find it far easier to believe they are also valued by God. When they find that they mean something to us, they can eventually believe they mean everything to God.

William Kaufman is a Jewish writer. In a short story called "The Day My Mother Changed Her Name," he writes of a time when he was in third grade. William was absent from class for two days that year to observe Passover. When he returned to class, he brought a note explaining his absence, as required by his teacher Mrs. Brady. The note was signed, "Sincerely yours, Rose Kaufman." Mrs. Brady, a stickler for details, asked William, "Did your mother write this note?" William explained that the note had been written by his sister Rose, not by his mother. His mother, William explained, could not speak or write English. But since Mrs. Brady required that all excuses be written and signed by a parent, William's note written by his sister violated her rule. She demanded that William bring his mother in for a reprimand.

The next day, Mama appeared for a meeting after school. Mrs. Brady scolded her while William interpreted. She then replied to Mrs. Brady while William interpreted. Mrs. Brady demanded that Mama at least sign her own name, even if the excuse was written by someone else, even if she had to sign her name in another language. William's mother agreed to the request. The next time

William was absent from class, Rose wrote the note and Mama signed it.

She did not, however, sign her name. Mama penned two Jewish words where her signature should have gone. The words were "Shalom Aleichem," meaning "Go in peace." Mama realized Mrs. Brady would think this was Mama's real name. And it would make Mama feel better about the conflict. For the rest of the year, every time Mama signed an absentee excuse for William, she wrote her new name: "Go in peace." It was her way of changing her relationship with that mean-spirited teacher.[9]

Esther is the story of a woman who refused to be known by only one name. It is the story of a woman who embraced a name that changed her relationship with others. Esther reveals how critical it is in a disenchanted time to truly value others, to make their cause our cause, to advocate for them. It's one of those practices that enables us to thrive even when God seems distant.

One way of moving in this direction is through the habit of intercessory prayer. "By means of Intercessory Prayer," Richard Foster writes, "God extends to each of us a personalized, hand-engraved invitation to become intimately involved in laboring for the well-being of others."[10] Intercessory prayer is our way of accepting this invitation and entering into the cares of others. This practice of praying for others changes us. Philip Yancey confesses, "When I pray for another person, I am praying for God to open my eyes so that I can see that person as God does, and then enter into the stream of love that God already directs toward that person."[11] God is the ultimate advocate. He takes up the cares of all. And as we pray for others, we take on the role of advocate. We make their name our own in the name of Christ.

Pay Out

I grew up near Holloman Air Force Base in New Mexico. My dad worked for the U.S. Air Force as a civil servant. For many years, we'd go on base and watch the Thunderbirds perform. They were the U.S. Air Force demonstration squadron. We'd see their jets fly tight, death-defying formations. Later in life, when I returned to the Southwest to preach, I was mesmerized by the F-117 stealth fighters stationed at Holloman. Every now and then while driving by the base on my way to visit my parents, I'd catch a glimpse of one or two of the unique fighters zipping through the air. They were surreal. I'd never seen anything like them before. No one in the world had either. Their technology was a watershed in military aircraft.

The BBC once ran a series called *Turning Points*. The program highlighted key moments when the storyline of history rotated in a revolutionary way. One episode featured air travel. They noted many turning points throughout history, like the stealthy technology I saw as I drove by Holloman in the 1990s:

- First heavier than air aircraft (1903)
- World's first nonstop flight across the Atlantic (1919)
- First flight by a jet aircraft (1939)
- First supersonic flight (1947)
- First commercially successful jet airliner (1958)
- First supersonic airliner (1968)
- B-2 stealth bomber enters service (1988)
- World's first hunter killer unmanned aircraft (1995)[1]

Each of these was a game changer. Each brought a paradigm shift, a new way of envisioning and practicing air travel or using aviation as a tool.

What's true with the story of aircraft is true with most stories. Most have a turning point, a fulcrum, on which important things pivot.

Consider your own life. There are probably key moments, turning points, at which the narrative of your life swung in a significant way. The day you broke up. The day you said, "I do." The day you moved. The day you graduated. The day you gave birth or adopted. The day you moved to the mission field. Your first day on the job. Your last day on the job. Your first home. Your first car. Your first kiss. Every story has turning points on which history rotates, sometimes in revolutionary ways.

The Evil Fulcrum of Finances

There are some decisive hinge points in the story of Esther. One of those is unexpected. It is a fulcrum upon which two primary narratives of Esther turn. The story pivots from (1) a scene where the Jewish people are disheartened but doing just fine in the kingdom of Persia to (2) a scene where they are desperate and about to die at the hands of Haman in Persia. In the first scene, the Jewish people are alive. They have homes. They are engaged in productive labor. But then their plot pivots radically. Sadly, tragically, they are faced with genocide. A decree is written on the request of Haman and under the authority of the king authorizing their extermination. Esther's story pitches from that first scene to the other like a rollercoaster suddenly hurling from its peaceful ascent down a scream-inducing plunge.

One text reveals the point on which this pivot takes place:

> Then Haman said to King Ahasuerus, "There is a certain people scattered abroad and dispersed among the peoples in all the provinces of your kingdom. Their laws are different from those of every other people, and they do not keep the king's laws, so that it is not to the king's profit to tolerate them. If it please the king, *let it be decreed that they be destroyed, and I will pay 10,000 talents of silver into the hands of those who have charge of the king's business, that they may put it into the king's treasuries.*" So the king took his signet ring from his hand and gave it to Haman the Agagite, the son of Hammedatha, the enemy of the Jews. And the king said to Haman, "The money is given to you, the people also, to do with them as it seems good to you." (Esther 3:8–11—emphasis mine)

Notice the two lines of Haman's argument. The first line is brief: "let it be decreed that they be destroyed." Haman's language is passive. Haman doesn't tell the king to decree it. He asks the king to *allow* it to be decreed.[2] Although this seems to be the worst part of Haman's proposal—asking for a decree for the end of the Jewish people—it's the briefest part.

The longest part of the proposal is found in the second line: "I will pay 10,000 talents of silver into the hands of those who have charge of the king's business, that they may put it into the king's treasuries." We find twice as much text about the loot the king will make compared to the lives Haman will take. In Esther, Haman is nearly successful with massacre because he convinces the king it will lead to more money. Haman nearly gets away with the annihilation of people because he gets the king fixated on the acquisition of profit. As is so often the case, if you can frame an action as prudent, pragmatic, or prosperous for those with power and privilege, you can get away with nearly anything—even murder.

Haman has a reason for linking his plan with profit. When this story began in Esther chapter one, the king was using a six-month feast to sweet-talk his fighters and financiers to support his quest to go to war against Greece. Nearly ten years have passed since then. In that time, the king has fought and lost a disastrous war with Greece, according to the historian Herodotus. The conflict and loss have emptied his treasury. Haman is thus now appealing to the king's need to replenish his dusty treasury.[3]

According to Herodotus, in a good year, the total revenue of the Persian Empire was 14,560 Eubonic talents or nearly 17,000 Babylonian talents (we don't know which measure would apply today). This revenue was generated by receiving tribute/taxes from the satrapies. For example, the satrapy of Media was assessed a tribute of 450 talents each year plus 10,000 sheep and pasturage for 50,000 horses.[4] Haman offers the king 10,000 talents—a huge amount of money. It's likely this is the money he will gain by plundering the Jews after he kills them.[5] Whatever acquisitions Haman might have acquired in the aftermath of the bloodbath, he now promises to deposit directly into the king's treasury.[6] The bribe shows just how obsessed Haman is with killing the Jews.[7] He's so passionate about it that he's willing to take a colossal personal economic loss. Haman knows the king is more likely to promote a plan that degrades the life of the Jews if he can stress how the same plan upgrades the life of the king. It's sad how quick we are to ruin others if, in the process, there's a reward to reap for ourselves.

Haman is right. The king swallows the bait, giving his signet ring to Haman so Haman can write a royal decree by the authority of the king calling for the execution of the Jews. The king punctuates the gesture with these words: "The money is given to you, the people also, to do with them as it seems good to you." When the king says, "The money is given to you," it may sound like he's saying, "Keep the money," and that he's refusing Haman's bribe. Instead, what's happening is similar to what we see in Genesis 23. There, Abraham asks to buy a field. The man selling it seems to give him the field for free, but then after a few more polite exchanges, an actual purchase price is set. This technique of polite refusals was standard for ancient Middle Eastern culture. What we hear from the king is simply his making the culturally expected gesture of appearing to turn down Haman's offer. In the end, he will pluck Haman's cash and Haman will press forward with his deadly plan.[8]

This story turns on money. Not simply racism. Not simply selfishness. The Jews are about to die because of a ten-thousand-talent bribe to the king. Evil pivots into the lives of the Jews through the fulcrum of finances.

That becomes even clearer through two more scenes that reflect on this conversation between Haman and the king. In the first scene, Mordecai has learned of Haman's desire to execute him and all like him. Esther hears that, in response, Mordecai has put on sackcloth and ashes and is in the center of the city weeping:

> When Esther's young women and her eunuchs came and told her, the queen was deeply distressed. She sent garments to clothe Mordecai, so that he might take off his sackcloth, but he would not accept them. Then Esther called for Hathach, one of the king's eunuchs, who

had been appointed to attend her, and ordered him to go to Mordecai to learn what this was and why it was. Hathach went out to Mordecai in the open square of the city in front of the king's gate, and Mordecai told him all that had happened to him, *and the exact sum of money that Haman had promised to pay into the king's treasuries for the destruction of the Jews.* (Esther 4:4–7— emphasis mine)

It's clear by Mordecai's explanation to Esther that the king has not turned down Haman's bribe. Mordecai has inside information about how much money Haman has offered to pay into the king's treasuries for the destruction of the Jews. What disturbed Mordecai was not only the news of the forthcoming extermination of the Jews, but the fact that it had been put into motion by money.

In a second scene, Esther approaches the king on behalf of her people. In describing what Haman has planned, she twice frames his plot in financial terms:

Then Queen Esther answered, "If I have found favor in your sight, O king, and if it please the king, let my life be granted me for my wish, and my people for my request. *For we have been sold*, I and my people, to be destroyed, to be killed, and to be annihilated. *If we had been sold* merely as slaves, men and women, I would have been silent, for our affliction is not to be compared with the loss to the king." (Esther 7:3–4—emphasis mine)

When Esther is finally able to reveal to the king just what a horror he has unleashed through Haman on her and her people, she describes it this way: "we have been *sold.*" This has been a cold cash transaction. Lives for loot. It's clear the king has accepted Haman's bribe.

Ten thousand talents.

Thirty pieces of silver.

Their story turns bad because of the bad use of money. This story turns on money. Not simply racism. Not simply selfishness. Evil pivots into the lives of the Jews through the fulcrum of finances. What persuades the king to allow Haman to flood evil into the lives of the Jews is Haman's money.

Esther's story reveals how much misery is unleashed when people are no longer seen as priceless but simply as profit. Esther laments that she and her people were not merely persecuted. They were peddled. They weren't only besieged. They were bartered.

The Good Fulcrum of Finances

Paul David Tripp writes that money has a similar effect on most of us:

> When we think of money, we tend to think first of ourselves: what do I need, what do I want, what dream can this money finance, what would I like to do that I have never done before, etc. I am not suggesting that we are never generous but that, for most of us, when it comes to money, generosity is a snapshot in a long video of self-interest.[9]

The biblical story, he argues, is just the opposite. It's a story of generosity.[10] Just as evil pivots into the lives of people through the fulcrum of finances, so good pivots into the lives of people through the fulcrum of finances. Repeatedly in Scripture, the story of people's lives turns for good through of the gracious use of goods.[11] Women with resources use their finances to support the work of Jesus and the disciples (Luke 8:2–3). Joseph of Arimathea and Nicodemus use their wealth in service to Christ (Matt. 27:57–61; John. 19:38–42). Barnabas uses his land investments to help the ministry of the early church (Acts 4:36–37). Cornelius gives alms liberally to people (Acts 10:2). Lydia invests her resources to benefit the cause of the early church (Acts 16:14). Paul collects money from multiple churches to assist people in crisis (2 Cor. 8–9).

The last example is noteworthy. In the Corinthian letters, Paul urges Christians to get in the habit of setting money aside each Sunday, and when he arrives in Corinth, he'll gather what they've set aside and take it to Jerusalem to help people who've been affected by a famine. Paul knows that the story of famine victims in Jerusalem will take a turn for the good if the church in Corinth will set money aside for their relief. He knows the church's finances will become a fulcrum for good.

I've preached for the Highland Church for the last twenty years. Each of those years, we've set aside money twice a year, in addition to our weekly ministry contribution, for use in outreach. Over my twenty years at Highland, these biannual outreach contributions have collected and sent out about seven million dollars in services and ministry to those outside Highland, especially to the poor.

Every time we hold one of these contributions, Larry McKenzie makes the same comment. Larry's been on our staff for more than fifty years. And for more than fifty years, he has continued to say: "I've got great news! God's already provided all the money that's needed for this contribution, all the money required to change the lives of people in our thirty outreach ministries. Now, here's the bad news: it's still in the wallets and accounts of those sitting in our worship service." God grants resources for renewing people's lives. He's always provided enough. But we must be willing to let it go for it to have its intended purpose.

One ministry partner we fund through those contributions is HopeWorks. They provide life-skills training and job-skills training for people in circumstances that make long-term employment difficult. Since its founding in 1990, more than nine hundred men and women have graduated from its Personal Career and Development Classes. One of those was Mildred Richard, whose story I recounted in Chapter Two.

She heard about HopeWorks through another program she had enrolled in. She knew she needed help with everything, from her posture to her dress to her speaking to getting a good job. HopeWorks promised to help with it all. "It was life changing," she said. Through the program's assistance, she went from being a seventh-grade dropout to advocating for HIV patients before the president of the United States. "I can't think of anything HopeWorks did not give me," she says. "I was ready for anything."

What made the difference in Mildred's life was the Spirit of God at work in her life and in the lives of men and women who believed in her and invested in her. And what made their work possible were funds directed toward their organization— HopeWorks. Finances were a fulcrum through which good pivoted into Mildred's life.

Esther's story reminds us of the ways unfathomable evil floods into the world through the enticements of economics. Mildred's story also reminds us of the ways immeasurable blessings flow into the world through the availability of funds. Generosity is a key discipline for those of us living in a disenchanted world. While we might wish God worked in less "secular ways," the truth is that he often chooses to use coins and cash and credit cards to accomplish his purposes in the world. While capable of snapping his fingers and creating a miraculous chain of events that brings about the good he wants, he seems to want to remain in the background, using the resources he's placed in our hands to change the world. The turning point our city, community, or neighbor needs may already be in our pantry, wallet, garage, or closet. It's up to us to identify it and share it joyfully and gratefully. Because when we do, God will use it powerfully.

Yet, as Richard Foster writes, "the great moral question of our time is how to move from greed to generosity, and from vengeance to magnanimity, and from violence to shalom."[12] In Esther, we see just how true this is. Greed bears destructive fruit. The key to moving from greed to generosity, James Bryan Smith argues, is a renewed view of God. Many operate from a false narrative suggesting that we must "earn favor" from God—that God is stingy and likely to grant favor and blessing only to the very best of us. This mind-set, in turn, creates people who are also stingy, taking rather than giving, because we find fault in all others. In truth, Smith proposes that Scripture presents a generous God. His favor and grace abound. His generosity thus necessitates an approach to others and to the world that is similar.[13] We find this in Esther's narrative. We witness a God with abundant care and provision for his people, even in Persia. We see a queen, therefore, who lives with liberality as she uses her power and authority for those who need her most. Generosity is a habit that allows us to mirror the generous nature of the God who is always at work.

9

POWER DOWN

In March 2015, I was sitting at a dinner table with a young student in the city of Qingdao, China. He became a Christian in China and was a member of one of the many house churches in the city. His English was far better than my Chinese, so we conversed in English while we plucked delicacies from a lazy Susan before us.

"I'm surprised to find so many in China so receptive to the message about Jesus and so involved in house churches," I said. I was part of a team from the United States surveying several Chinese cities. We marveled at the number of Chinese who were so open to Christianity and who willingly joined churches.

The student had just returned from a visit to the United States. He reflected on his time there in this way: "I was surprised to find so many in your country turning away from Christianity and the church." I nearly dropped my chopsticks. Here I was, the Westerner, the guy from the "Christian nation," supposedly bringing Christianity to the Chinese. Yet I found that so many of them had already embraced Christ and their churches were thriving.

He, on the other hand, found my own country anemic in terms of faith and our own churches dying.

This student was describing what one author, Charles Taylor, summarizes with the word "secular." Taylor defines "secular" in this way: "a move from a society where belief in God is unchallenged and indeed, unproblematic, to one in which it is understood to be one option among others, and frequently not the easiest to embrace."[1] Western culture is secular in that we've gone from being a country where it was once difficult to turn away from Christianity and the church to being one where it's much easier to turn away from Christianity and the church.

This creates a particular challenge for those who remain in the faith. It leads to what some have called the "culture wars." While, according to historian Stephen Prothero, a tension between Christianity and secular culture has existed for a long time in America, it seems to some the tension is far worse in recent years.[2] Many American Christians feel like the church has lost its place in American culture because culture has become increasingly secular. As a result, they want Christianity to regain its power and influence in American culture. Thus, this age in America is one when many in the church are concerned with cultural power.

This desire morphs into a wish for political power during midterm and presidential elections in the United States. Every election, but especially the presidential election, tempts Christians with the issue of political power. American Christians either wring their hands when they think of one person or one party winning power or they raise their hands when they think of "their" person or "their" party winning power.

In addition, each year, American Christians ponder military power. Memorial Day, known first as Decoration Day, grew out of the ashes of the deadliest military conflict this nation has known—the Civil War. After claiming more American lives than any other

U.S. conflict, the Civil War left grieving families and a grieving nation grasping for some way to honor the dead. Independently, towns and cities began a practice in the spring of taking flowers and decorating graves of the fallen.

By 1890, all the northern states had made May 30, Decoration Day, a state holiday. The date was chosen because no known battle had been fought on that date. But many states in the South refused to recognize May 30 and instead honored their dead on a different date. The Civil War continued to divide the country even on Memorial Day. It was only after World War I that there was unity between the North and South regarding Memorial Day.[3] It became a day not simply for honoring the fallen Union soldiers or the fallen Confederate soldiers, but for memorializing all who had died while fighting for the country.

And today, while the fallen are remembered, Memorial Day raises important questions about military power. When should our country's greatest power be put to use, especially when it costs so much? What responsibilities does a country like ours have when it possesses such a great military power? The day creates opportunities for Christians to reflect on the vast military power of our nation.

Carried Away

Esther's is a story of power. Early on, it's a tale of one-sided power. Esther does not have power. Everyone else does have power. This is artfully summarized in two verses in chapter 2: "Now there was a Jew in Susa the citadel whose name was Mordecai, the son of Jair, son of Shimei, son of Kish, a Benjaminite, who had been *carried away* from Jerusalem among the captives *carried away* with Jeconiah king of Judah, whom Nebuchadnezzar king of Babylon had *carried away*" (Esther 2:5–6—emphasis mine). Three times, the verb "carried away" is used to describe Mordecai. By virtue of his association with Esther, this verb also describes her. Esther has been carried away, carried away, carried away. Esther's family, and Mordecai's, was *carried away* from their home in Israel to the kingdom of Babylon, which is now the kingdom of Persia. She was then *carried away* from her home in Persia to the king's harem when he rounded up all the young virgins of the kingdom to find a new queen. Finally, Esther was *carried away* from the harem to the king's bed to see if she could please him more than the others.

Esther does not have power. Everyone else does have power. What does everyone else in the story do with their power? They carry Esther, and people like her, away.

The verb for *carried away*, Old Testament scholar Samuel Wells writes, is a symbol.[4] It's there to remind us that this is a tale shaped by plotlines of power. Esther begins the story as powerless as a commoner. She ends the story as powerful as a queen.

In the beginning, Esther is impotent. Xerxes (or Ahasuerus) holds all the cards. He can fire his queen with a word. Soon, he can authorize legislation that allows every Jew in his empire to be executed. He can declare that every young virgin in the land be abducted and brought to his bed. Esther, however, is defenseless. She can issue no decree. She can write no legislation. She has no voice. She is carried away, carried away, carried away.

But then Esther experiences an unexpected change of position. She is carried away—but notice just how far she is carried away. She doesn't stop until she's nearly at the top. The king, we are told, "loved Esther more than all the women" (Esther 2:17) and thus makes Esther his new queen, replacing Vashti. This Jewish orphan girl is now queen in one of the most powerful nations on earth. She is then made the guest of honor at a feast (Esther 2:18). This detail matters because feasts matter in this story. The story opened with the king hosting a feast for all the nobility of the kingdom. Then Ahasuerus threw a feast for all the men of the capital city.

Then the queen threw a feast for all the women of the capital city. Now Esther is the guest of honor at a feast.

As part of the festivities, the king declares an empire-wide holiday. It included the suspension of taxes, relief from military service, release of prisoners, distribution of gifts, and the proclamation of a general holiday.[5] This was no simple dinner party. This was an empire-wide celebration thrown in honor of Esther. It was a hint of just how high she'd risen.

Esther begins the story as powerless as a commoner. She ends this part of the story as powerful as a queen. If we were reading this story as a Jew idling in ancient Persia, we would be shocked. A Jewish woman has ascended the ladder to one of the highest positions in the land. She comes from the most disenfranchised population in the empire. Now this nobody is nobility. She was carried away by others. Now she's crowned over others.

The Purpose of Power

The big question we'd probably be asking once word of her coronation reached us is this: What's Esther going to do with her newfound clout? Will she use her superiority to strike back at the Persian power who snatched her from her neighborhood and her childhood? Will she utilize her royalty to grant herself limitless personal rewards after a lifetime of limitations? Will she grant her people kickbacks in response to their history of being been kicked down? What is Esther going to do with this power?

This is an especially critical question given what happens shortly after the coronation and the celebration. Two men, Bigthan and Teresh, become angry and scheme to harm King Ahasuerus. Mordecai finds out about the plot and shares the news with Esther (Esther 2:21–22). Mordecai may be part of the king's security force, and this may be how he's managed to learn about a plot against the king's life.[6] Rather than bring the information straight to the king, Mordecai passes it to Queen Esther. As a result, Esther now possesses the power of life and death over the king. If Esther sits on Mordecai's report, she could get retribution against the most powerful ruler on the planet. She could return upon him the pain and suffering he's inflicted upon her and her people. Esther finally possesses the power for payback. Best of all, Esther doesn't have to do anything despicable to rid the world of this disgraceful king. She can just slip under the covers of her bed and let the assassination plot unfold under the cover of night. When she wakes up, the dirty deeds of others will have made her dreams come true.

What is Esther going to do with her new power? It's easy to race past this moment. It's tempting to assume that the real test comes later with Esther's conflict over whether she possesses the courage to use her position to save her people from Haman. This moment, however, is just as critical a test. It's one of the most pivotal points in Esther's story. It concerns how the people of God wield power when living in a world that is not always to their liking.

This is a sober scene, given our own context. Our calendar, with days like Memorial Day and the Fourth of July, reminds us of the many times in history when military might has been called upon, and the complex questions and circumstances raised by the use of military power. Our midterm and presidential elections spark intense debates at dinner tables, on social media, and in church foyers about the proper use of political authority and those best suited to brandish it. Our changing culture, with its increasing secularization, leads many Christians to struggle with their desire for greater influence of Christianity and the church within the culture. All of this raises the same question we're asking about Esther: What would/could/should Christians do with power?

It'd be nice to think that we, being the nice people we are, would use power, once we got it, in nice ways and for nice purposes. Give a bad person power, and he's going to use it in bad ways. Give a nice person power, and he's going to use it in nice ways. Right? Wrong. Studies actually find that no matter how delightful we are, once we get a little authority, we become detestable.[7] Our admirable qualities lead the people around us to give us dominance over them. But once we're put in charge, most of us change. We lose the very characteristics that drew people to us in the first place. Sitting in the captain's chair, we become more impersonal and more hostile.

Power tends to bring out the worst in us. I experienced this when I was in middle school. My twin brother, Craig, and I formed a club called the Winter Stunt Club. I even made business cards—hand drawn and hand cut. It was a club whose sole purpose was to do the most daring and death-defying stunts in the heavy winter snow that blanketed our tiny town of Sunspot, New Mexico, from Thanksgiving through early March. When he learned of the club's existence, our friend Russell wanted in. He was the only other middle-school-aged kid living in Sunspot. Everyone else was in elementary school and thus couldn't qualify for membership. So, practically speaking, Craig and I had started a club whose pool for membership was extremely small: one. There was only one potential member beside ourselves. But we let being in charge go to our heads. When Russell asked to join, we came up with the most outlandish list of stunts for him to perform. I don't know how he didn't break a rib, a femur, or a wrist. We were terrible to him—simply because we could. That's what power can do.

Powering Down

And that's exactly what makes Esther's first power play as queen so surprising. It wouldn't be surprising to find Esther using her sovereignty in sickening ways. Instead, she brandishes it in surprisingly selfless ways:

> And this came to the knowledge of Mordecai, and he
> told it to Queen Esther, and Esther told the king in the
> name of Mordecai. When the affair was investigated and
> found to be so, the men were both hanged on the gal-
> lows. And it was recorded in the book of the chronicles
> in the presence of the king. (Esther 2:22–23)

Esther's been carried away, carried away, carried away. But what does she do as her first act as queen? What's her first step after gaining the upper hand over the man responsible for the darkest time in her life? She saves his life! She doesn't sit on the informa-tion. She tells the king. As a result, the assassins are stopped. The king lives.

Imagine how tempting it would be in Esther's disenchanted world to react differently. Picture in your mind how easy it would have been to look the other way since, it seems, God's been look-ing the other way all her life. Instead, Esther does just the opposite. She employs her position to love her enemy. She brandishes influ-ence in a way that benefits someone responsible for great pain in her past.

Esther models selfless sovereignty. Having ascended to a royal position from which she can now seek revenge upon a cruel king, Esther prefers to rescue him. Rather than take the life that has caused her great misery, she spares that life, showing great mercy. Esther demonstrates what can happen when the people of God gain influence, earn privilege, or ascend to greater authority wher-ever they work or live and remain faithful to God's call of selfless service. Clout can be used for compassion. Power can be used for philanthropy. Might can be used for mercy. Esther's saving actions after learning of the assassination plot against the callous king are an echo of the tone sounded clearly by Jesus. Jesus could crush his many enemies at any moment. Instead, he permitted them to slay him so that he might save them, and us. Empowered to pray, "Father, finish them!" Jesus instead pleaded, "Father, forgive them!" Jesus, and Esther, used power to deliver and defend, even when others seemed undeserving. So must we.

I met Terry when he enrolled in one of my online spiritual formation groups. Several years ago, Terry's twenty-seven-year-old son was killed when a drug addicted young man crashed his car into Terry's son's car. It took two years for the judicial system to finally send that young man to prison. A few months ago, the young man's prison sentence was brought up for review, and Terry and his wife were asked to attend the review. Terry brought a note that he had written and he asked that it be delivered to the young man who had killed his son. In summary, the note simply said, "We forgive you." The judge sent the young man back to prison. Terry is now making arrangements to visit the young man in prison. He wants to sit down face-to-face with him. Terry told me, "I want to express to him that God-given value he has and to use that value to turn his life around." And he wants to tell him, face-to-face, "I forgive you."

Every tragedy is unique. Every court case different. The survivors of victims have to find their own way. In this case, Terry is in a position of power over his son's killer. Terry's had to discern the best way to wield his influence. He's decided to be selfless with his strength. He's empowered to act in ways that say, "I condemn you." He prefers to respond in ways that say, "I forgive you." He's got the capacity to make the killer's stay in prison a greater burden. He's chosen to find ways to bring into it a blessing.

Andy Crouch has written an entire book on the use and misuse of power. He proposes that power is better than we can imagine and worse than we can imagine.[8] At its best, power is guided by love and thus brings refreshment, joy, and life. In truth, power is needed by love in order to turn loves wishes into reality.

But, at its worst, power is "the unmaker of humanity—breeding inhumanity in the hearts of those who wield power, denying and denouncing the humanity of the ones who suffer under power." This is what we find in Esther—one using power without love to unmake humanity and one using power with love to bring refreshment, joy and life.

Most of us have a degree of power over others. Older siblings over younger. Parents over children. Upperclassmen over lowerclassmen. Longer tenured employees over less tenured employees. Supervisors and managers over others. Locals over the newly arrived or the visiting. Those who've been members of a church for decades over those who just placed membership. One of the most important decisions you'll make this week concerns your power and influence. What will you do with it? Will it be infused with love or not? Follow the footsteps of Esther. Be a selfless sovereign, especially for those who may seem the most undeserving. For, in the end, we've all been on the receiving end of the loving power of the Mighty One, the King of Kings, the Lord of Lords, the one who still calls all the shots.

Work Wonders

Each summer in my elementary school years, just as I was beginning to run out of game shows to watch in the living room and games to play out in the woods, my family would take a three- to four-week trip. We'd drive thousands of miles from rural New Mexico to visit grandparents in rural Nebraska and Missouri. These trips occurred without the time-altering powers of smartphones or DVD players. All my twin brother, Craig, and I could do to endure the endless ribbons of interstates and highways was read our three-foot-tall stack of comic books or sketch on the piles of scrap paper we'd collected from the computer paper Dad brought home from his lab at work.

One of the things I often drew in the backseat of the station wagon as those miles meandered by was the jobs I imagined I'd have when I got older. My sketches focused on two careers: baseball and space travel. Those half sheets with computer gibberish on one side and pure white on the other were often filled edge to edge with my sketchings of a baseball stadium, every seat filled, with me at home plate, having just connected with a fast ball, watching a homerun sail over the back fence, the crowd standing and applauding because that one hit had just won the game, the series, the championship. Alternatively, my illustration contained a multistage rocket, me perched atop in the cockpit, flames surging out of the bottom, pushing the rocket and me toward the half-moon just visible in the top right corner of the paper. When I grew up, work was going to be wondrous. I'd be an applauded athlete or acclaimed astronaut.

And then I grew up.

One of my first jobs was at a New Mexico golf course. By day, I cleaned golf clubs. By night, I picked up golf balls on the driving range. It was hard and dirty work. I did not whistle while I worked. I had no sense of fulfillment or pride in my work. I quit after a few weeks.

I subsequently took a short-term job with the Otero County Electric Co-op. We provided the electric lines and utility poles for an entire county. It was a vast rugged and rural area filled with mountains and desert. On a typical day, I'd jump in a pickup truck with another employee. We'd drive for several hours to reach a new structure in the outland. Then we'd hammer down wooden stakes where new power poles should go, connecting the existing power line to the new structure, and we'd draw their location on a map. We would then drive back to the office and fill out forms detailing our work in the field. I was paid well for this work, but it felt like we got very little accomplished. All we had to show for eight to ten hours of work each day was a few stakes in the ground and some completed paperwork.

Sometimes, it may appear that only some positions—like that of a professional athlete or space explorer—provide the chance to do something substantial in life. Picking up golf balls or driving wooden stakes in the ground can seem unexciting and unfulfilling. The television drama *The Crown* portrays the life of young Queen Elizabeth. In one episode, depicting an infamous moment in the queen's life in the mid-1900s, Elizabeth visits a Jaguar car factory. Before the owners and workers, she delivered a terribly insensitive speech about the nature of their work.

"Many of you are living uneventful, lonely lives," she said. "Perhaps you don't understand that on your steadfastness and ability to withstand the fatigue of dull, repetitive work depends in great measure the happiness and prosperity of the community as a whole."

The queen didn't win friends that day among the blue-collar workers. To her, and perhaps to many of them, their assembly line workday was about as uneventful and dull as work could be.

A Tale of Two Heroes

This view of having a dull job could have been true for one of the key figures in the book of Esther. The book has two heroes. One looks like a hero. The other doesn't. Esther presents as a hero. She goes from Jewish orphan taken from her home to queen of one of the most powerful kingdoms on earth. And as queen, she uses her wit and grit to save an entire population from extermination by her husband's right-hand man.

Mordecai does not necessarily come across as a hero. Most of what he does from the story's start to its end is go to work. His "screen time" in the drama of Esther is devoted primarily to what he does at the office. It's not flashy. It's often forgettable. But God uses Mordecai's workplace routine for a remarkable purpose. By simply going to work, Mordecai ends up saving the world.

Working Hero

Let's track Mordecai's movements in the book of Esther. Seven times, Mordecai is mentioned doing the same thing in the book of Esther:

1. Now when the virgins were gathered together the second time, *Mordecai* was *sitting at the king's gate.* (Esther 2:19)

2. In those days, as *Mordecai* was *sitting at the king's gate*, Bigthan and Teresh, two of the king's eunuchs, who guarded the threshold, became angry and sought to lay hands on King Ahasuerus. (Esther 2:21)

3. And all the king's servants who were at *the king's gate* bowed down and paid homage to Haman, for the king had so commanded concerning him. But *Mordecai* did not bow down or pay homage. (Esther 3:2)

4. He [*Mordecai*] went up to the entrance of *the king's gate*, for no one was allowed to enter *the king's gate* clothed in sackcloth. (Esther 4:2)

5. And Haman went out that day joyful and glad of heart. But when Haman saw *Mordecai* in *the king's gate*, that he neither rose nor trembled before him, he was filled with wrath against Mordecai. (Esther 5:9)

6. Then the king said to Haman, "Hurry; take the robes and the horse, as you have said, and do so to *Mordecai* the Jew, who sits at *the king's gate.* Leave out nothing that you have mentioned." (Esther 6:10)

7. Then *Mordecai* returned to *the king's gate.* But Haman hurried to his house, mourning and with his head covered. (Esther 6:12—emphasis mine)

Over and over, the author describes Mordecai as "sitting at the king's gate" or simply at "the king's gate." To us, that sounds like the guy is just hanging out at some place. But Old Testament scholar

Adele Berlin points out that this language does not describe just a *place*. It also describes a *position*.[1] The phrase indicates that Mordecai holds a high position in the king's administration. It is a synonym for a government position. Mordecai works for the king. The "king's gate" is his office, his workplace. Again and again, what we see Mordecai doing is just going to work, Mordecai at the king's gate.

The author of Esther never gives us a glimpse of Mordecai going to the synagogue, the Jewish version of church—although we can assume that Mordecai does. The book never provides a peek of Mordecai at home. We can assume, however, that Mordecai spends many hours there. The camera in the story of Esther is generally only turned on Mordecai when Mordecai goes to work, to the king's gate. Yet by just going to work, by showing up day after day, Mordecai gains the opportunity to make a tremendous difference in his world.

Esther is the story of a person who saved his part of the world simply by going to work. By just punching the clock, by engaging in what appeared to be a secular profession, not a sacred profession, Mordecai gained the opportunity to participate in God's great work in the world. Mordecai's dedication to his occupation became collaboration with God's salvation of countless people on earth.

Notice the five fantastic things that happened when Mordecai went to work.

First, because Mordecai went to work, he was able to stay connected to Esther. The text tells us how the location of his vocation put him close to Esther after she was taken from him by the king: "And every day Mordecai walked in front of the court of the harem to learn how Esther was and what was happening to her" (Esther 2:11). When Mordecai took this job for this secular government, he could have never imagined that his boss would force his adopted daughter into a harem as part of the king's search for a queen. Yet once Esther was seized, Mordecai found that his job afforded him an office near the harem's residence and authority to access information about Esther within that harem during this critical time in her life.

Second, because he went to work, Mordecai uncovered a plot to kill the king. After Esther is crowned Queen, Mordecai arrives one day at the king's gate while an assassination plot unfolds:

> In those days, as Mordecai was sitting at the king's gate, Bigthan and Teresh, two of the king's eunuchs, who guarded the threshold, became angry and sought to lay hands on King Ahasuerus. And this came to the knowledge of Mordecai, and he told it to Queen Esther, and Esther told the king in the name of Mordecai.
> (Esther 2:21–22)

When Mordecai first applied for this government job, he could have never imagined the day would come when he might actually save the king's life. But because he clocked in every morning, the day came when he did just that.

Third, because he showed up at work, Mordecai was able to give Esther the encouragement that empowered her to play her part in God's providential rescue plan for the Jews. Once Esther learned of Haman's plot to eradicate the Jews, she initially shrank from marching into her husband's presence to spur the king to stop Haman. Knowing that an uninvited audience with the king had deadly consequences filled Esther with fear. But Mordecai brought her bravery with a short speech he was able to send due to the access granted by his profession:

> Then Mordecai told them to reply to Esther, "Do not think to yourself that in the king's palace you will escape

any more than all the other Jews. For if you keep silent
at this time, relief and deliverance will rise for the Jews
from another place, but you and your father's house will
perish. And who knows whether you have not come to
the kingdom for such a time as this?" (Esther 4:13–14)

The entire story pivots on this discourse. Without it, Esther cowers
in concern, Haman's scheme slithers on, and Jewish children,
women, and men are slaughtered. With it, Esther marches with
mettle and moxie, Haman's design deflates and he dies, and whole
tribes and clans are delivered. Mordecai's profession provides him
the opportunity to deliver this discourse.

Fourth, because Mordecai went to work, he gained the authority to write a letter to the Jewish people, allowing them to defend
themselves against Haman. Even though Esther halted Haman,
having him hung on a pole he intended for others, his attack of the
Jews still launched. Troops, preauthorized by the now-deceased
Haman, advanced on the Jews who were legally prohibited from
defending themselves. Mordecai and Esther, however, held positions that could abolish this prohibition. Mordecai thus sent an
edict freeing the Jews to fight for their freedom:

The king's scribes were summoned at that time. . . . And
an edict was written, according to all that Mordecai
commanded concerning the Jews, to the satraps and
the governors and the officials of the provinces from
India to Ethiopia, 127 provinces, to each province in its
own script and to each people in its own language, and
also to the Jews in their script and their language. And
he wrote in the name of King Ahasuerus and sealed it
with the king's signet ring. Then he sent the letters by
mounted couriers riding on swift horses that were used
in the king's service, bred from the royal stud, saying

> that the king allowed the Jews who were in every city to
> gather and defend their lives, to destroy, to kill, and to
> annihilate any armed force of any people or province
> that might attack them. . . . (Esther 8:9–11)

Because Mordecai had served so well at work, he earned the trust of the king and was thus able to send a letter carrying the weight of the king, which gave the Jewish people the right to defend themselves against Haman.

Fifth, because he just went to work, Mordecai brought prosperity and peace to his people. The long-term consequence of serving with character and excellence in a culture and administration that seemed to lack both at times was beneficial for all of Mordecai's people:

> King Ahasuerus imposed tax on the land and on the
> coastlands of the sea. And all the acts of his power
> and might, and the full account of the high honor of
> Mordecai, to which the king advanced him, are they
> not written in the Book of the Chronicles of the kings
> of Media and Persia? For Mordecai the Jew was second
> in rank to King Ahasuerus, and he was great among the
> Jews and popular with the multitude of his brothers, for
> he sought the welfare of his people and spoke peace to
> all his people. (Esther 10:1–3)

Because he went to work, day in and day out, eventually, Mordecai was in a position to bring "shalom," or peace, to every Jew in the kingdom of Persia.

Esther is the story of a person who saved his part of the world simply by going to work. The only picture of Mordecai we see in Esther is Mordecai at work. We don't see him at church. We don't see him at home. We just see him at work. It's through his secular work, in his position as a government employee in a corrupt administration, that Mordecai ends up making a difference in the world. Esther couldn't have done what she did if Mordecai hadn't come to work. The Jewish race wouldn't have been saved if Mordecai hadn't simply gone to work.

Meaning in the Mundane

God uses ordinary, mundane, and routine things like us just going to work to do his work in the world. You don't have to be an astronaut or a baseball player, like I dreamed of being, or a queen, like Esther became. Just doing the ordinary work God gives you provides you the chance to be part of the bigger work God is doing in the world.

In his book *Every Good Endeavor*, Timothy Keller writes this:

> Everyone will be forgotten, nothing we do will make
> any difference, and all good endeavors, even the best,
> will come to naught. Unless there is God. If the God of
> the Bible exists, and there is a True Reality beneath and
> behind this one, and this life is not the only life, then
> every good endeavor, even the simplest ones, pursued in
> response to God's calling, can matter forever.[2]

If there is no God, then even the best work, the thing you spend your best energy, creativity, and time doing, will eventually amount to nothing. But if there is a God, and if that God is doing something larger on this earth, then our work can become part of his work, and it can matter forever—no matter what that work is. That's what we see in the book of Esther. It's not just what we do at home that matters. It's not just what we do at church that matters. What we do at work can matter forever when it's pursued as part of a larger effort to participate with God's hidden work in the world.

Ben Witherington writes that if we want to move in the direction of what we see in Mordecai's example, where our employment and God's engagement come together, we need to make a significant change. We have to "stop working to make a living," and we have to "start working to make a life."[3] Working to make a living is employment to pay bills, earn money, and get an income. But working to make a life, a Christian life in particular, is employment to align what we are doing in the world with what God is doing in the world. We see our work as an extension of what God is doing in the world. Every day, we show up at the office, the classroom, the construction site, or on the road, and we strive to do our work with the faith that it too can contribute to what God is doing in the world. We trust that our work, even if it's for a corrupt organization and among a group of pagan people, can contribute meaningfully to what God is up to in the world.

Captain Chesley "Sully" Sullenberger and First Officer Jeffrey Zaslow piloted US Airways Flight 1549 from LaGuardia Airport. It was a normal day at work. For thirty years, Sully had been going to work as a commercial pilot. Day after day, flight after flight, he had been taking off, landing, taking off, landing. But on this day, three minutes into the flight, the plane struck a flock of Canada geese. Losing both engines, Sully made the decision to land the plane in the Hudson River. It was a risky decision—one only a pilot with three decades of experience could have made. It was a risky landing—something only a pilot of his expertise could have done. But because he had clocked into work, every day, flight after flight, the lives of 155 people were saved.[4]

It was called "The Miracle on the Hudson." The remarkable thing was not just the miracle, but the fact that it took place at work. This miracle that saved the lives of 155 people took place at Sully's workplace. Those passengers weren't in their workplaces. They were on vacation or traveling in between workplaces. But

Sully, First Officer Zaslow, and the flight attendants *were* at work. Their miracle took place when they showed up for another day at work.

Many days, miracles take place in the workplace. Big miracles take place like this one on the Hudson and like those in Esther where Mordecai worked. Little miracles take place as well. From the janitor who cleans toilets at the rec center to the cashier at the grocery store to the accountant to the teacher to the lawyer and everyone in between, miracles happen in the workplace. The office, the classroom, the cubicle, and the driver's seat become holy places where God does some of his best work in us, with us, and through us. Home and church are not the only places where God is at work. He is at your work as well.

Recently, a woman came into my office. Tragically, she shared a story of domestic abuse. She was fragile, overwhelmed, and wounded. Later, she made it to a doctor's office to have some of her wounds documented. She had chosen this particular clinic simply because it was close to her home. She had never been to the clinic. When the doctor entered, however, she was so relieved. She knew him from church. And he put her at ease right away. He hardly ever worked at that clinic. But when he came into work that day, a friend had called and asked if he could fill in at the clinic. "No problem," the doctor said. And just because he showed up at work that day, he gained the chance to comfort a woman in the worst situation she'd ever known. When the woman told me and others of her doctor's appointment, we told her, "You know, that was no coincidence." God was at work.

One of the most important practices in a disenchanted world is learning to see God where we've failed to see him. It may appear God has gone AWOL. The truth is far less sinister. God may be as invisible as the air you breathe, but he is also as immediate and inescapable as the air you breathe. He is everywhere you turn. And one place where he is showing up is at work—your work. So, no matter what you do, go do it. Go with eyes and heart wide open. Go with anticipation and conviction. Believe that God is at work. God is at your work, every single day.

THANK GOD

According to Richard Beck, a professor of psychology, *Scooby Doo* may be the perfect cartoon to summarize an important cultural shift. I used to watch the goofy murder mysteries over cold cereal when I was getting ready for 6:00 A.M. basketball practices in junior high. Most episodes unfolded in a similar pattern. Shaggy, Fred, Daphne, Velma, and Scooby Doo either stumbled into a mystery or were summoned to investigate one. On the surface, it appeared that a ghost, monster, or supernatural creature was causing chaos. After being scared to death, then regaining courage by scarfing some Scooby Snacks, Scooby and the gang finally figured out the thief wasn't some kind of specter. It was just an ordinary person pretending to be a poltergeist in order to scare others away from his or her hijinks. Once the gang revealed this, the authorities were called in and the person was arrested. What began as an instance of extraordinary supernatural activity was eventually disclosed as an instance of ordinary human activity.

This is what many are attempting to do in our Western culture, according to Beck. They are striving to reframe what we've understood to be supernatural as merely natural. A disenchanted, scientific worldview is replacing our enchanted one. In an enchanted world, the supernatural is present. Good and evil spirits fill the world. It's the world at the beginning of every *Scooby Doo* episode. In a disenchanted world, the supernatural is absent. No good or evil spirits fill the world. It's the world at the end of every *Scooby Doo* episode. And many today prefer to see things as disenchanted rather than enchanted.[1]

In the 1500s, the default belief for most people was enchantment. Most people believed that God and the devil were real and active agents in the world. But today, the default belief for many in the Western world is disenchantment. It's easier for many today to believe in the world *Scooby Doo* ends up with rather than the world *Scooby Doo* starts out with. This is true for Christians as well as for non-Christians. Even for followers of Jesus, life seems disenchanted. God may still be real for them, but he's no longer viewed as one who is intimately involved in the affairs of life and the world. How many Christians holding this book, I wonder, are afflicted with some form of disenchanted faith? The news cycle may lead us to feel this way. Reports of murders, wars and conflicts, political division, racism and sexism, and economic instability can leave us feeling as if our world, country, or city is disenchanted. Adversity can lead to this malady as well. Cancer, domestic abuse, job loss, mental health challenges, and relationship strains can cause us to feel as if there is no God involved intimately in life at all. Unanswered prayers lead some people of faith to disenchantment. When prayers rise unheeded one too many times, people sometimes conclude that God simply isn't involved anymore.

The book of Esther seems to have been written for this struggle. It helps us know how to connect with God when God seems out of range. It equips us to nurture intimacy with God in the midst of experiences that make us feel like God is no more than a stranger. The Hebrew words for God can't be found anywhere in pages of Esther. Yet God is written into the story of this book from commencement to conclusion—you just have to read between the lines. Esther explores an audacious assertion: even when God seems veiled or vanished, the truth is that he is still so tangled up in our tale, there's no telling where he ends and we begin.

Purim for the Disenchanted

Esther's story concludes by illustrating that when God seems absent, the best way to thrive is to celebrate the precious few ways in which he is clearly present. Esther does this through a practice known as *Purim*. Purim was a "day of feasting and gladness" (Esther 9:17, 18, 19). The holiday acknowledged that through the *purim* Haman cast—setting the date for the demise of the Jews—God had simultaneously cast the date for the deliverance of the Jews. The party of Purim would be a lasting practice, kept "throughout every generation" (Esther 9:28). In an epoch when so much of God's activity was undetectable, Purim was the party thrown for the work of God that was undeniable.

One word is used for Purim six times in Esther 9.

Instigator	Use of "Confirm" or "Obligate"	Verse
Mordecai and Esther	"confirm" Purim through the writing of a letter	vv. 29, 32
Mordecai and Esther	"obligate" the Jews to practice Purim	vv. 21, 31
The Jews	"obligate" themselves to keep Purim	vv. 27, 31

This word "confirm" or "obligate" does not refer to one person imposing his or her will upon another. It's not Mordecai or Esther imposing their will on the Jewish people. Instead, it refers to the confirmation of a decision that's already been reached.[2] It's as if, having reflected on all that's transpired, having considered this God who's been so concealed yet also acted so clearly, the people and Esther and Mordecai unanimously agree that what's called for is celebration and gratitude. Even when Esther appears to command the celebration, it seems to be a command resting on the reality that this was, in fact, what the people wanted to do in the first place. Their natural and voluntary response to now seeing what had previously gone unseen—God at work behind the scenes—is a joyous celebration. Thus, collectively, they bind themselves to this annual holiday called Purim.

This makes Purim radically different from the other five Jewish feasts in the Torah. Those were commanded by God and by Moses. They were imposed upon the people. Purim, however, was the "spontaneous response" of Esther and the people to the work of God.[3] It was the natural result of realizing that this world, so seemingly disenchanted, is, in fact, enchanted.

Five times, Purim is simply called a day of "gladness" or joy. It was a time to finally fete what at first was forgotten. This celebration, in turn, transformed their world. James K. A. Smith writes, "Worship 'enchants' our everyday lives, reminding us that the world we inhabit is not flattened 'nature' but rather a creation charged with the presence and power of the living Spirit."[4] In a world that seems disenchanted, habits like Purim help us see it as enchanted. One of the primary reasons for Purim in Esther's story was that the Jewish people needed practices that enable them to see the world as God-filled when it so often felt God-forsaken. And we continue to need practices like this today. We need a way to awaken ourselves to the fact that God is present even though it so often seems he may be absent. In a time that seemed disenchanted, Purim enabled people to see it once more as enchanted. Exercises like this that lead us to see and celebrate God's gift of the raindrop eventually train us to see the whole world as saturated with God's goodness.

This is why Jews read the scroll of Esther and kept the festival of Purim during the Holocaust, even in the death camps. If there was ever a time that felt disenchanted, it was then. But the words of Esther and the practice of Purim enabled them to see through the vile veil of violence and to once again realize that even there in the death camps, God was near. Worship and celebration ushered life into the camps of death.

Modern Day Purim

Purim's core is found in the spiritual discipline of celebration. Dallas Willard once noted that the spiritual discipline of celebration is the most overlooked and misunderstood practice among contemporary Christians. Most of us neglect it. Worse, most of us consider celebration "hedonistic" because we think we're not supposed to enjoy our Christianity.[5] Yet celebration empowers us to see the world as enchanted even when it seems disenchanted. Cultivating a habit of celebration, which is the substance of Purim, allows us to recognize that God isn't as far-flung as we fear.

Ann Voskamp writes about this in her book *One Thousand Gifts*. The book begins with the tragic tale of her sister's death. Ann remembers how that death rippled through her and her parents' lives. It created within her a bitterness and a great unease with God.

Eventually, Ann sought some way back to life with God. That way was celebration. The more she poured over Scripture, the more she realized that the fundamental call is for us to live lives of celebration. Although she still grieved the loss of her sister, she hoped that by intentionally seeking reasons for rejoicing, she could find light and life again. She determined to identify one thousand gifts given to her by God, even though her sister had been taken away. She began writing in a journal even the smallest gift of God received each day. Her list included things like the sound of book pages turning, boys humming hymns, wind rushing through an open truck window, or laundry flapping in the wind.[6]

She found that by actively looking for God in these gifts and by celebrating them, she experienced transformation. Not only did it lead her beyond the pain of her sister's death; it also helped her to experience a better way of living her own life. We might say she learned to see her world as enchanted when it once seemed so disenchanted.

James Bryan Smith urges people to take time each week, over the course of the week, to write down one hundred things for which they are grateful. They are not to write down the obvious things like friends and family and God and Jesus. They are to include the oft-forgotten items like warm cookies, a dog wagging its tail, and clean socks.[7] These, too, are the gifts of God's activity in our lives. As we celebrate these one hundred gifts weekly, our disenchantment becomes enchanted.

In 2007, Disney released a film entitled *Enchanted*. It told of a Snow White type of princess named Giselle. She was plunged from her idyllic, animated kingdom of Andalasia into the gritty, real world of New York City. There, she met Robert, a cynical divorce lawyer who was quite the realist and hardly a romantic. As Giselle spoke to Robert about things that were normal in her enchanted home of Andalasia (e.g., true love, trolls, fairies, talking animals), Robert dismissed her as demented. His mind changed, however, when he watched Giselle train doves to carry flowers to his girlfriend, as Giselle led all of Central Park in a song and dance number, and as a battle for good and evil played out around Giselle. This world of New York City, he realized, was far more enchanted than he'd ever known.

Mordecai was Esther's Giselle. Esther was the Jewish people's Giselle. What our world needs is more Giselles—people capable of lifting the curtain and revealing just how divinely enchanted the world around us truly is. What our world needs is people who can respond to crisis not with despair and not with violence but with abiding joy and hopefulness that comes through a conviction that there's far more going on than what we first see. The practice of celebration allows us to be those kinds of people.

LEND A HAND

Las Vegas, Nevada, experienced one of America's worst mass shootings in October 2017. The day after the bloodshed, Bishop Joseph Pepe of Las Vegas hosted a prayer service to mourn the fifty-nine dead and to pray for the more than five hundred injured. More than eight hundred people attended the prayer service.[1] It was a sobering reminder that when we are crushed by affliction, we instinctively cry out to the Almighty. We often do not know what else to do. Unable to make sense of what's happened on earth, we reach out to heaven. We empathize with the words of the psalmist: "With my voice I *cry out* to the LORD; with my voice I plead for mercy to the LORD. I pour out my complaint before him; I tell my trouble before him" (Ps. 142:1–2—emphasis mine).

When we are crushed by affliction, we instinctively cry out to the Almighty. More than eight hundred cried out to the Father the day after Stephen Paddock fired multiple rounds into the crowd of concertgoers in Las Vegas. Prior to the event, as hurricanes Harvey, Irma, and Maria slammed into cities and souls, thousands cried out to God. After the event, as fires stormed through California, thousands more cried out to God. When we are crushed by affliction, we cry out to the Almighty. It's our first move in times of misery.

The psalmist's words "cry out" are also found in the mouths of the Israelites who faced suffering. A category five hurricane slammed into their lives in the form of slavery. Afflicted, they cried out: "During those many days the king of Egypt died, and the people of Israel groaned because of their slavery and *cried out* for help. Their cry for rescue from slavery came up to God" (Exod. 2:23—emphasis mine). The Israelites cry out to God for relief, for rescue. They scream for divine assistance. That's their first move. It's often our first move as well.

But what does God do? How does God counter our cry?

God's Passover Reply

God responds to the plea of Israel with Passover. God promises to strike the firstborn in the land of Egypt as a way of executing judgment on Egypt and its gods for their treatment of the Israelites. But when God sees the blood the Israelites have painted on their homes, he will "pass over" them. Their firstborn will live. They will be freed forever from their enslavement from Egypt (Exod. 12:11–27).

The story of Passover is filled with the extraordinary ways in which God works against evil. God takes matters into his own hands:

- "*I* will strike all the firstborn in the land." (Exod. 12:12—emphasis mine)
- "*I* will execute judgments." (Exod. 12:12—emphasis mine)
- "*I* will strike the land of Egypt." (Exod. 12:13—emphasis mine)

In the Passover celebration each year after this, the Israelites would commemorate how the *Lord* struck the Egyptians. God operated in a supernatural way to defeat the source of their suffering.

This is often how we long for God to respond to our own cries during crisis. We long for God to take matters into his own hands and respond to us in ways that are mighty and miraculous. Occasionally, God does just that. In times of affliction, when we cry out to the Almighty, sometimes he responds with Passover—a personal and extraordinary means of addressing the source of our pain.

As Hurricane Irma was raging toward Florida in 2017, dozens of believers stood on the beach in Jacksonville and cried out for their own version of Passover. They prayed for God to miraculously still the storm in the same way Jesus stilled the storm on the Sea of Galilee. They begged God to literally turn the hurricane away from shore. They wanted a Passover response—a direct and divine intervention.[2]

Sometimes this is what God provides. He takes matters into his own hands in an unmistakable way. He cures the cancer. He diffuses the family division. He stills the storm.

God's Purim Reply

But many times, he doesn't. Irma roared ashore despite those prayers on the beach—it was one of the most powerful hurricanes in history, killing more than one hundred people, causing millions in property damage. Frequently, God does not reply to our cries with a Passover. More often, he responds in a different way. When we reach out in times of pain, we are more likely to find God reacting not with a Passover but with a Purim.

The psalmist's words "cry out," also spoken by the Israelites, are found again—this time in the mouth of a man named Mordecai who wailed his hurt to heaven:

> When Mordecai learned all that had been done,
> Mordecai tore his clothes and put on sackcloth and
> ashes, and went out into the midst of the city, and he
> *cried out* with a loud and bitter cry. He went up to the
> entrance of the king's gate, for no one was allowed to
> enter the king's gate clothed in sackcloth. And in every
> province, wherever the king's command and his decree
> reached, there was great mourning among the Jews,
> with fasting and weeping and lamenting, and many of
> them lay in sackcloth and ashes. When Esther's young
> women and her eunuchs came and told her, the queen
> was deeply distressed. (Esther 4:1–4—emphasis mine)

Mordecai has just learned that Haman, the second-in-command in Persia, intended to put to death every Jew in the land. Mordecai, facing a storm of suffering bearing down upon his people, cries out in agony. Just as the Israelites had cried out centuries ago in the face of their mortal enemy in Egypt, so now Mordecai cries out, presumably to God.

But God does not respond with another Passover. God does not treat his people in Persia as he did his people in Egypt. He does not handle Haman as he did the Pharaoh. Instead, in a bitter twist of irony, the news of Haman's death sentence for the Jews is sent out on the eve of Passover (Esther 3:7–14). On the eve of the holy day when they mark how God miraculously rescued them from the hand of a malevolent ruler, they learn that they are soon to be massacred at the hand of another malevolent ruler! As faithful and fraught people had done for centuries, Mordecai cried out while he was being crushed; but there would be no Passover to resolve his pain. He and the Jews could celebrate how God moved in personal and extraordinary ways to cease suffering in their people's past. But in the present, God would move in a far more mysterious way. This time, as the cry of the crushed reached God's ears, the eventual response would not be a Passover—it would be a Purim.

Just as Passover was the celebration of the way in which God delivered Israel in Egypt, Purim was the celebration of the way in which God delivered Israel in Persia. But if Passover commemorated the extraordinary, Purim commemorated the ordinary. God's deliverance, remembered in Purim, came simply through Mordecai and Esther writing letters authorizing the Jewish people to defend themselves against Haman's troops and the courageous Jewish people doing just that (Esther 8:9–12; 9:1–2).

In a Passover way, God could have sent a plague on the Persian soldiers as they slept the night prior to their battle with Esther's people. Instead, in a Purim way, God inspired Mordecai and Esther to write a letter granting the Jews permission to defend themselves against Haman's death squad, and God emboldened the Jews to fight for their survival. No Passover plague. No heavenly hands-on happenings. Just plain old Purim political maneuvering. Just popular-level Purim self-defense.

When we are crushed by affliction and we cry out to the Almighty, God may rarely respond with a Passover—an extraordinary and personal movement to cease our suffering. God may more routinely respond, as he did in Esther, with a Purim—an ordinary and more impersonal act to topple our tribulation. The book of Esther reveals that God's answer to our agony is more often ordinary rather than extraordinary, more frequently mundane rather than miraculous, more often secular rather than sacred.

This, however, makes it no less divine.

Anyone looking from the outside in at Passover would be led to believe it could only be the work of a divine Maker: a climactic plague that persuaded Israel's most vile villain to free them from slavery.

Anyone looking from the outside in at Purim would be led to believe it was only the work of mortals: a savvy queen, her astute adopted father, and dauntless Jewish soldiers—not a single mention of God. Yet Purim unapologetically suggests that this work of humans was nonetheless the work of heaven.

Exodus reveals those rare Passover ways through which God occasionally responds to our troubles. They are the Almighty's activities that are supernatural and easily seeable. Esther reveals those recurring Purim ways through which God often responds to our troubles. They are the Almighty's activities that are humdrum and often hidden. When they happen, the former seem unreal. The latter seem unamazing. But both are the labor of the Lord.

Our Lot in Life

This is especially seen in the meaning of the word "Purim." Purim comes from the word "pur," which is what Haman cast in order to determine when he would slay Esther's people (Esther 9:24–26). The words "pur" and "Purim" are not Hebrew words and are rarely found in the Old Testament. They refer to the lots Haman used, like die, to determine the will of the gods. There is a Hebrew word for "lot," and it is used often in the Old Testament. The Jews used this word in much the same way we use it today. For example, when we say, "That's my lot in life," we mean that God has willed a certain circumstance to occur—our "lot." God has worked in our life to bring us the particular situation in which we now find ourselves.

Similarly, in the festival of Purim, the Jews interpreted what had happened in their recent history in Persia as their "lot"—their divine assignment or portion, given them by God. Rather than being given a supernatural miracle, their lot had been a politically shrewd queen, a wise adopted father, and courageous soldiers. All of these were ordinary items in their ancient world. Yet the Jews interpreted this lot as a heavenly gift. It had not been their lot to get a Passover in the face of their pain. Instead, their lot had been to get something far more routine and mundane. To commemorate this, they called it "Purim" after the word "pur," or lot.

The book of Esther, through the festival of Purim, is saying that it is often our lot in life to have God address the sorrow in our life in ways that are ordinary and routine. This may be hard for us to swallow, especially in the face of suffering. We want a radical God. We desire an extraordinary experience of faith. When it comes to times of trouble, the lot we want is something more like Passover. Michael Horton writes about this in his book *Ordinary*:

> "Ordinary" has to be one of the loneliest words in our vocabulary today. Who wants a bumper sticker that announces to the neighborhood, "My child is an ordinary student at Bubbling Brook Elementary"? Who wants to be that ordinary person who lives in an ordinary town, is a member of an ordinary church, and has ordinary friends and works an ordinary job? Our life has to count! We have to leave our mark, have a legacy, and make a difference. . . . Today we feel the pressure to have our weddings look like the cover of a bridal magazine or movie set. Our marriages have to be made in heaven, even though we're very much on earth. Our presentations at work have to dazzle . . . nothing short of "brilliant" and "groundbreaking" will satisfy if you want a good job. When we do stop and smell the roses, it has to be an unforgettable package at an amazing resort.[3]

This hunger for the extreme and extraordinary also creeps into our faith. This may be doubly true when we face affliction. We long for God to respond to our cries with Passover. That's the lot we want. But Esther reveals that what God grants is more often routine and ordinary. Commonly, what God gives is Purim.

Gifts of Food

The book drills the point home by revealing how the Jews would give gifts of food during Purim. During this special season, the Jews would send savory presents to one another, especially to those who were in need (Esther 9:19–22). To appreciate the true significance of this offering of food, it's crucial to understand the word used to describe it. The foods given to the poor are called "gifts" twice (Esther 9:22). This word "gifts" is translated as "portion" earlier in Esther (Esther 2:9). This same root word is used by David and is translated "portion," a synonym for "lot": "The LORD is my chosen portion and my cup; you hold my lot. The lines have fallen for me in pleasant places; indeed, I have a beautiful inheritance" (Ps. 16:5–6).

David comments here about his chosen portion or lot—the circumstance given to him by God. This same word is used to describe the food given to the poor during Purim. In that regard, it is translated "gift," but it shares the root word of portion/lot.[4] Thus, during the festival of Purim (named after a word meaning "lot"), as the Jews took "gifts" of food to those suffering from poverty, those gifts reminded the Jews that it had been their "lot" in life to have God address their own affliction in simple and humble ways—through an orphaned queen, through her foster father, and through Esther and Mordecai's quick thinking and acting. But the "gifts" to the poor took it one step further. Each time Jews took these gifts of food to someone suffering in poverty, the giver and gift become part of that poor person's "lot" in life. They became part of the way God was continuing to work in simple and humble ways to address pain and sorrow in the world. In the offering of a routine meal to a hungry person, the giver and gift became part of God's ongoing yet unpretentious work to address agony and affliction in the world.

Passover celebrates the way God responded miraculously by working through wonders. Purim celebrates the way God responded mundanely by performing through people—Mordecai and Esther above all. But now each year, as celebrants give gifts to the poor, the flame of Purim leaps beyond the torch, sparking new candles in the dark. People in hardship experience their own lot in life change for the better through these gracious offerings and their donors.

The book of Esther teaches that God's normal approach to affliction is not to spectacularly still the storm, finish off the foe, or heal the hurt. God's routine approach to tribulation is instead to humbly send average folks into the fray to make a difference in their own simple yet significant ways. He has so often done this for us. He can so often do this through us.

A Flood of God's Love

This was the point, it seems, of the October 2017 edition of *The Christian Chronicle*, whose front-page headline read, "After Hurricanes, A Flood of God's Love." The paper carried stories of the devastation wrought by the hurricanes in Texas and Florida in 2017. It went on to discuss the ways in which ordinary people and churches had provided shelter and relief in the wake of the hurricanes in Florida and Texas:

> "I couldn't put it into words. They've treated us like we were royalty from some foreign country," retired Army Col. Chuck Emmerich, 81, said after spending four nights in the Belton Church of Christ gymnasium, about 200 miles northwest of Houston.
>
> Like the Belton church, the Champions Church of Christ—a Houston congregation that avoided flooding—transformed its building into an emergency shelter. . . .

"We were really homeless without any idea where we were," Toni Sinclair said. "The church was so over-whelmingly warm and friendly. It just made me cry. They had a little kennel for our dog, and they brought us food," she said through tears. "We hadn't eaten in a day and a half. And they just continued to give to us and love us and share with us what we needed to do. And they gave us clothes and a shower."[5]

There was no reporting of mighty miracles from heaven—just routine stories of average people and humble churches serving and making a difference. This was God's Purim reply to affliction.

Purim is not an answer to the why of evil. But it is an answer to the what. What God does in the face of evil is commission a man to take in an orphaned girl and raise her right, send an orphaned girl to become a queen, give courage to threatened Jews whose knees are weak, send givers with plates of food to those still hungry, and inspire ordinary church members to turn church buildings into shelters in the aftermath of mighty storms. When the trials come, he sometimes still responds with a Passover. More often, though, he responds with a Purim.

Bob Goff, in his book *Love Does*, puts it this way:

God . . . didn't choose someone else to express his cre-ative presence to the world . . . didn't tap the rock star or the popular kid to get things done. He chose you and me. We are the means, the method, the object, and the delivery vehicles. God can use anyone, for sure. If you can shred on a Fender or won "Best Personality," you're not disqualified—it just doesn't make you more quali-fied. You see, God usually chooses ordinary people like us to get things done.[6]

There's a bunch of bad stuff brewing in the world today. God has the capacity to bring all the marvels of heaven against it in a stunning display of sovereignty. At times, he will. And it will leave us speechless. Humbled. On our knees. But the rest of the time, he'll choose you and me to right the wrongs and treat the trauma—just as he chose Mordecai and Esther. Ordinary people. We're the means. The method. The delivery vehicles. A lot of the time, we are how God makes the lot in life a whole lot better for a whole lot of people. We are how God enchants the earth once again.

Starting.

Right.

Now.

Forty-Day Study Guide for the Disenchanted

To help you glean the most from each chapter and from this book as a whole, engage in these brief formation exercises and reflections over a period of forty days. You can complete these as a participant in a group or by yourself. This will be a way for you to embrace the practices of each chapter:

1. *Examen*
2. Waiting
3. Engaging
4. Humility
5. Radical prayer
6. Valuing others
7. Empathy
8. Generosity
9. Mercy

10. Purpose
11. Celebration
12. Service

DAY ONE

Read Chapter One: Refocus.

Draw a picture of a theatre stage. Put an X near the center of the stage. Write some dates or phrases that stand for times when God has been "center stage"—acted in your life in ways that have been clear, obvious, and unmistakable. Put an X near the very back of the stage. Write some dates or phrases that stand for times when God has been "backstage"—acted in your life in ways that have been hidden, distant, and hard to discern.

DAY TWO

Write a line of numbers from 0 to 10. Circle the 0. This stands for the number of times the word "God" appears in the written story of Esther. If someone were to observe an average day in your life and write a story about it, how many times do you suppose they'd write the word "God"? Circle that number.

In Chapter One, we see that, when it came to Esther, "God performed without visions and voices from heaven. He engaged without miracles and mystical appearances. God did it all in the midst of the most secular people and through the most secular means possible." Peer back over the course of your life. What are two or three ways in which these words ring true for you?

DAY THREE

Practice *examen. Examen* is an ancient practice designed to help us sight this secluded God. It slows us down, allowing us to revisit the previous day so we can see God's presence and activity where we may have missed it. Here's how it works: Find a quiet space. In a spirit of prayer, review the day that has just passed (yesterday, if you're doing this in the morning; today, if you're doing this in the evening). Let the entire day replay like a film in your imagination. The highs. The lows. The conversations. The times alone. The planned tasks. The unexpected things that happened. Here's what you're looking for: moments when God was present and active, though you may have missed it. Guidance he provided. Blessings he brought. Comfort he gave. Admonishment he delivered. Assume there were no "accidents" or "coincidences" during the day. Believe in providence—God's hidden hand at work in all things. Now, having recognized the many ways God was present and active in that day, though you may have missed it, give thanks to God for it.

Day Four

Read Chapter Two: Sit Tight.

Draw an oval running course with a finish line. Write a word or phrase on that finish line that represents something you've waited for or hoped for or worked for that didn't seem to materialize, at least not in the way you'd hoped.

Day Five

Look back over the tables in Chapter Two, representing the feasts and the reversals in the book of Esther. Now, consider a timeline of your life or a timeline of your community. When was a time when it seemed things were going to end very sadly and very badly, but God worked over time to reverse that ending and transformed it into something good and sacred? When was a time you could do nothing but wait on God and his slow work in a challenging time? What was the result of that waiting?

DAY SIX

Pray Psalm 30:11 throughout the day. As you move through the day, and you see God working out difficult situations, thank him using the words of the psalm ("Thank you, God. You have turned for me my mourning into dancing; you have loosed my sackcloth and clothed me with gladness"). As you move through the day, and you find situations that need God's attention, use the words of the psalm to pray ("God, turn my/their mourning into dancing; loose my/their sackcloth and cloth me/them with gladness").

DAY SEVEN

Read Chapter Three: Jump In.

Consider the various roles you have in life and the responsibilities and opportunities that come with each: child of God, family member, student/employee, citizen of a neighborhood/city/nation, etc. As you consider these roles, is there an invitation or opportunity in which God is calling you to engage, especially for the sake of others—even if it's risky? If so, complete this sentence: "In this role of my life (_____) and in this season of my life, God is calling me to engage his world in this way: _____

_____

_____."

DAY EIGHT

One study finds that we experience at least twenty-seven distinct emotions.[1] One of those is fear, which kept Esther from engaging in the opportunity to rescue her Jewish people. Here is the whole list:

Admiration	Entrancement
Adoration	Envy
Aesthetic	Excitement
Appreciation	Fear
Amusement	Horror
Anxiety	Interest
Awe	Joy
Awkwardness	Nostalgia
Boredom	Romance
Calmness	Sadness
Confusion	Satisfaction
Craving	Sexual desire
Disgust	Sympathy
Empathetic pain	Triumph

Draw and color a picture of at least one emotion that may be hindering you from engaging in God's invitation to be part of his work in the world. Think back through your life. Write down one time when you lived/acted without that emotion hindering you: _____

_____

_____

Day Nine

Live this entire day with this conviction: "I see God everywhere now!" Try to live as if you truly do notice God everywhere. And if God is indeed everywhere you are, try to imagine how God is inviting you to engage where you are. If God is in that supermarket you've run into for a gallon of milk today, how is he calling you to engage those who are also present? If God is truly present in the school or office you've entered for several hours today, how is he inviting you to engage those who are also spending the better part of the day there? End this day by reflecting on this exercise. Fill in these blanks: I was particularly aware of God today in these places and at these times: _____

_____

_____. Because I was aware of God's presence, I felt invited by him to engage in these ways today: ____

_____

_____.

DAY TEN

Read Chapter Four: Lie Low.

In the storyline, we see at least two pitfalls caused by pride and ego. What problems in the world today would you identify as being caused by the same kind of self-centeredness? How do those problems contribute to a sense that the world is disenchanted— void of God?

What problems have occurred in your own life as a result of ego and pride—your own or that of others?

DAY ELEVEN

Say this phrase out loud: "This is not about me." Keep saying it silently as you move through the day. And, as you move through the day, consider how that truth could/should change your behavior and attitude in each moment: as you interact with others on social media, as you talk to people at work or school, as you drive in traffic or walk among a crowd, as you deal with tasks and requests, as you watch or listen to the news. At the end of the day, write a paragraph about the way in which that phrase has affected your behavior and attitude.

Day Twelve

In her book *Glittering Vices*, Rebecca DeYoung proposes that one of the antidotes to ego and pride is silence.[2] Instead of always having to speak up in conversations, be quiet. Instead of asking everyone what they think of what you are wearing, be silent. Instead of drawing people's attention to what you are doing, have done, or will do, be quiet. Intentional silence can be a step away from ego and pride and toward humility. Today, practice silence in intentional ways that are designed to help you move toward humility.

Day Thirteen

Read Chapter Five: Pray Brave.

Using a timer or a clock, take the time to literally watch twenty seconds pass. Can you think of a time or two in the recent past when twenty seconds of courage would have made a significant difference in your walk with God and your service to him in the world? Write those down.

Day Fourteen

Identify one thing you need twenty seconds of insane courage to do. Perhaps it's something God is calling you to do in your neighborhood. Your family. Your school. Your work. Your personal life. And then, before you do anything, block out three days and simply pray about it. Pray and fast about it. You may find not only the courage you need. You may also find God doing things you never imagined he would or could.

DAY FIFTEEN

Take a step today to invite other Christians or your church to join you in radical prayer. Consider "praying the news" together—reading, watching, or listening to a recap of the day's headlines and then praying together over them. Call some Christians together to pray about a specific issue in your community or world. Sit down with a Christian leader to ask about planning a congregational time of prayer about weighty matters. Go with a small group to pray over those who are recovering in a hospital. Find some way to unite with others in prayer.

DAY SIXTEEN

Read Chapter Six: Treasure.

As Haman did, make two lists. List One should contain at least some of the things in your life for which you are deeply grateful: job, health, opportunities, loved ones, friendships, and so on. List Two should contain (potentially) the name(s) of people you may have mistreated or neglected or "considered as nothing" in your pursuit of a personal goal. Give thanks to God for List One. Confess to God the existence of List Two and accept his forgiveness for it.

DAY SEVENTEEN

Draw (and perhaps color) a simple picture of yourself. Write words on the outside of yourself that depict your instrumental worth—the external reasons some might love/value you. Write words on the inside of yourself that depict your intrinsic worth—the ingrained reasons God loves/values you. Give thanks to God for the way he loves you for your intrinsic worth.

Day Eighteen

As you move throughout your day, determine to treat each person around you with great value and worth—regardless of their contribution to you, their likeness to you (in terms of race, income, age, etc.), their familiarity to you, and so forth. You might silently say to each person, "You are beloved by God," and then allow that statement to dictate your attention to and treatment of that person.

Day Nineteen

Fill in these sentences: One thing that keeps my church from being a community that demonstrates value for all people is _____ _____. One thing I can do about this barrier/ challenge in my church is _____ _____. One thing my church does well in demonstrating value for all people is _____. One way I can better support and participate in this initiative in my church is _____. Spend time during the day praying for God to help your church be a community with a heart that acts with abundant love for all, especially those who are often neglected, mistreated, and undervalued in our communities.

Day Twenty

Read Chapter Seven: Advocate.

Write down some of the names you've been known by (including things like "boss," "mom," "kiddo," nicknames, and so on.). What do those names say about who you are? What other names do you wish you had been known by?

DAY TWENTY-ONE

Consider an imaginary diary. Day One contains an entry from Esther as she wears her Persian name Esther. "Today, I am a Persian, and my name is Esther," the entry begins. How might the rest of that entry flow? What activities might she have engaged in that day? What would her thoughts and feelings have been that day? Day Two contains an entry from Esther as she wears her Hebrew name Hadassah. "Today, I am a Jew, and my name is Hadassah," the entry begins. How might the rest of that entry flow? What activities might she have engaged in that day? What would her thoughts and feelings have been that day?

DAY TWENTY-TWO

Who has been one person to "wear your name"—value you and stand in solidarity with you? Write his/her name down: _____ . Give thanks to God for him/her. What person or group of people is God inviting you to stand in solidarity with? Write their name(s) down: _____ _____ . Ask God to show you what your next step should be. Practice intercessory prayer for those people or groups today.

DAY TWENTY-THREE

Read Chapter Eight: Pay Out.

What are two or three of the key turning points in your own life? Write them down here: _____

_____

_____

_____

_____

_____

Day Twenty-Four

Esther's story reveals the truth of what Paul writes: "For the love of money is a root of all kinds of evils (1 Tim. 6:10). What evils in your day can you identify that are taking place because of this love of money? Write them down here: _____

_____

_____

Day Twenty-Five

There's a long list of ways in which money and resources are used by people in Scripture to bless others and to build up the kingdom of God. What are some ways in which you've seen this happen in your own life? Write an example or two down here: _____

_____

_____

Day Twenty-Six

Draw a picture of some money—your money. What percentage of that money do you feel you are investing in positive, kingdom-building ways? Put a number to it. How might God be inviting you toward even greater generosity with your money and other resources? Write that down here. God is inviting me toward greater generosity in this way: _____

_____

Day Twenty-Seven

Read Chapter Nine: Power Down.

Draw an arrow pointing down. Can you think of a time in your life when you felt powerless? What was that like? Use a few words to describe that time: _____

_____

Day Twenty-Eight

Draw an arrow pointing up. Can you think of a time when a person with a certain amount of power used their power to benefit you? What was that like? Use a few words to describe that time: _____
_____. Give thanks to God for that person and their example.

Day Twenty-Nine

Every person has a certain amount of power or influence over others. What power or influence do you possess? What are some ways you can leverage that power and influence for the benefit of others, rather than for the benefit of yourself? Complete this sentence: Regarding many people in my life today, I have the power to _____, and I will use that power to _____
_____.

Day Thirty

Read Chapter Ten: Work Wonders.

Draw a picture of what you as a child wanted to be when you grew up. Why was that work or career important to you?

Day Thirty-One

Make two columns. One is "I work to make a living by . . ." The other is "I work to make a life by . . ." Consider your current occupation. Under the first column, write down some of the ways in which you approach your work solely as a means of making money, earning a living, paying the bills, and so on. Under the second column, write down some of the ways in which you do or could approach your work as a means of joining God in what he is up to in the world today, being part of his larger work.

DAY THIRTY-TWO

God is at work at your work. What is one thing you can do this week to better participate with him in that work at your work? Write that down here: _____

_____

DAY THIRTY-THREE

Read Chapter Eleven: Thank God.

What was the last party or celebration you attended? What sounds do you recall? What smells do you recall?

DAY THIRTY-FOUR

Dallas Willard wrote that celebration is one of the most over-looked and misunderstood disciplines of the Christian life. On this scale, how present is the practice of God-oriented celebration in your life? (1 totally absent; 10 very present)

1 | 2 | 3 | 4 | 5 | 6 | 7 | 8 | 9 | 10

What explains the presence or absence of celebration in your life?

DAY THIRTY-FIVE

See if you can write down one hundred things from the past week for which you are grateful. This may take a while. You may need to start this list and then come back to it later in the day. Include very ordinary things as well as extraordinary things. Once you complete the list, give thanks to God for these items.

DAY THIRTY-SIX

Draw (and perhaps color) three or four balloons. In each balloon, write one act or habit you could adopt that would enable you to be a more joyful, grateful, and celebratory person.

DAY THIRTY-SEVEN

Read Chapter Twelve: Lend a Hand.

Recall a time you "cried out" to God for help/relief/assistance. What was God's response?

DAY THIRTY-EIGHT

Draw a picture of a doorpost (doorframe) in order to represent Passover. Within the space framed by the doorpost, write a few words that summarize a time in your life when God did something that was direct, extraordinary, powerful, and, perhaps, even miraculous.

DAY THIRTY-NINE

Draw a picture of a plate in order to represent Purim. On the plate, write a few words that summarize a time in your life when God did something that seemed less direct and less powerful, yet was still clearly from him—a time he worked through others or through circumstances in routine and mundane ways for your benefit.

DAY FORTY

How is God inviting you to be his Purim response to people around you?

NOTES

Introduction: The Land of Disenchantment

[1]Junqiang Han, Yingying Meng, Chengcheng Xu, and Siqi Qin, "Urban Residents' Religious Beliefs and Influencing Factors on Christianity in Wuhan, China," *Religions* 8, no. 11 (2018): 244, doi:10.3390/rel8110244.

[2]Charles Taylor, *A Secular Age* (Boston: The Belknap Press of Harvard University Press, 2007), 3.

[3]C. S. Lewis, *Mere Christianity* (New York: HarperOne, 2015), 23.

Chapter 1: Refocus

[1]Charles Taylor, *A Secular Age* (Boston: The Belknap Press of Harvard University Press, 2007), 25–89.

[2]Karen Jobes, *Esther,* The NIV Application Commentary (Grand Rapids: Zondervan, 1999), 59. Ecbatana, Babylon, and Persepolis were the other capitals.

[3]Adele Berlin, *Esther,* The JPS Bible Commentary (Philadelphia: Jewish Publication Society, 2001), xv.

[4]Jobes, *Esther,* 21.

[5]Jobes, *Esther,* 60.

[6]Jobes, *Esther,* 59. In fact, the number 127 used to indicate the number of provinces in his empire is symbolic of this. Symbolically, twelve can refer to the number of the tribes of Israel. Ten can refer to the number of completeness.

Seven can refer to the number of perfection. Together, they make 127, a number symbolic of Xerxes ruling over the entire earth.

[7] Jobes, *Esther,* 62.

[8] Samuel Wells and George Summer, *Esther & Daniel,* Brazos Theological Commentary on the Bible (Grand Rapids: Brazos Press, 2013), 25.

[9] Jon D. Levenson, *Esther,* The Old Testament Library (Louisville: Westminster John Knox Press, 1997), 56.

[10] Jobes, *Esther,* 45.

[11] Jobes, *Esther,* 19–20, 43.

[12] Radley Balko and Tucker Carrington, *The Cadaver King and the Country Dentist: A True Story of Injustice in the American South* (New York: Public Affairs, 2018).

[13] Jim Manney, *A Simple, Life-Changing Prayer: Discovering the Power of St. Ignatius Loyola's Examen* (Chicago: Loyola Press, 2011), 3–4.

[14] Mark E. Thibodeaux, *Reimagining the Ignatian Examen* (Chicago: Loyola Press, 2015).

[15] Kevin O'Brien, *The Ignatian Adventure* (Chicago: Loyola Press, 2011), 75–77.

Chapter 2: Sit Tight

[1] Built off of comments by Michael V. Fox, *Character and Ideology in the Book of Esther* (Grand Rapids: Eerdmans, 2001), 156–60.

[2] Gregory Boyles, *Tattoos on the Heart* (New York: Free Press, 2012).

[3] Henri Nouwen, *You Are the Beloved* (New York: Convergent, 2017), 78.

[4] Mark Batterson, *Spiritual Rhythm* (Grand Rapids: Zondervan, 2010), 78

[5] Sue Monk Kidd, *When the Heart Waits,* (New York: HarperOne, 1990), 17

Chapter 3: Jump In

[1] Meghan Willet, "The Most Highlighted Kindle Quotes of All Time," *Business Insider,* June 10, 2014, http://www.businessinsider.com/amazon-kindles-most-highlighted-books-2014-6.

[2] According to Michael V. Fox, *Character and Ideology in the Book of Esther* (Grand Rapids: Eerdmans, 2001), 43–45, four reasons are often given for Mordecai's stand against Haman. Some see it as an act of arrogance. Some see it as a way of avoiding idolatry, thinking that kneeling before Haman may be an act of worship. Some see it as less than idolatry but still as an affront

to God. Still others see this as a matter of tribal conflict. This is most likely. Haman is called an Agagite (Esther 3:1). King Agag of the Amalekites was the first, the original, enemy of the Israelites (1 Sam. 15). So hated were they that God commanded King Saul to destroy them. Thus, for a Jew to bow down to someone like Haman who is called an Agagite would be quite difficult.

[3]Interestingly, Joshua used a similar device to cast lots before the Lord (Josh. 18:6).

[4]Fox, *Character and Ideology*, 47–51.

[5]Joshua and Caleb tore their clothes when they heard the people wanted to return to Egypt (Num. 14:6). David ripped his clothing after hearing of the death of Saul (2 Sam. 1:11).

[6]Karen Jobes, *Esther*, The NIV Application Commentary (Grand Rapids: Zondervan, 1999), 132.

[7]See James K. A. Smith, *How (Not) to Be Secular: Reading Charles Taylor* (Grand Rapids: Eerdmans, 2014), 22, 124.

[8]Shusaku Endo, *Silence* (New York: Picador Modern Classics, 2016), 203.

[9]For more on this language, see John Mark Hicks, *Meeting God at* The Shack (Abilene, TX: Leafwood Publishers, 2017).

[10]Leo Tolstoy, *Master, Man and Other Stories* (New York: Penguin Classics, 2005), 183–205.

[11]Brené Brown, *Rising Strong* (New York: Random House, 2017), xx–xxi.

Chapter 4: Lie Low

[1]For a thorough introduction to the origin of the seven deadly sins, see Rebecca Konyndyk DeYoung, *Glittering Vices* (Grand Rapids: Brazos Press, 2009), 28–29.

[2]Ryan Holiday, *Ego Is the Enemy* (New York: Penguin, 2016), xxiii.

[3]Hannah Arendt, *Eichmann in Jerusalem: A Report on the Banality of Evil* (New York: Penguin Classics, 2006).

[4]Hannah Arendt, *Eichmann*, 287.

[5]Phrase adapted from Sharon Hodde Miller in *Free of Me* (Grand Rapids: Baker Books, 2017).

[6]John Ortberg, *The Life You've Always Wanted* (Grand Rapids: Zondervan, 2015), 111–12.

[7]David Benner, *The Gift of Being Yourself* (Downers Grove, IL: InterVarsity Press, 2015), 22.

[8]Benner, *The Gift of Being Yourself*, 60.

Chapter 5: Pray Brave

[1]Bobby Ross Jr., "The Faith behind Disney's *McFarland, USA*," *Christian Chronicle*, February 6, 2015, http://www.christianchronicle.org/article/the-faith-behind-disneys-mcfarland-usa.

[2]Karen Jobes, *Esther*, The NIV Application Commentary (Grand Rapids: Zondervan, 1999), 110.

[3]Debra Reid, *Esther: An Introduction and Commentary* (Downers Grove, IL: InterVarsity Press, 2008), 106.

[4]Benjamin Mee, *We Bought a Zoo* (New York: Weinstein Books, 2008), 80.

[5]Mee, *We Bought a Zoo*, 36–37.

[6]*We Bought a Zoo*, directed by Cameron Crow (Los Angeles: 20th Century Fox, 2011), DVD.

[7]Michael V. Fox, *Character and Ideology in the Book of Esther* (Grand Rapids: Eerdmans, 2001), 63, 157.

[8]Richard Foster, *Prayer* (San Francisco: Harper, 1992), 243.

[9]"The Catholic Nun Who Tweets a Daily Prayer to President Trump," *All Things Considered*, December 16, 2018, https://www.npr.org/2018/12/16/677252495/the-catholic-nun-who-tweets-a-daily-prayer-to-president-trump.

Chapter 6: Treasure

[1]Adele Berlin, *Esther*, The JPS Bible Commentary (Philadelphia: Jewish Publication Society, 2001), 84–85.

[2]Charles Taylor, *A Secular Age* (Cambridge, MA: The Belknap Press of Harvard University Press, 2007), 25–89.

[3]Michael V. Fox, *Character and Ideology in the Book of Esther* (Grand Rapids: Eerdmans, 2001), 74.

[4]Karen Jobes, *Esther*, The NIV Application Commentary (Grand Rapids: Zondervan, 1999), 95.

[5]Kenneth Feinberg, "What Is the Value of a Human Life?" *This I Believe*, May 25, 2008, http://www.npr.org/templates/transcript/transcript.php?storyId=90760725.

[6]"Megillah 13a," *The William Davidson Talmud*, accessed June 18, 2018, https://www.sefaria.org/Megillah.13a?lang=bi.

[7]Lisa Wingate, *Before We Were Yours* (New York: Ballantine, 2017), 317.

[8]Paul Kalanithi, *When Breath Becomes Air* (New York: Random House, 2016), 198–99.

[9]Marilynne Robinson, *Gilead* (New York: Picador, 2006), 60–61.

[10]Henri Nouwen, "From Solitude to Community to Ministry," *CT Pastors*, accessed June 19, 2018, https://www.christianitytoday.com/pastors/1995/ spring/51280.html.

[11]Richard Beck, "At the Boundary of Holy and Unclean: The Church, Lady Gaga and the Little Monsters," *Experimental Theology*, October 18, 2016, http:// experimentaltheology.blogspot.com/2016/10/at-boundary-of-holy-and -unclean-church.html.

Chapter 7: Advocate

[1]"America's Wars," US Department of Veterans Affairs, accessed July 18, 2018, https://www.va.gov/opa/publications/factsheets/fs_americas_wars.pdf.

[2]Nash Jenkins, "How Paris Stood with the US after 9/11," *Time*, November 14, 2015, http://time.com/4112746/paris-attacks-us-september-911-terrorism/.

[3]Jean-Marie Colombani, "We Are All Americans," *Le Monde*, September 12, 2001, http://www.worldpress.org/1101we_are_all_americans.htm.

[4]Felicia Schwartz, "'We Are All Parisians,' Kerry Says in Unannounced Paris Trip," *The Wall Street Journal*, November 6, 2015, http://www.wsj.com/articles /we-are-all-parisians-kerry-says-in-unannounced-paris-trip-1447708994.

[5]Langston Hughes, "Let America Be America Again," *Academy of American Poets*, accessed July 1, 2016, https://www.poets.org/poetsorg/poem/let-america -be-america-again.

[6]Different Bible translations give the king a different name. Some call him Xerxes, a Greek transliteration of his Persian name. Some call him Ahasuerus, a Hebrew form of his Persian name. Karen Jobes, *Esther*, The NIV Application Commentary (Grand Rapids: Zondervan, 1999), 58.

[7]Jobes, *Esther*, 96; Jon D. Levenson, *Esther*, The Old Testament Library (Louisville: Westminster, 1997), 58.

[8]Adele Berlin, *Esther*, The JPS Bible Commentary (Philadelphia: Jewish Publication Society, 2001), 26.

[9]William Kaufman, *The Day My Mother Changed Her Name and Other Stories* (New York: Syracuse University Press, 2008), 45–59.

[10]Richard Foster, *Prayer* (New York: HarperOne, 2002), 211.

[11] Philip Yancey, *Prayer* (Grand Rapids: Zondervan, 2010), 303.

Chapter 8: Pay Out

[1] Stephen Dowling and Gavin Cammell, "The Greatest Turning Points in Aviation," accessed June 6, 2018, http://www.bbc.com/future/bespoke/great-turning-points-aviation/assets/images/great-turning-points-aviation.jpg.

[2] Michael V. Fox, *Character and Ideology in the Book of Esther* (Grand Rapids: Eerdmans, 2001), 51.

[3] Karen Jobes, *Esther*, The NIV Application Commentary (Grand Rapids: Zondervan, 1999), 94, 121.

[4] Fox, *Character and Ideology*, 51.

[5] Jobes, *Esther*, 121.

[6] Adele Berlin, *Esther*, The JPS Bible Commentary (Philadelphia: Jewish Publication Society, 2001), 41.

[7] Jon D. Levenson, *Esther*, The Old Testament Library (Louisville: Westminster, 1997), 71.

[8] Fox, *Character and Ideology*, 52; Levenson, *Esther*, 72.

[9] Paul David Tripp, *Redeeming Money* (Wheaton, IL: Crossway, 2018), 133.

[10] Tripp, *Redeeming Money*, 134.

[11] Richard J. Foster, *Money, Sex & Power* (London: Hodder & Stoughton, 2009), 38–39.

[12] Richard Foster, *The Challenge of the Disciplines Life* (New York: Harper One, 1989), 86.

[13] James Bryan Smith, *The Good and Beautiful God* (Downers Grove, IL: InterVarsity Press, 2009), 75–92.

Chapter 9: Power Down

[1] James K. A. Smith, *How (Not) to Be Secular: Reading Charles Taylor* (Grand Rapids: Eerdmans, 2014), 22.

[2] Stephen Prothero, "Why Conservatives Start Culture Wars and Liberals Win Them," *Washington Post*, January 29, 2016, https://www.washingtonpost.com/opinions/why-conservatives-start-culture-wars-and-liberals-win-them/2016/01/29/f89d0b2c-b658-11e5-a842-0feb51d1d124_story.html.

[3] "Memorial Day," *History*, last updated November 10, 2018, http://www.history.com/topics/holidays/memorial-day-history.

[4]Samuel Wells and George Summer, *Esther & Daniel*, Brazos Theological Commentary on the Bible (Grand Rapids: Brazos Press, 2013), 37.

[5]Jon D. Levenson, *Esther*, The Old Testament Library (Louisville: Westminster, 1997), 63.

[6]Adele Berlin, *Esther*, The JPS Bible Commentary (Philadelphia: Jewish Publication Society, 2001), 31.

[7]Jonah Lehrer, "The Power Trip," *The Wall Street Journal*, August 14, 2010, http://www.wsj.com/articles/SB10001424052748704407804575425561952689390.

[8]Andy Crouch, *Playing God* (Downers Grove, IL: InterVarsity Press, 2013), 24–25.

Chapter 10: Work Wonders

[1]Adele Berlin, *Esther*, The JPS Bible Commentary (Philadelphia: Jewish Publication Society, 2001), 31.

[2]Timothy J. Keller, *Every Good Endeavor: Connecting Your Work to God's Work* (New York: Penguin, 2014), 14.

[3]Ben Witherington III, *Work: A Kingdom Perspective on Labor* (Grand Rapids: Eerdmans, 2011), 83.

[4]Chesley Sullenberger and Jeffrey Zaslow, *Highest Duty: My Search for What Really Matters* (New York: HarperCollins, 2009).

Chapter 11: Thank God

[1]Richard Beck, *Reviving Old Scratch: Demons and the Devil for Doubters and the Disenchanted* (Minneapolis: Fortress Press, 2016), 13–15.

[2]Michael V. Fox, *Character and Ideology in the Book of Esther* (Grand Rapids: Eerdmans, 2001), 118.

[3]Karen Jobes, *Esther*, The NIV Application Commentary (Grand Rapids: Zondervan, 1999), 213–14.

[4]James K. A. Smith, *You Are What You Love* (Grand Rapids: Brazos Press, 2016), 130.

[5]Dallas Willard, *The Spirit of the Disciplines: Understanding How God Changes Lives* (New York: HarperCollins, 1999), 179–81.

[6]Ann Voskamp, *One Thousand Gifts: A Dare to Live Fully Right Where You Are* (Grand Rapids: Zondervan, 2011).

[7]James Bryan Smith, *The Good and Beautiful God: Falling in Love with the God Jesus Knows* (Downers Grove, IL: InterVarsity Press, 2011), 70–71.

Chapter 12: Lend a Hand

[1]Christopher White, "Las Vegas Bishop Leads Interfaith Prayer Service Following Shooting," *Crux*, October 3, 2017, https://cruxnow.com/church-in -the-usa/2017/10/03/las-vegas-bishop-leads-interfaith-prayer-service -following-shooting/.

[2]Joy Purdy, "Dozens Gather at Jacksonville Beach to Pray Hurricane Irma Away," *News 4 JAX*, September 7, 2017, https://www.news4jax.com/weather /hurricane-irma/as-some-evacuate-ahead-of-hurricane-irma-others-stay-and -pray.

[3]Michael S. Horton, *Ordinary: Sustainable Faith in a Radical, Restless World* (Grand Rapids: Zondervan, 2014), 11.

[4]Karen Jobes, *Esther*, The NIV Application Commentary (Grand Rapids: Zondervan, 1999), 216.

[5]Bobby Ross Jr., "After Hurricanes, A Flood of God's Love," *Christian Chronicle* 74, no. 10 (October 2017): https://christianchronicle.org/issue /october-2017/.

[6]Bob Goff, *Love Does: Discover a Secretly Incredible Life in an Ordinary World* (Nashville: Thomas Nelson, 2012), ix–xi.

Forty-Day Study Guide for the Disenchanted

[1]Alan S. Cowen and Dacher Keltner, "Self-Report Captures 27 Distinct Categories of Emotion Bridged by Continuous Gradients," *Proceedings of the National Academy of the Sciences of the United States of America*, September 5, 2017, https://doi.org/10.1073/pnas.1702247114.

[2]Rebecca Konyndyk DeYoung, *Glittering Vices* (Grand Rapids: Brazos Press, 2009), 75–77.

Awakening Purgation
illumination union

Spiritual Astrology

A Guide to the Twelve Zodiac Houses, Spirituality, Planets, Twin Flames, Soul Mates, Moon Phases, and Sun Signs

Your Free Gift (only available for a limited time)

Thanks for getting this book! If you want to learn more about various spirituality topics, then join Mari Silva's community and get a free guided meditation MP3 for awakening your third eye. This guided meditation mp3 is designed to open and strengthen ones third eye so you can experience a higher state of consciousness. Simply visit the link below the image to get started.

https://spiritualityspot.com/meditation

Table of Contents

Introduction

If you're interested in knowing how astrology can help you, this book is for you. I'll explain how astrology teaches you about the past and present, the future and the present, love, career, and more.

Astrology is a wonderful tool because it's complex and deep, incorporating the motions of planets and the changing seasons, positions of the moon, your zodiac sign, and much more. All these factors culminate to give you a complete picture of yourself in time. Astrology helps you make sense of what often feels like overwhelming diverse information. As a result, you'll put things into perspective and make sound decisions truly tailored to your specific needs.

Astrology has been around for thousands of years and is widely practiced by people in many cultures. It's a form of divination, meaning it attempts to understand the movement of celestial bodies. For example, astrologers study the positions and movements of stars to predict what events might happen on Earth and when. Many people believe astrology helps them predict their future (there's a good reason for this, as you'll soon discover), so it is a helpful tool to help you with decision-making.

This book is written in simple English, so it is easy to understand, unlike many other books on the subject. You won't be left scratching your head about the concepts in this book. It is chock full of the information you're bound to find useful, whether you've studied astrology for a while or are new to the topic. So, let's dive in if you're ready to take charge of your destiny and finally find your true purpose in life.

Chapter One: Spiritual Astrology 101

What Does Spiritual Mean?

To understand spiritual astrology, we must look at the two words that embody this concept- spiritual and astrology. What does "spiritual" mean? It refers to everything to do with the essence of life and all beings. Everything in our observable world is based on an energetic, nonphysical template known as spirit. Some people think of it as being dark matter. It is essential to note that there is more to this world than meets the eye. If you hope to understand what makes things happen the way they do, you must look past what you see and into the world beyond. I refer to the world of energy, the psychic and divine world from which every being and thing derives its existence.

What Is Astrology?

Signs.
https://pixabay.com/images/id-96309/

Astrology is the study of celestial bodies and how they affect us. The way the planets move and are positioned has a very real, perceivable effect on us. For instance, take the moon. When it's full, most of us observe odd behavior. This is no accident. Similarly, just as the moon affects us, so do other celestial bodies.

Putting It Together

So, let's talk about spiritual astrology. What does it mean? It's the study of the spiritual influences of the celestial bodies on our way of life. It determines how the placement of the planets affects everything from our careers to finances, relationships, and even health. This field of study aims to help you become more aware of the unseen strings being pulled by these influences and how you can work in tandem with them to live a rewarding life. The goal of the spiritual astrologer is to help you figure out your life path so that you can blossom and enjoy it.

As Henri J. M. Nouwen said, "*The spiritual life does not remove us from the world but leads us deeper into it.*" In other words, while looking into spiritual astrology seems an "otherworldly" endeavor that seems pointless to some people, the truth is that it will connect you with your world more strongly and give you an idea of your purpose. Far too many people live without knowing why they're here, and you can tell because they walk around with slouched shoulders and mopey faces on a path that isn't theirs.

You and Your Path

When you figure out what messages the spirit has for you through your astrological chart, you'll find clear pointers showing you what phase of life you're in and how best to work with it. For instance, you know it's time for some radical transformation when you've got a Pluto Sun transit happening, depending on whether it's opposite, square, or conjunct to your natal sun. The spirit of Pluto calls for development and growth, so this could play out in the best or worst of ways, like a new relationship, or the end of one, a job loss, health issues, or similar transitionary phases.

For most people, this is scary, especially when they don't see it for what it is. When you have many desires you'd like to manifest, the old must make way for the new. Sometimes, the only way for that to happen is through radical change, and, on the surface, it could seem rather a rough path to take.

When working with spiritual astrology, it doesn't mean that your life cannot change or you cannot craft it the way you want to because you're doomed to the spiritual energies of the stars in the sky. On the contrary, as you become a conscious co-creator of your life, knowing about the stars will help you create the life you want. It's easy to live life purposefully and powerfully when connected to the stars' energies.

Why Are You Here?

Even the best of us must wonder why we are on this little blue dot at some point in life. It doesn't take too much to notice that the world is in desperate need of healing. However, it can be incredibly difficult to figure out how to bring that healing about in a way that truly makes our souls sing.

Thankfully, this is not something you have to continue scratching your head over because you can work with the ancient wisdom embodied in the stars to find your path. In this book, you'll find your road map and discover how to use your one-of-a-kind skills and gifts to leave an indelible mark on the world forever. At present, you're possibly working in a thankless, boring job you know you're not fit for, or you're considering striking off and doing your own thing. You may even be at retirement, contemplating the next steps in life because you don't intend to remain idle. Whatever stage you're at, you can find the answer in the stars and planets. They will tell you what you can do with your time and resources to fulfill your dreams and bring back the meaning and joy you experienced as a child.

Perhaps another point that needs to be made is that "no one is an island." In other words, life is set up so that we have no choice but to have relationships with one another, whether they're personal or professional, casual or deep. You simply must relate to others. Sometimes, the process is messy, especially since humans are complex people with so many layers of emotions and thought patterns. So, as you work with the planets, you'll determine where you stand concerning other people around you. You'll learn about your desires and dreams and what others yearn for. You'll understand people on a level so deep it can only be described as "*soul-deep.*" Combined with the knowledge you learn about yourself from the planets, you'll also learn your place among others and how best to work with them to achieve the best outcomes.

Your Calling: More than Just Work

It's a sad state of affairs that, for the most part, most of us merely "accept the hand we're dealt" without pausing to get in touch with our authentic selves. We fall into these roles society has picked out for us, knowing fully on the inside that we are meant for so much more. It is how we become stuck in draining relationships, situations that suck the life out of us, and jobs we hate. We do this because it is easier to get stuck in a rut or continue saying "yes" to bosses, friends, and others, even when we die a little each time we acquiesce to their demands. We justify this in so many ways, but we know we're not honoring our calling. What is that? It is whatever you truly want the most in your heart.

We all have a true calling we were sent onto this Earth to accomplish. It's what your soul is supposed to do and considers your natural gifts and the things that bring you joy and fulfillment, emotionally and spiritually. It's the key to your ultimate success in life precisely because it is the perfect blend of your dreams, drive, and gifts. Hence, it is why spiritual astrology is so important. Think of it as being plopped down in the middle of a great, big city. You want to go to the Everton Hotel, but how do you know how to get there when you don't even know where you are, let alone what roads to take? You need a map and a sense of direction. This is what your astrological chart offers you.

This natal chart will map out your entire life and contains the solar system's state as related to when and where you were born. Your birth date and time are crucial because they're not random. Your soul chose them on purpose because they intended to express themselves specifically in your present incarnation. Your chart is the blueprint to understanding your essence. Ultimately, we all have the same goal; to fully embody who we truly are. The chart uses the gifts we've been blessed with while doing our best to work around the obstacles naturally to see our life's mission through to completion.

Now is as good a time as any to clarify that your career is not necessarily the same thing as you're calling. The reality of the world we live in is that to be able to afford things, you must have a job. So we spend every second of every day of our lives thinking about work or working and don't pay much attention to what's happening spiritually or personally. In other words, we become sellouts for the sweet, sweet nectar of capitalism — money. If you think about it, money is not necessarily the goal. It's purely about the freedom it can bring you. So we continue to work hard, slaving away day and night while, paradoxically, the freedom we labor for never happens. Things are set up to have just enough money to feed yourself and stay alive long enough to go to work the next day, but no more than that. That is not freedom.

We are so wired to focus on the process of making a living that we do not consider that there are other aspects to being human. We don't think of our personal and spiritual lives as priorities but as luxuries. In other words, instead of spending time with loved ones connecting, bonding, and forming meaningful memories, it's more important to take that time to eke out another dollar. It's such a sad state of affairs, and few of us realize that we cannot take our possessions with us when we pass on. There isn't one person on their deathbed who was busy thinking about how much money they had managed to accrue in their bank account. Yet, for the most part, we do not think about this. We continue to live as though tomorrow is a given, and there will always be time until we realize we've committed most of our lives to all the wrong priorities one day.

So, here and now, dear reader, I call on you to take stock of what you've been doing so far and ask yourself, is this what you see yourself doing until the day you die? Don't you think your life could be something grander? Think about the fact that your career makes up at least 60 percent of your entire existence, and realize how great it would be to make your career line up with your soul's highest goals. Do you want to give the best of your day slaving away for something you do not believe in? Do you want to spend every last drop of blood, sweat, and tears invested in something that does not bring you joy or fulfillment? I want to believe your answer is a strong and vehement "no."

Soul's Blueprint vs. Status Quo

The argument that we should continue doing things the way we do them because "That's just the way things are" is flawed. Not everybody is fortunate enough to realize the game is rigged unfairly, that you do not have to play the game at all but could create a fulfilling life that's good for your heart. Deciding to focus on what makes your heart sing rather than sell out for a paycheck can be incredibly daunting. But I put it to you today that this is far more important than anything else you could strive for in life. Discovering your true calling and following it until the end is far more important than any degree or job position you could ever hold.

A good first step in the right direction is to get in touch with your intuition on what is right for you. For instance, when you were asked to take on more than you could handle, you could check in with your intuition whether this is a good time to say yes or no. You can also ask yourself, "Why am I here, and how can I accomplish what I'm here for?" The truth is, you can only find what you were looking for. The fact that you chose this book rather than any other, dear reader, tells me you're ready to break free of the shackles holding you back. You're ready to step into your own, and I must applaud you.

Understand that you must know who you are first and be in touch with your gut feelings before realizing the true success that has remained elusive to you all this time. Doubtless, you understand that success is not about how much money you have in your bank account. Indeed, you cannot claim to be successful if you do not enjoy what you are doing. True success is finding and following your calling, which will inevitably support you financially and spiritually (spiritual support being more important here). Aligning yourself with your spiritual cause is far more meaningful than any accolades, awards, certificates, or honors that anyone else can bestow upon you for following a path that is not your own. When you decide you're going after your calling, you create significant changes in the world for the good of one and all, which counts.

Chapter Two: Sun Signs — Personality

"What's your sign?" often gets answered with a sun sign because few people know more about this ancient divination method than simply the sun sign. Let's focus on sun signs before getting into the other aspects of understanding your astrological roots.

Your sun sign is the one that tells you the truth about who you are. It's the representation of the sign the sun happened to be in when you were born. This sign gives you intricate details of who you are, making it easier to work with your strengths and weaknesses to create your desired life outcomes.

Think of your sun sign as being the very essence of your life. It is what drives you — and all astrology, too, because the other planets and celestial bodies need the sun to orbit around it. You can find this symbol on your astrology chart as a dot with a circle around it. The sun sign isn't the be-all and end-all of your chart, but it's the central focus around the other elements that affect you. It colors the way you see life.

When finding your true path in life, the only way to achieve total satisfaction and harmony is to do things the way you want to, attaining freedom, growth, and joy congruent with your inner being's desires. You can use your sun sign to piece together the puzzle of why you're here. Many of us go about the process backward, forcing ourselves to fit into containers that were never meant for us instead of choosing to be expansive and daring enough to go after that which is ours. Then, we get worked up when we find that nothing we do is good enough despite our best intentions.

It is also terrifying to allow ourselves to be our best versions because we're scared of rejection. Furthermore, many of us struggle with beliefs that put us in a cage. Society places some of these beliefs upon us, while others are of our own making. With your sun sign, you can shine a light on the way your soul chose to represent you in life so that you can be true to your path and express yourself with no fear or limitation.

A Quick Note about Dates

You should know that you must consider that what you see in the papers or on various websites with zodiac signs is usually very inaccurate. A certain date can be one sign in one year and another in a different year because each day, the sun moves through the astrological wheel a bit more than a degree, resulting in each year there could be a change in the dates. So you could easily be born right on a cusp, between two signs. The only way to tell for sure is to look at your astrology chart. Here are the 12 zodiac signs:

- Aries
- Taurus
- Gemini
- Cancer
- Leo
- Virgo
- Libra
- Scorpio
- Sagittarius
- Capricorn
- Aquarius
- Pisces

Modality

The zodiac signs fall under one of three modalities and deal with the way their lives or approaches differ:

- Cardinal — Aries, Cancer, Libra, Capricorn
- Fixed — Taurus, Leo, Scorpio, Aquarius
- Mutable — Gemini, Virgo, Sagittarius, Pisces

Cardinal signs are born leaders, always initiating things and willing to encourage change and transformation. Fixed signs are firm in all they do. They persevere no matter what, and their focus is unlike anyone else's. The mutable signs are the most adaptable. Regardless of what you throw at them, they are flexible, and it is this trait that makes them some of the most resilient people you'll ever meet.

Elements

Zodiac signs are also connected to the four classical elements — earth, water, air, and fire.

- Earth signs — Taurus, Virgo, Capricorn
- Water signs — Pisces, Cancer, Scorpio
- Air signs — Libra, Aquarius, Gemini
- Fire signs — Aries, Sagittarius, Leo

Earth signs are cautious, but that shouldn't be interpreted negatively. They think before they act. They are some of the most productive people you'll meet in life, and are quite materialistic (in a good way), meaning you can trust they will do everything they can to ensure all relevant needs are taken care of, including the state of nature. They see things as they are and are great at ensuring things aren't just started but seen through to completion. People with earth signs are also pretty sensuous.

Water signs are all about their emotions and are very aware. They are some of the most sensitive people you'll meet, very in touch with how they feel. Their intuition is off the charts, and they're usually empaths. They're also very interested in spiritual matters and vulnerable — which can be a strength in the right circumstances.

Air signs are very intellectual people. They are about being social and some of the brightest minds you'll ever encounter. They are fascinated by life, curious about everything, and always gathering information like it's running out. They love to test different ideas and enjoy rubbing their minds with others. Conversation and communication are important to them.

Fire signs are full of desire and explosive, creative power. They are some of the most restless people you'll meet because they feel the need to do more, be more, and have more. They're not particularly patient and don't do well with limits, so they ironically burn out from all that fire. However, you can rely on them to bring energy and fun into the room and make things more interesting.

Considering the Planets

Each planet has its unique energy that affects each sign differently. Before we go over each one, let's link each zodiac sign to its ruling planet:

- Aries — Mars
- Taurus — Venus
- Gemini — Mercury
- Cancer — Moon
- Leo — Sun
- Virgo — Mercury
- Libra — Venus
- Scorpio — Pluto (according to modern astrology), Mars (according to traditional astrology)
- Sagittarius — Jupiter
- Capricorn — Saturn
- Aquarius — Uranus (according to modern astrology), Saturn (according to traditional astrology)
- Pisces — Neptune (according to modern astrology), Jupiter (according to traditional astrology)

Now let's look at the effect of each celestial body.

The Sun: This is the ruler of all things, and it is an energizer. It drives everything we are at our core, so when we embrace our sun sign, we feel happy and content with life. The sun is in charge of your true purpose, creativity, conscious mind, masculine energy, and sense of self.

The Moon: The sign associated with the moon changes every 2.5 days, so it's possible to find Cancers are ruled by or connected to any of the other signs born in the same year. The moon is all about emotions and sensitivity. It is where you get the empathetic aspect of yourself, and the emotions it is tied to are the ones we have trouble expressing. It represents our shadow side, which we are only vulnerable enough to reveal to those we feel safe with. It rules feminine energy, all emotions, and instincts.

Mercury: There's more to this planet than it's in retrograde, which everyone and their grandma like to blame for their bad choices. However, there's more to this planet than flipping your life upside down. It's in charge of your intellect, sense of timing, communication style, how you reason and express yourself, and how you juggle several different conversations and lines of thought at once. It's also all about traveling and sharing information.

Venus: This planet, like the goddess, is all about love and pleasure. It's about romance and beauty in all things. Those under its influence have a great sense of aesthetics. This planet is also connected to money — especially what we spend on things that make our hearts sing. It's about sensuality and luxury in all its forms.

Mars: This planet is about tempers, aggression, how you take action, and your sexual drive. The energy of this planet is very unrefined, but this is a good thing in the right context. It's about how one asserts their dominance, goes after their goals, and deals with their libido. It's not the red planet for nothing, red being the color of passion, fire, and intensity. This planet drives our primal desires.

Jupiter: This planet rules positivity and optimism. It's in charge of good luck, abundance, and true growth. When you have this planet influencing your life, you'll likely experience amazing benefits. It's about travel and the exploration of philosophy through learning and teaching. It asks you to become more expansive by learning from life, books, and spirituality. It's the planet that inspires you to go after your grandest ideas.

Saturn: Think of this planet as the dad energy to the moon's mom energy. This strict planet is about discipline, love expressed in tough situations, drawing boundaries, and angst. Its energy could represent a challenge, but it will help you evolve into more of who you truly are and learn to take more responsibility in your life. It's about hard work and persevering to overcome your challenges.

Uranus: This planet is about upsetting the status quo and breaking away from ruts. It's all about progress, thinking outside the box, and creativity. The trouble with this planet is that it is very hard to predict what comes next. It's not a planet that cares for nostalgia. Innovation is the game's name and often smacks us in the face with profound, sudden inspiration. It's a good kind of unpredictability. Think of it as the planet of revelation and awakening.

Neptune: Neptune is the planet that rules all things ethereal. It's about your intuition and dreams, and psychic abilities. It influences your ability to connect with the spiritual and express those aspects through art. This planet is also about escapism since it is the furthest from the physical reality we know, and it's what influences our desire to run away from the harsh realities of life. Working consciously with its energies will help you become more sensitive to your spiritual side.

Pluto: Pluto rules the subconscious mind and the underworld. It is connected to great changes. This planet's energy is rather dark and heavy, and it handles the transitions from day to night, darkness to light, and endings to beginnings and back. Regardless of the spectrum, it's in charge of extremes and everything beneath the mind and heart's surface.

Now you know the planets and their effects, let's move on to the sun signs.

Sun Signs

Aries — The Ram (March 20 to April 18)

Aries sign.

This sign is full of spirit. People born under this sign happen to be some of the frankest and most straightforward people you'll ever meet. They have the courage that defies logic, just like the ram, and are not afraid to start new things. The essence of this sign is fresh starts, and little wonder that it happens to be the first sign. If this is you, your ruling planet is Mars, the god of war to the ancient Romans. Mars makes you a person full of desire and anger. It also imbues you with energy and a desire to take concrete action. People with Mars influences are assertive and unafraid to state what they think or want.

Symbol: The symbol of this sign is reminiscent of a ram's head, with its long face and curvy horns. It also brings to mind the idea of a fountain with water springing forth on either side. The ram is a stubborn creature that will tenaciously see what it wants and go after it. The same can be said of Aries people.

Strengths: The great thing about you, Aries, is that you are quite a formidable force to be reckoned with. No one could ever accuse you of not being bold and going after what you want with a tenacity of equal parts admired and envied. You have quite an exhilarating energy around you. Whatever your attention, you are very enthusiastic about it. You can't be considered a true individual who is unafraid of being authentic. You know who you are, and you are the least likely to allow other people to dictate how you should be.

You don't waste time figuring things out because action and progress are the same things to you. You have no trouble speaking up for what you truly believe in, even though your opinion may be at odds with what the world thinks. So, you make an excellent leader indeed. You're not afraid to take necessary risks, and you're often the first person to try new things.

Weaknesses: You tend to think of yourself a little too much and too often, and, for you, it's, "My way or the highway." You can get very competitive in a bad way, to the point where you don't care who you hurt or sacrifice in the process. You're so eager for what you want that you see rules and actively think of ways to break them to obtain what you want — and, of course, this doesn't always work out well for you.

Sure, you're very passionate about several things, but the trouble is that you don't settle down long enough to see all of them through, and, as a result, you find that your initial spark dies out. When it comes to your emotions, it's not easy for you to put yourself in another person's shoes, making people think you're very insensitive. Additionally, it takes very little to get you to blow your lid. Thankfully, your anger is over as quickly as it sets in, but that doesn't make it less scary.

Famous Aries People: Reese Witherspoon, Sarah Jessica Parker, Kiera Knightley, Elton John, Jonathan Groff, Fergie, Mariah Carey, Quentin Tarantino, Ewan McGregor, Jonathan Van Ness, Alec Baldwin, and Robert Downey Jr.

Taurus — The Bull (April 19 to May 20)

Taurus.

There's no one as dependable as you, Taurus. You're the person who will stick around through thick and thin. You also love to enjoy yourself, and you're given pleasure since Venus rules you. Like the bull, you have stamina, unlike others. You're the person who is comfortable with taking on responsibility and one of the more loyal and devoted signs.

Symbol: The glyph for this sign looks like a bull's head, a circle with two horns on top of it. It is also reminiscent of a woman's womb with its fallopian tubes.

Strengths: You're the one who takes the Aries energy and grounds it, in reality, to be applied to practical matters that bring forth actual results. Security matters to you in all ways, so you're very cautious about making hasty decisions. You're the sort to hold on fiercely, and when you've decided something, no one can change your mind. Tenacious is your name, and you accomplish your goals by remaining determined, no matter how long it takes. You're gentle, kind, a romantic, and a lover of all things sensual. You also love beauty and look for ways to bring it to life in your environment.

Weaknesses: You take your time with things, which is usually a struggle for others to deal with. You're likely to find yourself stuck in a groove, and on top of that, you're beyond stubborn. When applied to your morals or goals, it's a good thing, but it also means you're resistant to change even when it would be good for you. You can hold on to old ways of doing things even at the cost of your own joy. You can also get greedy and jealous and engage in quite the pity party for yourself. Sometimes you're insensitive and possessive and have no qualms exploiting people. You don't get mad like Aries, but everyone in your path will feel it when you do.

Famous Taurus People: Jack Nicholson, Harry S. Truman, Mark Zuckerberg, Dwayne Johnson, Che Guevara, Adolf Hitler, Stevie Wonder, Kirsten Dunst, Tina Fey, and Adele.

Gemini – The Twins (May 21 to June 20)

Gemini.

You're bright. You have a way with your words, and you can persuade the Saudis to buy sand. This is due to Mercury's influence on you. You're a very lively person to engage with and agile too.

Symbol: Gemini's glyph resembles two pillars, or the number eleven, with curved lines connecting them at the top and bottom, facing outward. They represent the two sides of this person.

Strengths: You're always in touch with your inner child, happy and gregarious. Your intelligence knows no bounds and is further boosted by your thirst for knowledge. Nothing excites you more than new people, the latest news, and new things. You're the type of person who probably has more than one job simultaneously. You probably have more than one book you're reading right now and more than one lover. Spontaneity is very important to you. Sure, you may commit yourself to many things at once and complain about it, but the truth is you love it.

Weaknesses: The downside of being a Gemini is that you are hyperactive and cannot focus. You care more about instant gratification rather than taking your time with things. Your attention span is very short, which causes you trouble more often than not. Sitting still isn't something you do well. As much as you get excited about things, you talk yourself out of them with equal energy. Other people may find your intense fascination with them a bit of a drain. Your worst traits are superficiality and deceit, and some people will say you're full of hot air and have no depth to you emotionally. You're the sort of person who would rather adapt to a bad situation than do something about it, and you may even rewrite the situation to suit yourself. All consequences can be dealt with — just much, much later.

Famous Gemini People: Donald Trump, Angeline Jolie, Nicole Kidman, Arthur Conan Doyle, Marilyn Monroe, Prince, Kanye West, Allen Ginsberg, Anne Frank, Queen Victoria, John F. Kennedy, Aaron Sorkin, Salmon Rushdie, Alanis Morrissette, and Kendrick Lamar.

Cancer — The Crab (June 21 to July 22)

Cancer.

https://pixabay.com/es/illustrations/c%c3%a1ncer-astrolog%c3%ada-firmar-s%c3%admbolo-2551431/

Being ruled by the moon makes you very in touch with your intuition if you're a Cancer. You look within yourself a lot and are very aware of your emotions. You're security conscious, too. While you may sometimes feel like an emotional mess, there's more to you than that, and you don't allow your vulnerabilities to get in the way of attaining your desires.

Symbol: The cancer glyph is reminiscent of the yin yang symbol, the numbers 6 and 9, with their curved tails on the top and bottom, respectively, while the circles are side by side. The symbol is also said to represent the breasts and the fluidity of emotions.

Strengths: Due to the water element, you have no trouble allowing your emotions to be open, and, at the same time, you are deeply reflective. You have ambition and are deeply connected to the world around you, making your moods go up and down when combined with your emotions. You can be as shrewd as you need to be, trusting your emotions and intuition to guide you through all situations. You're connected to your past and history and love nothing more than family and a sense of belonging. You're a supportive friend, very loyal, and rather affectionate, and never give up on the people you care about. Regardless of how you feel, you ensure that your goals are attained. Even when your journey toward your goal causes you to cry, you continue to put one foot in front of the other.

Weaknesses: You appear tough on the outside, but you're also soft on the inside like a crab. When something scares you, you tuck yourself back into your shell. You're not a person to deal with issues head-on. However, you'll stick up for yourself when you need to, but usually wind up putting your foot in it and then go into denial about the truth, making it hard for others to connect with you. You will inevitably overcome powerful emotions because of the moon, which means that sometimes you won't deal with them well. Your fear of being abandoned or having no resources to fall back on makes you fiercely hold on to things that you need to let go of.

Famous Cancer People: The Dalai Lama, Ariana Grande, Nelson Mandela, Kevin Bacon, Wendy Williams, Pablo Neruda, Florence Ballard, Chiwetel Ejiofor, Priyanka Chopra, Kevin Hart, Khloe Kardashian, Mindy Kaling, Alan Turing, Mike Tyson, and Robin Williams.

Leo – The Lion (July 23 to August 22)

Leo.

You're one of the friendliest people anyone will ever meet as a Leo. You collect friends like the Kardashians collect plastic surgeons. You're a very warm person, and people love to be around you because you're so outgoing and how good you make them feel. It also doesn't hurt that in everything you do, you demonstrate flair.

Symbol: The glyph of this sign looks like a circle with a tail that swirls out of it, just like a lion's tail.

Strengths: You're friendly, joyful, and loyal to a fault. You go after what you want with passion, and your social life is brimming with fun activities. Your goal is to live your best life, and you do a good job of having fun with it. You are usually the entertainer in a group because, naturally, you're the center of attention, like the sun that shines. Your sense of humor is amazing, and you know how to share the best of yourself even when others can't find theirs. Charisma is your name, a fact you know and are proud of. You love luxury, respect, and honor. You enjoy glamor, consider yourself royalty, and are willing to put in the work. You're also generous.

Weaknesses: You have trouble letting people know just how vulnerable you are. You can be quite the people-pleaser because you want to be liked, so you speak for people's approval instead of your truth. In other words, you are quite at home, lying and manipulating others. Sure, your intentions are pure because you don't want to hurt people, but this isn't the way to do things. You're not a person to be silenced for long, and eventually, you'll let the truth out — even if you might exaggerate a bit. Your worst traits are being vain, overly dramatic, and controlling. However, you're hardly ever at your worst, so you don't have to worry too much about that. The acknowledgment you seek will come to you naturally when you relinquish your need to control and just be your bright, sunny self.

Famous Leo People: J. K. Rowling, Charlize Theron, Alfred Hitchcock, Carl Jung, Robert De Niro, Madonna, Mick Jagger, Andy Warhol, Steve Martin, Neil Armstrong, Fidel Castro, Usain Bolt, Sandra Bullock, and Viola Davis.

Virgo — The Virgin (August 23 to September 22)

Virgo.
https://pixabay.com/es/illustrations/virgo-astrolog%c3%ada-firmar-s%c3%admbolo-2552259/

There's no mind sharper than a Virgo. You have Mercury to thank for your quick wit and communication skills. You're a person who sees what most others don't, and your level of insight is unmatched. You're also rather articulate and critical. People may whine about that, but they don't know you're more critical of yourself than anyone or anything else. You don't believe in being perfect, so you constantly want to improve yourself.

Symbol: The glyph of Virgo looks like the letter M, with an extra "prong" that crosses over the bottom of the third one. It's a sign representing the female genitalia.

Strengths: No one can put one over you because you see the devil in the details. You're efficient, can read between the lines, and glean what's not being said and what is meant. You're funny, smart, and can hold a conversation very well. You're very analytical, think clearly, and concentrate better than most. You love to learn "new things." Yet, despite all you know, you're a modest person, making you rather attractive. No one knows better than you that you're not perfect, but you know you'll always strive to be better. The difference between you and the other earth signs is your efficiency. Discipline and organization are your wheelhouses, and there is no limit. You won't push to become who you want to be and are open to helping other people. Sometimes you help them to the point of disregarding your own needs. However, it is no shock since Virgo is the sign of service.

Weaknesses: You need to go easy on people — meaning yourself, too. Sometimes, you can't distinguish between what's just okay and a grand idea. When what you want doesn't happen, your disappointment knows no bounds and can bring you down to the point of depression. While you may play the martyr to uplift other people, you struggle deeply with anxiety, shyness, and not belonging or inferiority. You struggle with guilt and worry about many things, even what isn't yours to be concerned about.

Famous Virgo People: Beyonce Knowles, George R. R. Martin, Dave Chapelle, Amy Poehler, Sean Connery, Ivan the Terrible, Agatha Christie, Stephen King, Amy Winehouse, Warren Buffet, Louis C. K., Sophia Loren, and Michael Jackson.

Libra — The Scales (September 23 to October 22)

Libra.

You are one of the most rational people on the planet, Libra. You love all things beautiful, you adore love, and you're an exceptionally fair person, making it easy to hang out with you. You're all about being civilized and proper.

Symbol: The glyph looks like the equal sign, with the top dash curving upwards in the middle. This represents justice and the sun setting on the horizon.

Strengths: You're refined in all your ways, and, additionally, you're the definition of cool. Your temper is balanced. You notice things and were born a diplomat. You want nothing more than peace wherever you are and have a deep appreciation for music, art, and aesthetically pleasing things. You're an easygoing person with a charm that draws many to you. You're also quite a flirt, but that doesn't mean you're not loyal in your relationships. Your intellect is excellent, and you're sensible in all you do. You're a person who wants to hear all sides of the story before drawing your conclusions. Hence, you love debating, doing your best to be objective, and balancing your emotions with careful logic.

Weaknesses: You let people make you feel like you're not worthy, worry a lot, and when you don't know who you are, you lack confidence. You are very critical of yourself, especially if some of your planets are placed in Virgo. You're anxious about making a good impression and doing everything to make people happy, which doesn't always work out well. On the flip side, sometimes you don't do as much as you should. When you don't feel great, you crawl into your shell, choosing to be vague and indulging yourself only. You don't do well with squabbles, yet you don't have a problem causing them. You seek balance in your life but don't do well keeping it. Your tendency to overanalyze things can be problematic when deciding on something important.

Famous Libra People: F. Scott Fitzgerald, Cardi B, Gwyneth Paltrow, Gwen Stefani, Mahatma Gandhi, Kate Winslet, Brie Larson, Kim Kardashian, Eminem, Matt Damon, Friedrich Nietzsche, Ralph Lauren, Oscar Wilde, Neil deGrasse Tyson, and Will Smith.

Scorpio — The Scorpion (October 23 to November 21)

Scorpio.

This sign is all about intensity. You're ruled by Pluto, making you a very extreme and interesting person. You're not afraid to take a walk on the wild side.

Symbol: The glyph is the letter M with a tail at the end of the third prong, representing the scorpion's tail.

Strengths: You're a magnetic person with a deep passion for everything you do. Your sensuality and vibrancy are enthralling. You're a complex person who takes life into your own hands, and you tend to do what you want, which makes you interesting. You're in tune with body language, words, love drama, and drawn to all things mysterious. Your mood goes from heavenly highs to hellish lows because you feel everything deeply. You love your privacy, but you're very good at getting others to open up to you about their dark secrets. Your willpower and self-control are worth commending, and you always execute your plans at the right time, not a moment before or after.

Weaknesses: You have some of the nastiest traits, so watch out for them. You're manipulative, quite adept at lying, and arrogant. You keep secrets to lord them over others or manipulate them. When you have no other options, you have no qualms about hurting people deeply, and you are horrible at forgiving people. You can be very cold, full of spite and jealousy at your worst. For the most part, Scorpios do well at not letting that dark part get the better of them, and they struggle with a lot of depression.

Famous Scorpios: Bill Gates, Joe Biden, Roseanne Barr, Drake, Julia Roberts, Leonardo DiCaprio, RuPaul, Kelly Osbourne, Jonas Salk, Albert Camus, Robert F. Kennedy, Neil Young, Matthew McConaughey, and Caitlyn Jenner.

Sagittarius — The Archer (November 22 to December 21)

Sagittarius.
https://pixabay.com/es/vectors/sagitario-zod%c3%adaco-se%c3%b1ales-36395/

You're full of energy, and you're your own person and ruled by Jupiter. Your mind is always full of possibilities, and you love nothing more than to explore all of life through travel and new people with new ideas.

Symbol: This glyph is an arrow pointing upward and to the right, with a dash going through the bottom of the arrow, making it look like a cross. It is the centaur's arrow and represents lofty goals.

Strengths: You're a cheerful soul and love to wander. You have amazing wit and are always ready for some excitement. You're fun to have as a friend and think about the deep things of life with those you care about. You think life is about growing in wisdom and experience, and you don't care to hold yourself back for the sake of security. You don't do well being restricted, and you'd rather be your own person. You're open-minded, easy to get along with, and spontaneous. You're fearless in your approach and passionate about religion and philosophy.

Weaknesses: While you love to have a good time, an aspect of you wants nothing more than to grow mentally, and this makes you flounder. You're not the most organized person and sometimes very impractical. You aren't careful with your money and are not the most reliable person, making promises you could never hope to keep. Also, you're the most tactless sign. You don't know how to tell the truth with love and blurt things out before you know it. Other times, your silence gives you away.

Famous Sagittarius People: Mark Twain, Frank Sinatra, Sarah Paulson, Sarah Silverman, Jon Stewart, Steven Spielberg, Jane Austen, Zoe Kravitz, Winston Churchill, William Blake, Tiffany Haddish, Lucy Liu, and Pablo Escobar.

Capricorn – The Goat (December 22 to January 19)

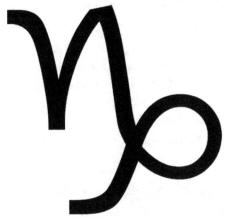

Capricorn.

You love tradition, and if there's anyone who's a stickler for the rules, it's you. You love rules because you thrive with them.

Symbol: This glyph resembles a combination of numbers 7 and 6, showing you the goat's horns.

Strengths: You love competition and are very productive. You could never be accused of being immature. Even when you were a kid, you were a rather serious person, which most of your peers didn't understand. As an adult, you come into your own and have learned to be a happier person. You have ambition for days and are patient while achieving your goals, no matter how far away they may seem. You don't have a problem with other people's needs and will also help them achieve their goals. You're calm in the face of trouble and know how to discipline yourself without going to the extreme. You carry a natural air of dignity and authority. You're also sensual, like the other earth signs.

Weaknesses: You're quite conservative, so you don't do things spontaneously. You worry about money and how you're perceived, and, at your worst, you're quite the pessimist. You repress your real self because you're worried about being judged. You don't know how to relax because you feel you always have to be on the go and there's so much still to do. You sense that you'd do much more if you could be alone. You tend to work too hard, and even now, as you read this, you think it's a good thing to be proud of. However, it's vital to relax. Also, you're not good with feelings because you don't like to show people how vulnerable you are or how much you're hurting. It would serve you to deal with the truth as it is.

Famous Capricorn People: Carlos Castaneda, Shona Rhimes, Jim Carrey, Haruki Murakami, Kate Middleton, David Bowie, Dolly Parton, Christian Louboutin, Orlando Bloom, John Legend, Zooey Deschanel, Muhammed Ali, Denzel Washington, Martin Luther King, and J. R. R. Tolkien.

Aquarius – The Water Bearer (January 20 to February 18)

Aquarius.

You're a person considered original, all about your future and how to make progress. You gain insight into many things, and you're peculiar.

Symbol: The glyph is two zigzagging lines stacked on top of each other, representing water waves or light.

Strengths: You're a true humanitarian, theoretically speaking. Your principles are very benevolent, and you do your best to live by them. For you, everyone is equal and should be treated that way, so it bothers you when you see things to the contrary. You love to create things, technology, and all things science. Your finger is always on the world's pulse, and the stranger and more unconventional, the better. You're warm and full of charisma and make friends with people from all walks of life.

Weaknesses: Sometimes, you are very immature, refusing to get along with others. You're stubborn about ideas you hold dear, even when they don't work out well. Your altruistic viewpoint is often thought of as fake or for appearance purposes. Your actual self is often detached, and you'd rather deal with ideas, not feelings. You may appear warm and welcoming, but when people get closer, they sense you're cold, insensitive, and, ironically enough, it's easy to get under your skin. When you're at your lowest and worst, you're pretty much a robot. You're also a tad insecure, although it's not immediately obvious to everyone.

Famous Aquarius People: Sheryl Crow, Ellen DeGeneres, Oprah Winfrey, Paul Newman, Ashton Kutcher, Charles Darwin, Wolfgang Amadeus Mozart, The Weekend, Dr. Dre, Vanessa Redgrave, Paris Hilton, Michael B. Jordan, Cristiano Ronaldo, and Virginia Woolf.

Pisces — The Fish (February 19 to March 19)

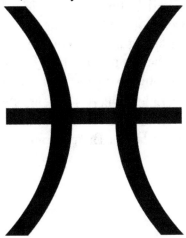

Pisces.

https://pixabay.com/es/vectors/piscis-zod%c3%adaco-firmar-astrolog%c3%ada-36394/

You're all about your imagination and dreams. This sign is about everything spiritual and true compassion. Your biggest challenge is learning how to ground yourself in the world despite your penchant for wanting to escape it.

Symbol: The glyph looks like two letter Cs backing each other, connected by a dash. This represents the connection between the inner and outer worlds.

Strengths: You're sensitive, and you pick up on everything emotionally. You are rather psychic, but it's hard to stay safe because you're not the best at setting boundaries. You sense when things are off between people, which bothers you deeply. You love it when your people win and celebrate with them because your heart is big and full of compassion. Your imagination knows no bounds, and you love to daydream, which helps you with creative solutions and ideas that prove useful in life. You're open to change and have a level of faith many only hope to achieve. Even when things don't work out, you trust it was for your greater good.

Weaknesses: Sometimes, you get lost in your head. When you're at your lowest, it's easy to deceive you. You lose touch with rationality, and it's easy for people to hurt you and for life to beat you down. You are often incredibly entitled to the nth degree. You also aren't good at decision-making, and, more than anyone, you deceive yourself the most, sometimes to the point of not acknowledging your part in finding yourself where you are. When things aren't going well, you wait for someone to take care of you or save you rather than taking action. You can be full of anger, self-pity, and resentment when things don't go your way and are likely to give in to drugs and alcohol to escape yourself and your troubles.

Famous Pisces People: Albert Einstein, Rihanna, Rob Lowe, Kurt Cobain, Queen Latifah, Chelsea Handler, Trevor Noah, Ruth Bader Ginsburg, Victor Hugo, Bryan Cranston, Glenn Close, and Erykah Badu.

Chapter Three: Sun Signs — Compatibility

Your sun sign is responsible for how you see yourself and others see you. It's responsible for your sense of self-worth and confidence, but more than that, it has a strong influence on your life path. When you know what your sun sign is and how it affects you, you can further discover how your sun sign interacts with others.

What Is Compatibility?

Some sun signs are more compatible with each other than with others. If you want to know how to get along with others better in love, friendships, and at work, it's worth looking into their sun signs to see how well you are likely to get along. You shouldn't immediately assume that because someone has a sign known to be incompatible with yours, you should automatically assume you'll never get along. Regardless of their sun sign, even if they are one of the three dark personalities – Machiavellians, psychopaths, and narcissists - you should be able to get along with them when needed.

I'd like to note that the various combinations we will look at depend on other factors besides the particular sun signs, like the moon sign. So you must consider other factors besides the sun signs if you want to figure out a specific relationship. Now without further ado, let's look at each sign and how it fares with other signs.

Aries' Best Match

Leo is the one for you, Aries. Of all the signs, you won't tame this lion, and it is why you're drawn to them. You're drawn to that regal aura around them, and you love their boldness. It is an especially great combo when the Aries is a woman and the Leo is a man. Leo's going to be the one in charge here. You're both fire signs, which means you're compatible. It also means there will be a fair bit of drama, but don't worry about it because you can work your way through any trouble — usually in the bedroom. You both make each other better. Leo can learn to deal with an Aries' temper and need to fight, while Aries will have an energizing effect on Leo.

Aries' Worst Match

You and Taurus will often lock horns because you share little or nothing in common. Building a relationship together is a futile exercise. Aries is all about opportunity, taking every shot they can to do courageous things, which means stepping outside of one's comfort zone. On the other hand, Taurus only wants peace and stability as it's comforting for them, so they'll think Aries is too much work, and the latter will think the Taurus much too boring.

Taurus' Best Match

Capricorn is made for you, Taurus. You mesh well together, being earth signs and have the same thought patterns. You're grounded individuals who are always practical, and thankfully there's enough difference between your characters to give you the balance to make this union work. Taurus is quiet and enjoys peace, reveling in materialism and pleasure. When this goes too far, they are indulgent or downright lazy. Capricorn is a diligent sign, very resourceful, and always putting things in place to ensure their success. They can be quite the workaholic. Together, these signs balance each other out, with Capricorn lighting a fire under Taurus and Taurus teaching Capricorn just to chill.

Taurus' Worst Match

Sagittarius absolutely won't jive well with you. Sagittarius likes to travel and enjoys new things, while Taurus is resistant to change and prefers routine. They want nothing more than comfort, great sex, delicious food, and a comfy bed to end the day. This doesn't work for Sagittarius because they crave nothing more than travel, and that's far too chaotic for Taurus. Also, Taurus gets jealous easily, an unattractive trait to the archer, who certainly doesn't want to be possessed.

Gemini's Best Match

You would do wonderfully well with a Libra. You work well together socially and love hanging out with each other. You both are lifelong learners, making it easy for you to connect with people across all spectrums of life. You could never be bored with each other because you have loads to talk about. Gemini understands Libra's indirectness in communication because you're intuitively connected. They are both quite flirtatious and don't get jealous or insecure because they understand this about each other.

Gemini's Worst Match

Gemini has no business being in a relationship with a Scorpio. Where Gemini is happy to be involved in several things at once, Scorpio focuses on doing only one thing and giving it their all. To Gemini, that's an obsession. As for Scorpio, they see the Gemini as a shallow person. They don't find it easy to connect. Scorpio can't stand how much Gemini can change, while Gemini doesn't understand how Scorpio focuses on one thing. Gemini is a social butterfly, and Scorpio can't handle this because they're prone to jealously. Add in Gemini's propensity for flirting, which could be a problem. Also, Gemini may not always know when Scorpio doesn't want other people to know something, and it could tick the latter off when the former accidentally spills the beans.

Cancer's Best Match

Pisces and Cancer work beautifully well together, both being water signs, so the emotional bond they share is incredible. They understand each other so well that they don't even need to say a word to each other to pass a message. They know how to offer comfort and warmth to each other, and where they diverge in character, their differences are actually good for the union. Cancer is a practical sign, a homebody that loves to care for others. They can get a little too worried and nervous as a result. Pisces is a spiritual sign with a gentle soul, and they're some of the most compassionate people on Earth who understand human nature. Despite this, they're usually not grounded in reality and have issues being practical. So Pisces will learn this from Cancer, and they help

Cancer find peace.

Cancer's Worst Match

Cancer would do horribly with Aquarius, assuming they even manage to find each other attractive, to begin with. Cancer comes from an emotional and intuitive place, while Aquarius is a logical person who holds reason above all else. They don't get each other, so they cannot connect, let alone make peace with what makes them different. No one can make Aquarius feel deeply, and no Cancer can change that. Cancer will find Aquarius too cold. It's rare to find a successful connection between these two.

Leo's Best Match

Besides Aries, Leo is also compatible with Libra, who is quite the diplomat, flirt, and conversationalist. Libra naturally makes Leo want to be extra charming and smooth, and they do this without threatening to snatch the limelight from the lion, making them even more attractive. They're the couple you enjoy observing. They're very social and give the best parties, with Libra as the most gracious host and Leo the center of attention. Even behind closed doors, they're like this. Now and then, it's wise for them to take a break from performing and just relax. Libra could be the cooler of the two when they're alone, but the love is still strong between the two.

Leo's Worst Match

Leo and Virgo couldn't possibly work together. They're adjacent to each other on the zodiac circle, to begin with, meaning they have trouble connecting. Sure, there are rare exceptions, but rare is the keyword. Leo loves to take center stage, while Virgo is a modest person who prefers being at home behind the scenes. Leo loves to be adored, but Virgo doesn't do so well with this, even though they appreciate sincere compliments when they count. Virgo tries to be helpful with their constructive suggestions, but this doesn't go down well with the vulnerable Leo, who feels criticized. It doesn't help that Virgo will not offer a compliment unless it is well earned.

Virgo's Best Match

Virgo and Capricorn are wonderful. They're both earth signs and practical people with a healthy sense of materialism. They do well working together and intuitively know what each other needs for support. The odds are they fell in love at work. If you're in this relationship, you both share a great sense of humor, and laughter is the norm for you two. Your mutual joy allows you to relax with each other and be more sensual. Your differences also work well together. For instance, Capricorn has little time for nonsense in their career and ambitions and always considers their future in all they do, but this makes them forget important things like health. On the other hand, Virgo sees all the details everyone else misses and reminds Capricorn to take care of themselves. Capricorn also helps Virgo when they become scattered and unfocused.

Virgo's Worst Match

Aquarius and Virgo are a no-no. These signs are intellectual but not compatible. Virgo is grounded and practical. They like to file things in the appropriate boxes. As for Aquarius, they don't care for the box, and that's the problem. However, they recognize each other's intellectual prowess, so they could work well in other ways, just not romantically. To Aquarius, Virgo fusses far too much. To Virgo, Aquarius is a rule-breaker, and not in a good way.

Libra's Best Match

Other than Leo and Gemini, Libra does well with Aquarius. As fellow air signs, they're very compatible. Libra is the social one who has no trouble fitting in anywhere. Aquarius is usually the odd one in groups. They're both turned on by intellect, and this is what pulls them to each other. Libra is intelligent, but they downplay this trait because they understand some people can't handle it. However, they know a lot about everything and can hold their own in conversations on any topic with any person. Libra is a just and fair sign, so it honors rules and follows social cues, but deep down, there's a bit of mischief that peeks out now and then, which draws them to Aquarius.

Libra's Worst Match

It could never work out between a Libra and a Scorpio. Scorpio's always spoiling for a fight, and Libra doesn't have time. Libra is a courteous person who loves honesty, peace, and harmony, all of which Scorpio struggles with. Libra will tell "white lies" for the sake of peace, but lying isn't in their nature. Scorpios values honesty too, but when they're at their worst, they can pull a complete 180 and manipulate and lie to their heart's content. This trait is rather ironic, given that they're very intuitive and can tell when they're being lied to. They're driven to get down to the bottom of things, but it unsettles Libra because the truth may not be something they can handle. Libra loves to learn about people, but they don't want to get into the dark stuff, and they're not in the mood to share this either - something Scorpio desires deeply.

Scorpio's Best Match

Scorpio and Pisces work well together, being water signs. They're both incredibly intense and sensitive to emotions. They are intuitively connected and can even share telepathy. Pisces is the more free-flowing person, while Scorpio has the drive and is more intense. Pisces is the more flexible one. Scorpio is always the leader in the relationship, being protective and in charge regardless of gender. Pisces brings their softness into the relationship to bring Scorpio the tranquility they need. Pisces's innate understanding of humans makes them one of the few signs that see past Scorpio's misbehavior, making it hard for Scorpio to hide the truth of their vulnerability. They work well in the long haul.

Scorpio's Worst Match

Other than Gemini, Sagittarius is another sign that Scorpio does not do well with. These two signs share no common traits. Scorpios want intimacy, and they want a deep relationship. This is at odds with Sagittarius's desire to be free. There's no room for negotiations here. Nothing will ever be enough for Scorpio in this pairing, and Sagittarius will feel there's a noose around their neck that grows tighter each day they spend with Scorpio. Fortunately, it's rare that these two ever connect.

Sagittarius' Best Match

Aries is the best match for the archer, and there's a lot of fire going on here. They both love to go on adventures together, and this is a relationship full of fun times. Sagittarius' love for travel is something that Aries is fine with, and Aries doesn't need Sagittarius to be emotionally over-invested in the relationship. Also, Aries respects Sagittarius, making them even more sexually attracted to the archer. They think of Sagittarians as strong people and are drawn to strength. Aries isn't the easiest person to get along with, so Sagittarius' laid-back attitude is a positive for this union. Being laid back doesn't mean the archer isn't strong, though. They're a lovely combination of relaxed and powerful, which means they can handle whatever Aries throws their way.

Sagittarius' Worst Match

Besides Scorpio and Taurus, Sagittarius doesn't do well with a fellow Sagittarius because while they may both get along, they won't remain together for the long haul. Sagittarius people are afraid of committing because it means having to settle down, the complete antithesis of their desire to explore. If they had their way, they'd be happy to live a single life until they pass away. Neither partner will be able to really drive the relationship forward because they're not inclined to settle.

Capricorn's Best Match

Capricorn goes with Virgo very well. They're both earth signs and can be with each other harmoniously. There's more tension here than you'd have with a Taurus and Capricorn pairing. In this case, Capricorn has to bring balance to the relationship. They're supportive of each other, with Capricorn considering the long term and Virgo able to handle the short-term stuff. There is romance, but there's also work. This relationship would be even more beautiful if they got into business together.

Capricorn's Worst Match

Leo and Capricorn don't do well together because they're always competing to be on top, and they couldn't be more different. Leo exudes that regal aura, and they won't let you forget it. They have to be adored and want to be in the lead. On the flip side, you have Capricorn, who's more interested in getting things done. They couldn't care less about how cool Leo is, which infuriates the latter. Capricorn comes off as a bore to a Leo, so it's not common to find a working relationship between these two.

Aquarius' Best Match

Aquarius and Sagittarius work well together. They may seem distant, and they don't need emotional closeness, but somehow this is what makes them work. They get each other. They know what it's like to feel overwhelmed or sick of neediness from a partner, so they don't mind being with each other. They're also the couple who would love to live in their own homes, have separate bedrooms, or have an open relationship. Aquarius is aloof but friendly and quite emotionally stable, and Sagittarius brings an exciting energy to the relationship.

Aquarius' Worst Match

Aquarius wouldn't do well with a Virgo, even though they may share the same friends since they have a flair for intellectual matters and events. However, they go after their passions differently, with Virgo being all about the details and Aquarius about the big picture. Aquarius is also a rule breaker, which doesn't sit well with Virgo. These two will inevitably frustrate each other.

Pisces' Best Match

Other than Cancer, Pisces does well with Virgo. They are opposite signs, which means they work well together as partners. They're both about offering service and understanding the value of staying humble. However, they serve others differently. Where Virgo is a practical helper, Pisces is more into helping people with spiritual matters. Pisces has a better view of the bigger picture than Virgo, but they're not the best with details. However, Virgo can see the details that Pisces misses, and this is where they meet each other halfway and work wonderfully well together.

Pisces' Worst Match

Pisces and Leo do not work. They don't have enough similarities, and their differences do not complement each other. When Pisces is a man and Leo is a woman, she may have a problem seeing his strength, which is present but not the sort the Leo woman cares for. They could probably work if she could only look at him from a different perspective. The opposite is true when it's a Leo man with a Pisces woman. She'll be absolutely in love with how much of a charmer he is, and he'll love her for adoring him. However, they'll see that they don't have much in common with time.

Chapter Four: Sun Signs at Work

Each sun sign leads to a different work personality.
https://pixabay.com/images/id-2562325/

While every person has their unique individual flair, your sun sign can indeed shape aspects of your personality and work style while also providing insight into how others react to you based on your birth date. There are certain qualities that the sun sign determines when assessing individuals that are beneficial for you and your colleagues to understand.

For example, if you are an Aries, you may be described as strong-willed and confident. However, it is also common for people with this sun sign to be impatient and temperamental. These characteristics make interacting with others difficult. But if you know these potential personality struggles, you can work toward avoiding being considered difficult.

Your sun sign can give you a glimpse into your personality, but it is not the only influencing factor. When you consider your job or career path, take advantage of the insight your sign offers.

Aries at Work

The Aries sun sign is bold and outspoken. In the workplace, this means you are direct and, at times, bold with your comments or words.

Aries people are known to be competitive and determined, so working with a like-minded group of individuals will be like a game of one-upmanship. Avoid allowing yourself to be defined by your colleagues' opinions to avoid getting caught in this cycle.

In some cases, Aries leaders make insensitive comments when frustrated or annoyed with the situation. This is a trait that will cause problems if it continues. Remind yourself to take a moment and calm down before you respond to a co-worker's comment.

Strengths

- Energetic and enthusiastic

- Ambitious and confident

- Creative and energetic

Weaknesses

- Impatient and temperamental

- Dominant and demanding.

Best career choices: Stock trading, entrepreneur, advertising, media, entertainment, security, politics, sports, disaster management, emergency services.

Worst career choices: Anything that is tedious and repetitive, such as banking, cleaning, and data analysis.

Taurus at Work

The Taurus is serious and capable. The confidence Taurus brings to the table can inspire others, but it can also drive them to develop a lack of communication or otherwise unnecessary work-related arguments. The Taurus personality type is often perceived as calm, steady, and dependable, but these individuals take a moment to put themselves in other people's shoes before speaking up.

The best way for Taurus people to avoid conflicts with co-workers is to identify the feeling behind others' reactions to you. Understanding how their reactions differ from yours will help you communicate better with your colleagues and have easier interactions overall.

Those with the Taurus sun sign are known for being practical and reliable. This is good for being respected by your colleagues. But this sign is also known for being stubborn, so it is important to balance your professionalism with your need to get things done your way.

Taurus people also lean toward materialism, which means they spend as much time thinking about what they want as they think about the available possibilities. This characteristic makes them appear self-centered and impacts how Aries interacts with a Taurus.

Strengths

- Methodical and patient
- Abiding and tenacious.

Weaknesses

- Stubborn and complacent
- Materialistic and inflexible.

Best career choices: Medicine, pharmacy, art direction, interior design, accounting, banking, nursing, project management, real estate brokerage, architecture, music, cuisine, and scientific research.

Worst career choices: Jobs that require quick decision-making, like being in the police force, being a firefighter, or a trauma surgeon.

Gemini at Work

Those with the Gemini sun sign are enthusiastic, talkative, witty, versatile, and adaptive. Interacting with them is a challenge because they have an opinion on everything, making it difficult for others to get a word edgewise. To get along well with those who have your sun sign, you must be willing to listen while also offering your thoughts when necessary or appropriate.

Geminis are known for being intelligent and unorthodox. So, they will frequently challenge conventions and rules and question why they are even necessary in the first place. This can make them a welcomed addition to any team, particularly if they provide an innovative edge or creative direction to a project.

However, your colleagues may see you as a little flighty when taking criticism.

Avoid making the mistake of assuming that everyone wants the same things or appreciates your unique work style. You will question why you are there in the first place since it may feel like everyone is doing the same thing.

If you are a Gemini, it is important to take a moment before responding to a co-worker's feedback or criticism.

Strengths

- Unconventional and creative
- Able to find solutions to problems
- Brilliant and quick-witted.

Weaknesses

- Cynical and defensive
- Naive and lacking basic skills.
- Self-centered
- Sensitive

Best career choices: Diplomacy, acting, journalism, travel, blogging, event management, language translation, advertising, media, short course creation and teaching, sales, information technology management, and tour guide.

Worst career choices: Since you're not the best at committing to a single decision, you should stay away from jobs focused on long-term matters and projects. Also, if it's a job that won't let you socialize, it's not for you.

Cancer at Work

Those with the Cancer sun sign are nurturing and caring. This works well for you in the workplace since your co-workers will know how much commitment and effort you put into each project or assignment. However, you have a harder time breaking away to make new connections because of this sign's loyalty.

Cancer people can often work alone due to their affinity for privacy, so they are not always made aware of the project's progress since they miss out on opportunities for recognition and advancement. This can cause frustration when they do not receive the same attention as others. Ensure everyone is involved in the decision-making process and communicates as much information as possible throughout a project.

Strengths

- Committed and detail-oriented
- Accomplished with a meticulous nature.
- Empathetic and understanding.

Weaknesses

- Defensive and guarded
- Demanding and opinionated.
- Loyal to the point of being oblivious to others' needs.

Best career choices: Therapy and counseling, human resources, baking, psychology, nursing, nutrition, hospitality, medicine, catering, real estate, anthropology, archeology, teaching, and social work.

Worst career choices: You're very emotional, so you will likely not do well with any job requiring practicality. Stay away from marketing because you are not a person who likes to take risks. Also, stay away from politics, insurance, and stock trading.

Leo at Work

Leos seek recognition and appreciation, even when they are in the workplace. They are known for their good looks and confidence, making them great leaders and potential influencers. However, this is also a sign prone to being overly dramatic at times. So, when things don't go as intended, Leos have a hard time not taking it personally.

If you are working with someone who is a Leo, make sure you take a moment before responding to their comments or criticism. Sometimes, Leos will be too self-centered in their decisions, causing others to feel they are not involved in matters concerning them.

A Leo sun sign's presence can seem larger than life, which is beneficial for those around them. But it can also be a challenge to maintain diplomatic relationships with other people due to Leos' tendency toward being overbearing and arrogant. If you're a Leo, it is important to remind yourself that others may not be as pleased with how well you are doing as you are. It could cause your colleagues to question whether they are truly committed to the project and believe in how hard they worked on a particular project.

Leo people are temperamental and competitive, making them successful at work, but they need help learning to work more collaboratively with their co-workers.

Strengths

- Witty and charming
- Intelligent and ambitious
- Innovative and forward-thinking.

Weaknesses

- Volatile and unpredictable
- Dictatorial and overbearing
- Resentful of others' success.

Best career choices: Politics, ambassadorship, acting, modeling, fashion, diplomacy, entrepreneurship, event managing, media strategy. You can also be a spokesperson, civil servant, minister, or chief executive.

Worst career choices: You don't do well with authority and taking orders, so stay away from backend jobs. Also, avoid work where you can't interact with the public.

Virgo at Work

The Virgo sun sign is organized and efficient. They are ideal employees but can also cause others to mistake Virgo's efficiency for stubbornness. Virgo people are deeply analytical, which means they will frequently question every decision or action, making it difficult to interact with their colleagues.

It takes a lot of hard work to make it in the workplace, and Virgos often have more than their fair share. Moreover, this sign struggles to get along with others because they struggle with criticism. This can create friction in a team since only one person can get their point across. Virgos must learn how to effectively communicate when they feel frustrated or neglected by the lack of recognition for their hard work.

Remember, your co-workers are humans too and are only doing what they think is best for the organization. So, work out your differences by approaching your colleagues respectfully.

Strengths

- Methodical and detail-oriented
- Thorough and attentive to details.
- Efficient and practical.

Weaknesses

- Impractical and pessimistic.
- Critical of others' work.
- Resentful of the praise others receive for their work.
- Overly analytical to the point of being inflexible or indecisive.

Best career choices: Investigation, translation, editing, designing, detective work, statistician, hospitality, nutrition, veterinary medicine, quantity surveying, auditing, accounting.

Worst career choices: You won't be successful working in security or any job involving adventure.

Libra at Work

The Libra sun sign is diplomatic, which can be a good trait in the workplace. However, this sign struggles with decision-making, taking on responsibility, and being assertive. It makes them appear wishy-washy to their colleagues because they try so hard to be liked by everyone.

Ensure that your Libra co-worker understands the demands of their position within the company and the importance of reaching deadlines. Allow them to provide input on a project before starting so that they are engaged and committed. They will feel that their ideas and needs are considered before taking any action.

Watch for signs of frustration or disappointment in your co-worker. This could indicate they are uncomfortable with the amount of responsibility placed on their shoulders, which should be discussed to avoid future issues.

Libra people are also indecisive and uncomfortable discussing new ideas or difficult decision-making. Typically, Libra is happy to work as part of a team since they appreciate other opinions and viewpoints for decision-making.

Strengths

- Diplomatic
- Able to juggle different responsibilities
- Sensitive to others' needs

Weaknesses

- Impractical
- Wishy-washy and indecisive
- Malleable and lacking in commitment or focus
- Easily disconnected from project goals or timelines
- Unrealistic regarding deadlines, budgets, or expectations for the project

Best career choices: Law, negotiation, detective work, human resources, counseling, styling, interior design, diplomacy, negotiation, mediation, event planning, lobbying.

Worst career choices: Stay away from jobs that require you to make critical decisions on the go.

Scorpio at Work

The Scorpio sun sign is passionate, imaginative, and highly intuitive. They can analyze data and make quick decisions easily since they can look at situations from multiple angles.

Scorpios often have difficulty asking for help since they believe that seeking assistance makes them seem weak. This causes them to struggle with delegation since they are afraid of how others will react if they can't handle everything themselves.

Scorpios are usually overly critical and hurt or upset others because of the way they interact with the Scorpio in the workplace.

Scorpios must remember their co-workers are also human, even if they don't agree with their opinions or actions. Listen to your co-workers and remember they only want to help you.

Strengths

- Brilliant and inventive
- Dedicated and passionate
- Likable
- Intuitive and insightful

Weaknesses

- Possessive of their territory or achievements.
- Overly dramatic or moody
- Quick to anger or resentment.
- Ruthless when dealing with competition or threats to their success.

Best career choices: Engineering, spy work, surgery, science, research, engineering, fertility matters, market analysis, business analysis, occultism, secret service, psychology, financial advising, astrology.

Worst career choices: Stay away from jobs without any deeper meaning. For instance, translation, cooking, statistics, and mathematics.

Sagittarius at Work

The Sagittarius sun sign is enthusiastic and optimistic, making them great colleagues since their sense of humor lightens the mood in tense situations. However, they are open-minded, making them seem flaky or disorganized in the workplace.

Sagittarius people need to learn to be more organized and focused at work to use their time more efficiently and get the recognition and advancement they seek.

Sagittarius is also drawn to the opposite sex, so it could be difficult for them to concentrate on their work in the office with their colleagues. Sagittarius people must learn to resist temptation and concentrate on their careers. It will allow them to make great connections at work and foster relationships to help them in the future.

Strengths

- Ambitious
- Persistent and tenacious.
- Adventurous and daring.
- Creative and lively.

Weaknesses

- Naive and erratic.
- Irrational and impractical.
- Impractical, inconsistent, or unreliable.
- Wishful thinkers or overly optimistic.

Best career choices: Travel sales, public relations, administration, entertainment, recreation, adventure, tourism, theology, life coaching, politics, public speaking, piloting, sports, spirituality, entrepreneurship, detective work.

Worst career choices: Stay away from everything mundane. Also, you don't do well working where your efforts aren't recognized, or you're shackled to a chair, like a ghostwriter, copy editor, or any other desk job.

Capricorn at Work

Capricorns are pragmatic and disciplined, making them a great fit for the workplace. However, they are also overly analytical and critical of others, which makes it difficult for them to relate to others in the office since they seem cold or distant.

Capricorns must avoid being critical of their colleagues or appearing aloof or uninterested in others. Instead, they should recognize that this is their natural tendency when under stress and learn to deal with it so that it does not affect their effectiveness in the office.

This sign is serious, disciplined, and efficient in whatever they do, making them ideal employees and great leaders. They are very goal-oriented and can also motivate others to succeed. However, watch for signs of frustration from your Capricorn co-worker since they bottle up their feelings rather than address them. Capricorn people must be given feedback on their performance regularly. This allows them to reflect on where they can improve.

Also, give your Capricorn co-worker any praise and recognition they deserve, especially in a public forum where it will be noticed by everyone else, too.

Strengths

- Efficient and effective
- Disciplined and organized
- Entrepreneurial and innovative.

Weaknesses

- Unemotional or cold.
- Controlled or aloof.
- Reserved or indifferent.
- Lacks focus or follow-through.
- May intimidate others with their cool demeanor.

Best career choices: Banking, law, information technology, medicine, science, accounting, administration, business execution, physics, financial planning, business, consultancy, logistics, science, and supply chain management. You can also be a physics scholar or a CEO.

Worst career choices: There is nothing you love more than financial excellence, so you must take a job where you are adequately compensated. Stay away from all jobs requiring adventure or having to make decisions in the heat of the moment.

Aquarius at Work

Aquarius is hardworking and determined. They are also open-minded and accept differing opinions, making them a great asset to the office environment. However, they struggle with accepting criticism, so it's essential to give them feedback so they can evaluate their work performance.

Aquarius people are too emotional in the workplace, which can cause them to act carelessly or fall prey to their emotions when dealing with co-workers. They cannot focus on one particular thing all day long as other signs do. It causes difficulties for them in their career and prevents them from meeting their goals.

The Aquarius sun sign is quite independent and unconventional, making it difficult for Aquarius people to work with their colleagues since they often don't fit into the company culture.

It is important to watch for signs of dissatisfaction from your Aquarius co-worker since they could be struggling with isolation or rejection. It is hard for them to talk about their problems if they are afraid you'll think they are just complaining about everything. As an Aquarius, if you feel something does not seem right, it is best to speak up about the situation rather than wait until something negative happens before you can intervene.

Strengths

- Innovative and original
- Independent and dedicated
- Persistent and tenacious

Weaknesses

- Overly critical or cynical.
- Prone to depression.
- Unstable and changeable.

- Aloof, distant, or uninterested in other people's lives.

- Suspicious, paranoid, or untrusting of others.

Best career choices: Music, invention, exploration, science, concept-building, computer development, electronics, photography, communication, astrology, agriculture, aeronautics, environmental activism, and market research.

Worst career choices: It is not for you if your job does not allow you to use your innovative gift. Stay away from the conventional, and do not attempt to become an officer of the law.

Pisces at Work

Pisces people are moody and fickle, so it is difficult to concentrate in the workplace. They do not have the focus required to succeed in a job setting. They will become overwhelmed and distracted by everything around them.

Pisces people often have trouble communicating their emotions, and they seem distant and cold in the workplace. Pisces people must learn to express their feelings more often to be taken more seriously.

The Pisces sun sign is very sensitive and intuitive. You are difficult to offend, but you can be easily overwhelmed by the emotions of others.

Pisces people need to learn to take things less personally and focus on the bigger picture instead of getting bogged down with animosity or jealousy from their co-workers. Be sure that your Pisces co-worker understands their role in the company and what is expected of them before starting any new projects or tasks.

Strengths

- Warm and compassionate
- Highly intuitive
- Great team player.

Weaknesses

- Torn between the demands of personal life and work.
- Can be a victim of mistreatment.

- Subject to being emotionally manipulated by others or giving in to peer pressure.

Best career choices: You can be an artist, animator, social worker, philanthropist, psychic therapist, recruiter, hairstylist, nurse, theme park designer, psychologist, physiotherapist, or teacher.

Worst career choices: Financial gain isn't so important because you're not practical. You don't care much for jobs that are restrictive with your time. Do not attempt to join the armed forces or become a stock trader or banker.

Chapter Five: Zodiac Houses and Their Meanings

The zodiac is split into twelve parts known as houses. Each house is led by one sign and connected to very specific qualities, starting with your personality and extending outward to society and the universe. Every celestial body is in set houses and signs when you're born. So, interpreting your natal chart involves factoring in the influence of each planet, noting their houses and the signs, to help you determine your hidden gifts and future struggles in this incarnation.

When a planet is in a house, it imbues that house with its energies and inevitably affects your life. This is how an astrologer knows which aspects of life need attention at a particular point and how you can effectively deal with the things that happen to you. Houses one through six are personal houses, while houses seven through twelve are interpersonal houses.

The Houses

The first house is the house of all things "first." It's about fresh beginnings, the self, and how you look. It's about first impressions, your body, and how you identify in life. It's the way you deal with things in life. Aries governs this house.

The second house: This house deals with your physical surroundings and senses. It is associated with your line of work, how you attract finances, your values, the things that matter most to you, and your habits. It's ruled by Taurus.

The third house: This house governs how you communicate and think. It's about your interests, your education, and your neighbors. It's about schools, teachers, and travel in your immediate environment and community. Gemini governs it.

The fourth house: Ruled by Cancer, it's the house of home. It's all about foundations, connected to your roots, how you care for yourself, your emotions, children, motherhood, and everything pertaining to a woman.

The fifth house: This is Leo's turf. It's about your love affairs and romantic life. It's also in charge of the way you express yourself, childlike exuberance, play, creativity, joy, and the drama in your life.

The sixth house: It's Virgo's territory. It's about the organization, work ethic, systems, fitness, general health, and the desire to be useful and service to everyone.

The seventh house: Libra's house is about your connections to others in relationships, business, marriage, and contracts. It's about how you relate and share with other people.

The eighth house: This house concerns merging with others, intimacy, mystery, and sex. It's also in charge of your property, assets, loans, inheritances, and how you share finances and resources with your partner. It is Scorpio's house.

The ninth house: This house is in charge of travel, discovery, learning, philosophy, wisdom, religion, and law. Sagittarius rules it, so it's about relating to people from different cultures.

The tenth house: Capricorn reigns here. This house is about your career, expertise, long-term goals, public perception, status, and reputation. It's also connected to masculinity and fatherhood.

The eleventh house: Governed by Aquarius, this house is in charge of connection to groups, friendships, and your society's awareness. It's also about your future dreams and hopes, your eccentric side, and how you deal with sudden changes.

The twelfth house: This is the house of endings. It's all about wrapping things up, the afterlife, getting old, and surrendering. It's a house that also involves separating yourself from the rest of the world, hidden plans, hospitals, imprisonment, and other institutions. Ruled by Pisces, it's also in charge of your subconscious mind, the arts, and imagination.

Now that you know what all the houses are about, let's look at each zodiac sign in each house and how it's likely to affect you.

The Signs in Each House

Aries

Aries is the first house: You have a highly developed sense of individuality and self-awareness. You don't like being told what to do but prefer being in charge of your life. Your personality is open to new ideas and opportunities, so you're always searching for something that makes you feel more alive or brings a spark back into your life.

Aries in the second house: The people in your friendship circle may not consider you very social. You have strong desires and interests but prefer a private life. You may get along well with your cousins, who share some personality traits.

Aries in the third house: Some time ago, you may have gone through a very difficult personal situation that caused you to change your life. Thankfully, you overcame this obstacle and learned an important lesson about common sense and staying connected to other people. Being separated from people makes you lonely and depressed.

Aries in the fourth house: You have a great memory and excellent sense of direction. There's a place inside you that you might keep hidden from most people. It's your inner place, perhaps your retreat or sanctuary. Only you have access to this hidden place, where you go to take a break from the rest of the world and recharge your batteries.

Aries in the fifth house: The main lesson you've learned since coming into this world is that it's healthy and necessary to enjoy life fully. You want to live with more spontaneity and fewer restrictions from other people to express yourself more freely. This lesson may be difficult for you to learn, so you do something silly in an attempt to make a point.

Aries in the sixth house: Your environment, especially your neighborhood, has a tremendous impact on your personality. You have an inherent sense of security and well-being when surrounded by people you know and who like being with you. You feel so comfortable that it's hard to imagine stepping outside those boundaries.

Aries in the seventh house: A unique quality about your life expresses itself through money made and used daily. You are prone to saving money in anticipation of an unexpected event, like an illness or a new car. You probably believe that keeping a certain amount of money aside is more important than spending it.

Aries in the eighth house: Your home is your primary source of security, comfort, and love. It represents stability and security, so you're very protective of it. Although you may find yourself frustrated with a situation related to your home, you take comfort that it's always there whenever things get rough, or life gets too difficult to handle.

Aries in the ninth house: Your mind is always filled with ideas and thoughts. You like to keep busy, so it's important to organize your time to allow you to do what you truly enjoy. Many things interest and spark your imagination, but you get bored and lose interest quickly once you get started on something.

Aries in the tenth house: You naturally take charge of things. When others start panicking, or the situation seems too difficult, you jump in and take command of the situation. This is beneficial in many ways, but you have to be careful not to let it go too far. You don't want to get so involved that you become a dictator, especially if you're in a leadership position.

Aries in the eleventh house: You define your personality and vitality by the friends surrounding you and the activities you participate in together. You may get emotionally involved with people and like or dislike them based on silly things they say or do. This creates problems since other people react in kind, creating tension between you.

Aries in the twelfth house: Your spiritual growth is directly connected to your mental state. You become obsessed with things that don't matter or want to convert people when it's inappropriate. Your efforts in this area often come from your core beliefs or religion, so you're coming from a place of strength.

Taurus

Taurus is the first house: You have a great ability to attract people with your sense of security and stability, but this is not always the best thing for you. You have an inner strength that's always there, even when things look bad on the surface. You know how to relax and enjoy life, so you're usually surrounded by good friends you love.

Taurus is the second house: You know how to get what you want. Money is important, but not for the usual reasons. You're not interested in being rich but rather having enough money to do what you want to do. You have a very practical approach to life, but it's often wiser than it first appears to be.

Taurus in the third house: You're very stable, and people depend on you for advice or a place to stay when they're in a bad situation. Your powers of concentration are almost superhuman, and you're an expert at focusing on one thing at a time. Nothing will distract you when your mind is focused with laser-like intensity on something until it's done.

Taurus in the fourth house: Your home will likely be a very solid, comfortable, and secure place. You're sensitive to your family members and therefore make a great parent. Many family members turn to you for help with their problems, so you need to learn when to say no.

Taurus in the fifth house: You are a sensualist and love physical pleasures like food, drink, sex, and touch. Your love life is always important, but it's best if you don't make it too complicated, or jealous situations may be the result. Your ability to look at things sensibly will help keep jealousy at bay.

Taurus in the sixth house: You are very attentive to your home and will do everything to keep it feeling comfortable and attractive. Your sense of aesthetics is strong, and you use it to ensure the place looks pleasing.

Taurus in the seventh house: You approach things practically, but there's always an artistic streak that makes you want to sit down with a pen and paper and create. You express yourself best through music, painting, or writing because these are ways you communicate your feelings, which sometimes go unspoken between friends.

Taurus in the eighth house: Money isn't as important, but you are tempted to take advantage of someone else's finances sometimes in your life. Protect your money from others, and don't let anyone borrow from you.

Taurus in the ninth house: You have a strong sense of justice and see things as black or white. Most people think of this as a spiritual house and feel drawn toward religion, philosophy, or metaphysics. You're very patient with people and love showing them new experiences.

Taurus in the tenth house: You have a lot of drive and organizational ability needed for success in your career. You're willing to work hard for what you want and will achieve it in time.

Taurus in the eleventh house: Friends are very important, and you do anything to help them if needed. Your friends find you very dependable and responsible, but at times they also find you a bit stubborn, even lazy, because you're more comfortable than ambitious.

Taurus in the twelfth house: You're very good at concealing the things you want to hide. People can't tell what you want to hide, but you know. Your love of secrets makes you vulnerable and insecure, so don't let anyone see the real person behind them, or they could hurt you.

Gemini

Gemini in the first house: You are a very intelligent and quick-witted person. You often have many ideas simultaneously, but you can't put them into action all at once. So, it is hard for you to get things done, and sometimes you find yourself not doing what you want to do. You need a structure for things to move forward.

Gemini in the second house: You take a lot of risks with what you do and say, mostly because your mind is constantly moving incredibly fast. Often, people don't always understand you, so they think your unpredictability will cause problems sooner or later. When decision-making, keep this in mind because it won't always work out as expected.

Gemini is the third house: You are a very curious person and never let anything stand in the way of true knowledge. You find it very hard to make decisions, especially financially. It is easy to lose your money by spending frivolously or wasting time on unimportant things.

Gemini in the fourth house: You have many friends who know what is best for them because of your levelheadedness. However, they soon become interested in other things that have nothing to do with you, and your thoughts get lost in the shuffle. You need to know when to stop and focus on yourself.

Gemini in the fifth house: You are an optimistic person always looking for the good in things. You may not be as practical as other people, but you are always open and honest. You love learning new things and having a good time, but this doesn't mean that you don't work hard during the day.

Gemini in the sixth house: You love to travel, even if this means leaving your home for vacations or business trips. Your mind is very active, so it is easy to get distracted, so traveling keeps you very busy and stimulated.

Gemini in the seventh house: You are a very social person and love to be with people. Your love for human interaction is hard to resist, but this makes it hard to stay focused on one thing at a time. You always want to keep your mind busy, and sometimes it conflicts with other people who want to work alone.

Gemini in the eighth house: Even though you are a very intelligent person, you don't always make the wisest decisions with your finances. You like putting yourself into situations that make your heart race or cause you stress. For example, you often spend more money than you should and then feel bad about it.

Gemini in the ninth house: You are a very curious individual who loves learning new things and can learn from other people's experiences. You are also very easy to get along with, making it easy for friends to trust you with their lives. It makes you a very reliable person and causes others to hold back information too important to reveal.

Gemini in the tenth house: You have a lot of ideas that surface from your subconscious mind, and these ideas are hard for people to understand at times. It isn't easy to get your ideas and plans approved by others. If you want to succeed, you need to learn to explain yourself for people to get your message.

Gemini in the eleventh house: You are the life of the party and don't mind going out at night to a place filled with people. You love being around people who have new information or new thoughts, but sometimes this is overwhelming when you have to focus on a single thing.

Gemini in the twelfth house: You have a very active imagination when awake and when dreaming. It is difficult to make decisions, especially when it negatively affects your life's direction. You need to learn how to overcome this by talking about your thoughts and plans.

Cancer

Cancer in the first house: You are an emotional and sensitive person who holds everything in. You want to express yourself but find it hard to put your thoughts into words. This is also true when you want to remember things; they often seem vague or foggy.

Cancer is the second house: You are a very generous person, and you like buying people presents or giving them money because of how they make you feel. You can earn a lot of money because you are smart and hard-working. However, this could cause financial problems because you spend more than you earn. You also find it difficult to save your money for future goals or emergencies, but this can be overcome with discipline and organization skills.

Cancer in the third house: You love to communicate and express your thoughts very easily, and you enjoy writing letters and reading novels. You are intelligent and have a great memory, but you struggle to concentrate on important things or constructive work.

Cancer is the fourth house: This position gives you a great appreciation for home comforts and security. You love having your own space, so your surroundings must make you feel comfortable. You worry about security and safety, even though you are a careful person.

Cancer in the fifth house: You have a very strong sense of justice and fairness, especially with money issues. You like to judge people, which makes you very intolerant of others, often leading to a bad temper. Crime and legal issues usually interest you.

Cancer in the sixth house: This position reveals many facets of yourself and makes it hard to put yourself into one category or type. You have an emotional mind that goes from anger one minute to happiness the next. You also have difficulty getting along with co-workers, often causing you much stress.

Cancer in the seventh house: This position makes you want to get married and have a family, even though you're very shy around people. You are loving but also very moody. You make friends easily, but sometimes this leads to jealousy from friends or rivals. You like spending time with your partner or spouse, and you want them to be happy above all else.

Cancer in the eighth house: You have a strong sense of material wealth and assets you need to protect. These are very important because they represent security and safety. Even though you are a careful person, you enjoy spending a lot of money on unnecessary gadgets and objects.

Cancer in the ninth house: This position makes you very happy and energetic, but it also causes your moodiness to worsen. You have strong personal beliefs and morals that guide your life, and you worry about your health because you're anxious about it being too good or too bad. You will likely get involved in political issues since this is where you feel the most energy and get the most pleasure.

Cancer in the tenth house: This position gives you an analytical mind that is critical of other people at times, so you struggle to communicate with others. You are a very sociable person and love to spend time with others, but if someone is not being friendly or civil, it will make you very angry.

Cancer in the eleventh house: This position makes you good at decision-making, and you can clearly see what needs to be done. You are very logical and have no emotions, so you don't always experience true happiness in your life or with others around you. Often, you make enemies because people cannot understand you or the logic in your decisions.

Cancer in the twelfth house: This position gives emotional intelligence that causes your moodiness to worsen. You will likely get involved in legal issues because of your passion for making the wrongs right in your head. You prefer privacy and ensuring that your emotions are in control around other people, even though they may be very difficult to hide.

Leo

Leo in the first house: You are very much a leader and highly ambitious. You want to be the best in everything, which could cause many challenges. Even though people like being around you because of your warmth and goodwill, others dislike you for your direct personality.

Leo in the second house: You struggle with financial problems because of your lack of organizational skills or money discipline. You love spending money on luxurious items, causing financial problems because you keep spending more than is sensible. There is also a good chance that you'll be involved in a scandal.

Leo in the third house: You are very popular, and people like being around you because of your warmth and goodwill. You are extremely loyal to people who have been kind to you, as long as they treat you well, making it easy for the wrong people to get close to you.

Leo in the fourth house: People have a problem with your leadership ability or views on life, especially if those views are contrary to what everyone else thinks and does. This possibly causes a great deal of difficulty when making friends because people will avoid you for being too forceful about your beliefs.

Leo in the fifth house: You have trouble achieving romantic goals and maintaining a happy relationship because your approach to things is very direct. Others more reserved or quiet will feel alienated. Your love life may not be great, but it will,

Libra

Libra is the first house: You go overboard with your hobbies or interests, which often causes social embarrassments. Exercise self-control before spending your hard-earned money on things that only bring you negative attention.

Libra is the second house: You love having things around you that make you feel especially good, like beautiful artwork or expensive jewelry. It's essential not to be addicted to these things and limit your spending because you'll eventually run out of money for necessities.

Libra is the third house: You put others down in their appearance, which is not very attractive when people look at a romantic relationship between you and another person. Be more humble; you'll get further in life.

Libra is the fourth house: You push things away and keep them a secret. Maybe it is because of your resentment toward your parents or their values, or maybe you are hiding something from yourself. Whatever the case, don't bottle up your true feelings.

Libra in the fifth house: You have a lot of fun with others and make life exciting whenever you hang out. Remember, other people might not be as outgoing as you, so don't judge them.

Libra in the sixth house: You value beauty and harmony, which is good for your work ethic and how you handle yourself in the workplace. However, don't get too caught up with the aesthetic of your workspace, and focus more on finding a balance between beauty and productivity.

Libra in the seventh house: You want others to be happy and make them feel beautiful, which is great. Just don't forget about yourself when you're doing things for others because you also deserve happiness. If someone doesn't appreciate you for who you are, they aren't worth your time.

Libra in the eighth house: You are very judgmental towards others, even when those you judge are your friends. Be more understanding and not so quick to judge people behind their backs.

Libra in the ninth house: You have a fondness for beauty and harmony that causes you to make rash decisions or give in to your desires without thinking them through. Sometimes it's better to say no rather than yes.

Libra in the tenth house: You can easily get overwhelmed by everything that needs fixing around your home or workplace; you shouldn't impose yourself on these issues immediately if they don't need you. Instead, focus your energy on things you can control or are good at doing.

Libra in the eleventh house: You are self-conscious when around others and take criticism personally. It's better for people to be honest with you about their feelings than to hide them from you.

Libra in the twelfth house: Your artistic abilities will likely get overlooked because you feel you must blend in with others. Don't be afraid of expressing yourself, even if it means being a little eccentric now and then.

Scorpio

Scorpio in the first house: You want to use your attention to attract people in your life and to know how beautiful you think they are. However, it may be difficult for others to see that beauty because of how you treat them. Be a little more patient.

Scorpio is the second house: Your energy is overwhelming and intimidating when socializing, so hold back on your energy when meeting new people.

Scorpio is the third house: Your mind is always on the go, and you are always contemplating how to make people fall in love with you. However, your best bet is to tell them who and what you are so they can make their own conclusions. Be a little more authentic.

Scorpio in the fourth house: Your energy is sometimes hard for people to handle because you are deeply spiritual, mysterious, and intense. Fortunately, this doesn't bother you much because you don't care what anybody thinks about you anyway. The problem is that it doesn't work with your interests and passions.

Scorpio in the fifth house: You are deeply charismatic and quite magnetic to others. Your attention is a bit more of a burden than it would seem, so be less intense with people. There is nothing wrong with being attentive, but sometimes it overwhelms others.

Scorpio in the sixth house: You care about how you treat other people around you, so it might come off as controlling. Let go of your emotions and admit when something bothers you. People won't have to guess what is on your mind.

Scorpio in the seventh house: Intimidating and mysterious, you give people a hard time by the way you present yourself. The only way you'll enjoy a good relationship is if you are more open. You have nothing to worry about.

Scorpio in the eighth house: Your intensity can be too much for some people to handle, but that doesn't stop you from being who you want to be. Your intense energy is very intimidating, but people are drawn to it anyway because it is you they are attracted to.

Scorpio in the ninth house: Your intensity isn't easy for people to handle because you want to control everything. You need to lighten up and realize your intensity is probably one of your biggest strengths. However, don't push it on others.

Scorpio in the tenth house: You have a lot of potential for your future goals because of your intensity and focus. You will further reach those goals if you are more flexible with people and don't push so hard.

Scorpio in the eleventh house: You are intensely passionate about everything you do, which is positive. However, your intensity may be a bit much for some people, so be more subtle with your passion and intense energy.

Scorpio in the twelfth house: You're intensely focused on what you want out of life. You are drawn to deep mysteries and life secrets because of who your energy attracts. It's good to have those interests but focus less on them for stronger relationships with people.

Sagittarius

Sagittarius in the first house: You are a bit of an adventurer, and being around new people and exploring your surroundings. However, your adventurous nature can get in the way of making friends.

Sagittarius in the second house: You aren't afraid to be notified for socializing and meeting new people, but people may not know what you want from a relationship. Spend more time alone with your thoughts before looking for a person who will match them.

Sagittarius is the third house: You are free-spirited and spontaneous around others. You have a positive attitude toward life and don't mind joking around. You're an extrovert who loves to talk.

Sagittarius in the fourth house: You may have difficulty making your downtime feel like something much more important than relaxing. However, be careful not to let your imagination run wild and consume all your energy. Make sure you stay active to release that extra energy and not feel guilty about being inactive for a while each day.

Sagittarius in the fifth house: You have a good ability to see the bigger picture and are not afraid to explore people who aren't as well-liked. You are a people-pleaser and want to please everyone around you. You cannot get stuck on making your friends happy all of the time as it will cause problems making new friends or developing new interests.

Sagittarius in the sixth house: You have a good ability to connect with others, making it easier for you to build relationships. However, your fondness for being around people may lead you to do counterproductive things when you find someone special. Don't feel pressured to have a connection when you meet someone. Rather open yourself to the world and new things instead of building connections familiar to you.

Sagittarius in the seventh house: You may feel like people do not trust you, but it's better to stay than change how others see you. This sign is at its most relaxed before making a long-term commitment in a relationship. You may not feel comfortable in the spotlight, but you must let people see your bright side so they see your potential for success in life.

Sagittarius in the eighth house: You are prone to committing yourself to projects you feel responsible for, but don't let this stop you from reaching your full potential. You're a person eager to take what you are doing and finish it yourself, and that's fine, but don't lock yourself in your room. Release your energy, so it helps you focus and make new friends.

Sagittarius in the ninth house: You love experiencing new things and being around people who enjoy adventuring as much as you. However, you are prone to taking too many risks in things that interest you. You often feel like you've already experienced life at its best. Take a step back and see what else life has to offer.

Sagittarius in the tenth house: You're a romantic and always looking for someone special that will make you feel they are worth your time and attention. However, you are often unsure how you feel about people in your life. Spend more time with people you don't consider your ultimate match until you determine how interested you are in them.

Sagittarius in the eleventh house: You look at things differently and see things others do not. You have a great memory, so it's hard to forget the past, especially in relationships.

Sagittarius in the twelfth house: You like experimenting, but this excitement for life can be difficult to control. Whatever you are interested in, be careful not to go off the deep end. Be more open-minded about new experiences and people.

Capricorn

Capricorn is the first house: You have a sharp mind and are always looking for ways to make quick money. You also don't mind putting in some extra work to get what you want and will probably start working at a young age.

Capricorn in the second house: You likely spend time understanding how the world works and how to invest your funds. You've probably learned to save money from an early age.

Capricorn is the third house: You like being around people but are prone to shyness and feel too much pressure when first getting involved with others. However, don't think about why people aren't talking to you.

Capricorn in the fourth house: You have been the child to get chores done early, which means you have a good understanding of managing your money. You value security and like things to be in order. Sometimes it is difficult to tell others what's wrong or how you feel.

Capricorn in the fifth house: As a child, you probably found it easy to concentrate on your studies or hobbies for an extended period and preferred not to have been disturbed. You are tidy and organized, so living in a mess is an uncomfortable experience.

Capricorn in the sixth house: You are ambitious and disciplined but find it difficult to make time for yourself. You are serious in everything you do, so sometimes you come across as cold and uninterested.

Capricorn in the seventh house: You were likely the one child with few friends due to your shyness or awkwardness around others, or you were more interested in things other than people.

Capricorn in the eighth house: You may have grown up a little more timid and reserved than other children and had less-than-welcoming relationships. You like to control your surroundings and are likely to be established early in life.

Capricorn in the ninth house: As a child, you preferred not to participate in fun or exciting things. You probably even went as far as to avoid any opportunity for fun, lest you were left with no choice but to join in.

Capricorn in the tenth house: You had few friends growing up, as you were more interested in being serious than people. You most likely wanted to be grown-up early in life and preferred responsibilities over playtime.

Capricorn in the eleventh house: Your childhood could have been insecure or difficult, as you never felt completely secure regarding your place in the world. You may have been teased or disliked by others for merely being who you are.

Capricorn in the twelfth house: You are very responsible and reliable and don't need much encouragement to get started on anything. You grew up feeling like you didn't fit in and were probably teased for being different.

Aquarius

Aquarius in the first house: People tend to think of you as a fun-loving and positive person who doesn't let anything get them down. You probably spent time with others your age and were quite the social butterfly as a child.

Aquarius in the second house: You are a frugal person and don't mind hard work to buy what you want. The first things you bought were probably practical or would last a long time.

Aquarius in the third house: You are something of an oddball, as even from an early age, you had different interests from others. It probably started with your first love, whatever that was. This brought about your social awkwardness among others as you portray yourself differently.

Aquarius in the fourth house: There's nothing better than indulging your curiosity by learning more about people and their quirks. It leads to meeting like-minded people and forming strong bonds.

Aquarius in the fifth house: You are someone who isn't afraid to stand up for what you believe in and make it known across town. It can result in heated debates and also a lot of admiration from people who appreciate your determination.

Aquarius in the sixth house: People may consider you a health freak due to your obsession with staying healthy. You'll likely go above and beyond what is required to keep yourself or those around you healthy.

Aquarius in the seventh house: You're a unique person when it comes to love. You often fall for unpopular people much different from yourself and even with opposing points of view. This causes disputes between friends and other loved ones, but they don't last long because of your strong bond.

Aquarius in the eighth house: You are a very generous person, always willing to help those in need, even if you don't know them personally. The only problem with this is that when you need help, people are not willing to repay the favor.

Aquarius in the ninth house: You are one of the most interesting individuals and never cease to surprise those around you. Your determination to solve problems and discover what makes things tick makes interesting conversations with others. Your impulsive nature will lead others astray if they follow your example.

Aquarius in the tenth house: You are someone with a strong sense of spirituality and morality. Although you can be eccentric, you do not choose to act this way on purpose. Instead, it is because you can't help but think things through to their conclusion.

Aquarius in the eleventh house: You have a very well-developed intuitive nature between people and yourself. You struggle to believe if things about others are true or not, but you'll find out soon enough through what people say about you in public.

Aquarius in the twelfth house: You are a very realistic person having little trouble living and dealing with the realities of life. Your intuition is very strong, and you can easily tell if you're being lied to or if a person is truly trying to help you. You can usually differentiate between what's important and what's not.

Pisces

Pisces is the first house: You have a very strong personality, which sometimes makes it difficult for people to relate to you because you are so stubborn. You have a hard time being wrong, and it is often impossible to admit that you are.

Pisces in the second house: Due to your dreamy nature as a child, many of your early interests and hobbies revolved around fantasy and not reality. It doesn't mean you didn't learn to do things in real life, but instead, you struggle to comprehend something until you see it.

Pisces in the third house: You are highly creative and imaginative. When you get an idea, you have to act on it. You also have a very high pain tolerance and are very good at finding ways to make things work or take care of things that go wrong.

Pisces in the fourth house: You have a great love for entertainment, so you have a hard time with real-life responsibilities and problems because your mind needs something more interesting than reality to occupy itself.

Pisces in the fifth house: You have problems in romance and relationships because you are too idealistic with unrealistic expectations.

Pisces in the sixth house: You struggle with authority due to your larger-than-life imagination, which puts you in the positions of authority figures, and then you rebel against them.

Pisces in the seventh house: You have difficulty with marriage and partnerships, whether business or personal. You battle to confide in people, and people find it hard to confide in you, resulting in a lack of communication between partners.

Pisces in the eighth house: You are very mercenary-like with your money and possessions. However, this quality is not for self-gain but rather for the benefit of others.

Pisces in the ninth house: You have a great deal of trouble believing in religion. You cannot comprehend something that can't be proven or isn't entirely concrete.

Pisces in the tenth house: Settling down or even committing to your job is a struggle because it is too hard to focus on one thing for extended periods. Your mind just keeps wandering, making you restless and desiring to be somewhere else.

Pisces in the eleventh house: You have a very hard time with friends due to your extreme sensitivity. This sensitivity makes it difficult to form relationships because you are too quick to take things other people say about you personally.

Pisces in the twelfth house: Discovering anything about yourself is extremely difficult because it requires self-awareness, which is rare in Pisces. However, when you learn something about yourself, it can be extremely profound and affect every aspect of your life.

Chapter Six: Planetary Placements

Planetary placements are precisely what they sound like. It refers to where the planets are positioned during your birth or at any point in time, like an important event in history or in your life. These placements are why we can get information about our lives through astrology, what determines our character, and why two people with the same sun signs can be very different. Let's get into the various planet positions in each of the twelve houses without further ado.

The Planets in Each House

Sun

Sun in the first house: You're a very active person, a person to start new things and who takes pride in what you've accomplished. You have a personality that shines, and when needed, you can be assertive with grace and dignity. You're a natural leader and a pretty successful one at that.

Sun in the second house: The spotlight shines especially bright for you. You're self-assured, strong, and capable of great things. You have the drive to excel, and this translates into your career.

Sun in the third house: This is the house of your appearance, social standing, and good judgment. You're observant and have a knack for quick decision-making based on what you observe first thing in the morning.

Sun in the fourth house: Your home is your haven, where you shed yourself of troubles by submerging yourself in family life. Your home will represent everything that makes you happy or feel safe and at peace. You place romance high on your priority list.

Sun in the fifth house: You're sociable and fun to be around. It's easy for you to make friends because of your approachable demeanor, and it's equally as easy for you to get along with people at work. You love yourself, but you also love helping others.

Sun in the sixth house: As your home is your haven, this is also where you go when you want to retreat from all the hustle and bustle of city life. It's a place of solitude that allows you time to think things through carefully and rationally.

Sun in the seventh house: Successful relationships await your notice. Something worth noting here is that the relationship you have with your spouse, partner, or life partner will be very important. So, pay more attention to this aspect of life, especially a long-term committed relationship.

Sun in the eighth house: You draw strength from your family and friends. Your home is also a place of comfort and serenity, and that's the way you like it. You're very close to the money, as you're fiscally responsible.

Sun in the ninth house: It's time to change scenery. You seek out freedom from all your problems, particularly from the rigors of city life. This is where you should take some time off to travel for fun and relaxation, or sometimes just for enjoyment's sake.

Sun in the tenth house: You have a lot to offer others through your expertise and experience. You can also connect with others through your words. But amid all this, it's perfectly fine for you to be alone every once in a while.

Sun in the eleventh house: It's easy for you to relate to others, and they'll come to you when they need a shoulder to cry on. Helping people gives your life purpose, and achieving goals gives you satisfaction. You're very "people" oriented right now.

Sun in the twelfth house: It's time for self-reflection and introspection. You take time off by yourself, whether at home or elsewhere, so you can fully explore the depths of your mind and soul.

Moon

Moon in the first house: You're very passionate and emotional. You're the first to know when you're feeling down, and you own your feelings without caring what others think. Your emotions highly impact how you take care of yourself.

Moon in the second house: Your emotional state affects how much money you spend, so knowing how to gauge or balance your moods is important. You could learn to be more frugal with yourself.

Moon in the third house: There's nothing like comfort food to give you a sense of security. You're very loyal to your friends, and their friendship is important. You clearly understand what makes someone happy and what doesn't, so it's easy for you to judge other people on their happiness levels.

Moon in the fourth house: If you haven't already started doing it, consider getting a pet. There's a strong emotional connection between you and your pets, especially because they're loyal to their master. This is also the house of family and home, so take good care of both. You're very passionate about love and romance, and don't hide it from anyone. Your ambitions drive you.

Moon in the fifth house: You have many friends and acquaintances, and you can relate to anyone. Those who care for you are bound to have a very special place in your heart. You have a knack for making others feel comfortable.

Moon in the sixth house: You're empathetic and feel other people's feelings. You're also sensitive to criticism. But even though you have a knack for helping others, someone has to be there for you as much as everyone else.

Moon in the seventh house: You're very observant. When judging others, you don't just jump to conclusions. You consider all the evidence before concluding. This is the house of healing, so if there's anything that ails you, do whatever it takes to make yourself feel better. You care a lot about your family and friends, but you're also very self-sufficient. You can handle yourself without the help of anyone in love and romance.

Moon in the eighth house: You're emotional, passionate, and possessive in romantic relationships. It may be tough to find the right person who understands you, but at least you know you can balance your emotional state by being alone. You feel safe and secure in your home.

Moon in the ninth house: You're very intuitive and have a keen way of taking things apart to see what they're made of. You're also very romantic, and it's always a great time for romance and love. People who live with you are bound to feel safe and secure, especially in romance.

Moon in the tenth house: You're a very social person, so your connections with others are pretty strong. You may meet unfamiliar people at work or through your community activities, so be actively open to new people.

Moon in the eleventh house: You're very popular, and you can connect with everyone in one swoop. You have many friends, including acquaintances and even strangers, who are kind to you. If you're feeling lonely or down, many will comfort you.

Moon in the twelfth house: You are very introspective and reflective about your life. You start asking yourself questions about what makes your life meaningful and where you go from here. It's time for you to leave that place for a better place—yourself.

Mercury

Mercury in the first house: You think and talk very fast, so naturally, you're clever. You're ready to take on the world at a moment's notice. You like to be in the spotlight, and it's easy to stick out in a crowd.

Mercury in the second house: Your mind is always working at 100%, so you can't sit and relax. You have plenty of ideas often occurring simultaneously, but there's nothing worse than having nothing to do.

Mercury in the third house: One way or another, your words always get out into the world through phone calls or texting with friends, work colleagues, or family members.

Mercury in the fourth house: Your mind is always working, and you have a knack for making connections that make sense. You're also very patient, observant, and methodical in your approach to problems.

Mercury in the fifth house: Your communication skills are strong, so it's no surprise you're good with everyone, even children and animals. You're very entertaining and have a way of making people laugh.

Mercury in the sixth house: You're very imaginative and creative, always thinking of new ways to make a living or an income. You're also good at making money, though in your own methods.

Mercury in the seventh house: You're very interested in learning more, so you're quick to pick up new skills when they come along. You're an excellent communicator, and you'll make a great lawyer or teacher.

Mercury in the eighth house: You are a good listener and know how to get information out of someone without making them feel uncomfortable. You also have a knack for learning how and why people act the way they do and use the knowledge wisely.

Mercury in the ninth house: You're curious about life, so you always have new things to learn. Your intellect is sharp, and your mind never works at less than 100%. Your interests are varied, and you're always interested in what's going on.

Mercury in the tenth house: You talk a lot, but you hate it when other people give their input without knowing the full story. Talking is your way of obtaining more information. Talking with someone who asks questions that prompt your thoughts and feelings is best for you.

Mercury in the eleventh house: You have a way of making connections with people and people like you. You're good at presenting your point of view so they can understand. You have a knack for communicating with children, but be careful not to break their trust or treat them without cause.

Mercury in the twelfth house: You're very curious about life, and this curiosity helps you connect with people. But with romantic relationships, too much curiosity leads to deception or betrayal. Be careful of others' motives from now on. It's best to rely on more concrete information than your instincts when choosing a partner in love and romance.

Venus

Venus in the first house: You have a wonderful time with friends and are also very good at talking to friends and family. You'll find yourself in trouble if you fall out of love with people. You like to keep friendships, but don't forget to put your own needs first.

Venus in the second house: You enjoy being around friends, so this is an excellent time for socializing and making new connections. This is a very friendly planet, so you'll be popular wherever you go. As long as you know how to relax, it's easy to find the right balance between work and play in your daily activities.

Venus in the third house: Your relationships often seem unreal compared with your work life. You get involved with people more emotionally than you should. You're also very honest and straightforward, so you can't stop yourself from speaking your mind and being completely honest.

Venus in the fourth house: Your desire for harmony makes your friendships perfect for inner peace and stability. You never want anything to change. However, the rest of the world is moving forward rapidly, so keep up with the times.

Venus in the fifth house: Your friendships are highly important, and you're very nurturing and supportive of others. However, you know how to take care of yourself, including your needs. You would gain a lot from starting a relationship with someone who has a lot in common.

Venus in the sixth house: You think about your problems and how to solve them in various ways, so naturally, you're good at making connections between thoughts and ideas. Keep an open mind about what you learn about yourself and other people.

Venus in the seventh house: You're optimistic about your future, so you have a good chance of starting a positive new relationship during this period. You also have a knack for telling others what they need to hear to keep up with their lives and treat them well.

Venus in the eighth house: There's an emotional connection with people, making it easy for you to connect and understand people's emotions. But, if you do too much, it could lead to deception or betrayal with your partner in love or business.

Venus in the ninth house: You may develop a strong desire to travel or learn more about other cultures. You're excellent at making friends and can talk to anyone, even strangers. Your curiosity about other people and situations leads to a greater understanding of how things work in the world.

Venus in the tenth house: Your social life is very important, so you want to spend time with friends and family. Going out for entertainment becomes more important than staying home alone. You need friendly support from others, but make sure the people around you are on your side, not only after material advantages.

Venus in the eleventh house: You'll meet someone who shares your interests and will be a good friend. You'll enjoy talking with people and often feel like being with your friends more than anything. Talking with someone who asks questions that prompt your thoughts and feelings is best for you.

Venus in the twelfth house: You have a strong emotional bond with family or close friends, so it's not practical to take on any new responsibilities. Travel also helps you learn more about yourself but ensure you don't overlook important responsibilities at home. Don't let others' needs affect yours too strongly during this period.

Mars

Mars in the first house: You have a competitive nature. You want to win every argument, and you don't like losing. You're also quite determined, and you have an eye for detail in your career and other important activities. Watch out for accidents, injuries, or illnesses while traveling.

Mars in the second house: There's certainly no lack of energy with you, so you love doing physical activities with friends and family. You're also very clear about what's in your best interests with money and possessions. However, if you don't take care of yourself, it could lead to trouble.

Mars in the third house: It's important to have fun with friends, relatives, and even strangers. You're very aggressive, but that's not necessarily a bad thing. Fight your own battles whenever you have an argument or a conflict, and don't let others take advantage of you.

Mars in the fourth house: Mars energy helps you decide more quickly. You can achieve more things than normal if you work hard enough. Feeling good about yourself is important for helping others feel good about themselves.

Mars in the fifth house: Your competitive nature could lead to arguments, especially with people you're close to. You feel competitive with others and have a strong will to succeed. There's also an attraction to people doing well financially.

Mars in the sixth house: You like being around friends or your romantic partner. Guard your health and finances firmly because it's important to be healthy and wealthy. You need to be careful with spending money on luxury items. It's imperative to live within your means.

Mars in the seventh house: You have an active social life, which can be very positive when well-led and organized. You're excellent at making friends, officiating at parties, and hosting activities to help people get to know each other better.

Mars in the eighth house: You strongly crave material gain, so often take on more responsibility than you can handle. You also spend too much money or even get involved in financial fraud and embezzlement. You need to control your anger and aggression or risk going to jail.

Mars in the ninth house: Your desire to learn more about the world by traveling is very strong. You enjoy learning about everything from travel to food to people's activities in different regions. You're good at making friends, even if others don't realize it at first.

Mars in the tenth house: There's a strong desire to spend time with people and not only for social reasons. You need to invest your time in friends and family. You feel a strong need to earn money if you're out of work. Doing something that keeps you actively involved in the world is best for you.

Mars in the eleventh house: Your desire for action is apparent, and you like having fun and talking about interesting things with friends. You can enjoy spoken or written debates when someone makes a logical argument on an issue or topic that interests both parties.

Mars in the twelfth house: You are secretive or even deceptive with your plans and ideas, so don't expect others to understand where you want to go or what you want to do with your life unless you are open with them.

Jupiter

Jupiter in the first house: You are a friendly and optimistic person who enjoys spending time with friends. You like being a role model for younger people and a mentor or teacher. Spending time outdoors as much as possible is best for you.

Jupiter in the second house: You are generous with your wealth and ensure that family members are taken care of financially. The circumstances around you lead to financial opportunities, but it's best to live within your means.

Jupiter in the third house: You have a very outgoing personality and enjoy talking with people about anything. You're quite social and get along with everyone easily. You're also intelligent and could be a teacher or academic.

Jupiter in the fourth house: You have a strong family bond and enjoy spending time with relatives and people you're close to. Overlooked activities like home improvement projects could give you a boost in energy that lasts for many days.

Jupiter in the fifth house: You want nothing more than to be with your partner, spouse, or children, and it's important to spend more time together. Your interest in sports is strong, and there's an attraction to outdoor activities like golf or tennis. Spending time enjoying yourself with other people is best.

Jupiter in the sixth house: Your sense of humor is strong, and you enjoy laughing and joking with people. You could be a teacher or work for a charity. Some concern must be given to travel or relocating plans in the near future because it could affect your work.

Jupiter in the seventh house: You love being with your partner or spouse, and it's important to spend more time together. You're also very friendly and enjoy helping others solve problems they have difficulty dealing with independently.

Jupiter in the eighth house: You have an optimistic and positive outlook on life and like being around active people. There's an attraction to the elderly, especially if they're active. You may deal with health issues, but you can lead a very healthy lifestyle with good nutrition, exercise, and a positive attitude.

Jupiter in the ninth house: Your desire to learn more about the world is strong, as is your interest in philosophy or astronomy. You enjoy talking with people who care about far-reaching topics larger than life or even small topics like gossip. Spend time traveling and possibly attending lectures or classes at a college.

Jupiter in the tenth house: You like being active and can get along with almost everyone. You might want to be a public figure or performer. You do very well in the arts and academic fields considered liberal arts – like writing and philosophy.

Jupiter in the eleventh house: Your desire to help others is very strong. You like talking with people who have individualistic ideas and are open to new things. You might travel or work with people with similar interests.

Jupiter in the twelfth house: Others recognize your desire to help them when they need advice for life situations. There's an attraction to scientific studies and people interested in the occult or psychic practices.

Saturn

Saturn in the first house: Your desire to be an authority is strong, and you enjoy being a role model for others. There's an attraction to philosophy and an academic field with very strict standards.

Saturn in the second house: You are a bit of a perfectionist. You worry about spending too much money. However, you handle money responsibly and will likely have many savings for your retirement years.

Saturn in the third house: Your ability to learn is excellent, and you're an avid reader of books or magazines that contain interesting facts or teach you something new. You like to teach others about the world around them.

Saturn in the fourth house: You enjoy being with people and are quite social. You enjoy being around others in groups and talking about your interests. Your need to be involved in traveling activities is strong, and you have an adventurous spirit.

Saturn in the fifth house: You handle money responsibly but are not particularly generous in sharing your wealth or helping family members financially. There is a higher probability of illness related to health issues like joints, bones, or skin.

Saturn in the sixth house: You love to be of service and choose to work in a service-oriented industry, like teaching or helping those having difficulty getting around. You may deal with health issues, but you can manage your symptoms effectively with proper nutrition and exercise.

Saturn in the seventh house: You have an attraction to older people you admire or share similar interests and possibly an attraction to someone already married. However, it's best to spend time with someone you love and who loves you back.

Saturn in the eighth house: You handle money responsibly, but there's a higher probability of being involved in legal matters, like contracts and legal settlements. There's an attraction to risky or taboo activities, like gambling or even illegal activities.

Saturn in the ninth house: Your desire to learn more about the world is strong, and you enjoy learning from books or lectures by people with great knowledge. You could work for someone well-known and respected for their skills. Keep an open mind about your beliefs, and don't be so closed off to people's ideas.

Saturn in the tenth house: You are drawn to authority figures and love to be a mentor or someone looked up to. You set the best examples for those following in your footsteps.

Saturn in the eleventh house: Your desire to be helpful is strong, and you enjoy mentoring others, especially younger people. You could teach at a college or university or teach other people new life lessons.

Saturn in the twelfth house: Your need to be involved with travel activities involving travel and having visitors is strong. But there's also an attraction to strange subjects and people fascinated with the occult or psychic practices.

Uranus

Uranus in the first house: You love to be different and are quite eccentric. There's an attraction to unusual or controversial subjects that people appreciate, and you've done much research on those subjects. You're creative, innovative, and freedom-loving.

Uranus in the second house: You dislike routine and have a strong desire to explore the world. There's also an attraction to the new subject matter, since what interests you is new and different each day. You're also innovative and free-thinking.

Uranus in the third house: You have a knack for discovering secrets and would enjoy traveling through space. If you're lucky, you'll work for NASA or a similar organization. You like being different, which attracts quirky or eccentric people. There is an attraction to older people who know subjects that interest you.

Uranus in the fourth house: You're very creative and unconventional and have a strong desire to seek fame or money from your ideas that others might appreciate. You could be involved in the arts. However, spending time with someone you love and who loves you back is best.

Uranus in the fifth house: You don't like regular routines or repeating the same activities each day. You have an unusual desire to travel to other countries and learn about their customs. There's a higher probability of you having health issues related to your bones, joints, or skin.

Uranus in the sixth house: You're innovative and unconventional, but your desire to be different also attracts you to bizarre subjects others might find humorous. Be open-minded about religions, philosophies, and politics.

Uranus in the seventh house: You handle money responsibly, but there's a higher probability of being involved in legal matters related to contracts or settlements. You could be involved in the arts and be a performer, an actor, or even a director.

Uranus in the eighth house: Your desire to be different is strong, but there's also an attraction to unusual or controversial subjects people appreciate. You're creative and innovative.

Uranus in the ninth house: You love to learn new things and enjoy learning new life lessons. You could work for someone, like teaching or mentoring. Keep an open mind about other people's beliefs, and don't be so closed off to your ideas.

Uranus in the tenth house: You have an unusual desire to be different and unconventional. There's a higher probability of being involved in legal matters like contracts, contracts, or settlements.

You could be involved with the arts, like acting, directing, or even writing.

Uranus in the eleventh house: You crave authenticity and originality. If you go against society's expectations, you could get into trouble with the law or out of place among your peers. Stay true to yourself, and don't sacrifice who you truly are for anyone else's expectations.

Uranus in the twelfth house: You're different and unconventional, and there's also an attraction to strange people and occult practices. You could be involved with the arts or work for someone with connections with people from other cultures.

Neptune

Neptune in the first house: Your need to be different is strong, but you also want to rebel or explore new things. You could become involved in various mysticism and alternative religions contrary to what your family or other members of society believe. There's an attraction to unusual subjects like occult practices, astrology, and fortune-telling.

Neptune in the second house: You have your own ideas about handling money. You're creative and have many original ideas, but there's an attraction to unusual subjects like occult practices, astrology, and fortune-telling.

Neptune in the third house: You are a person who loves to explore new subjects, especially those controversial or even illegal. You may be drawn to subjects relating to the arts or theater.

Neptune in the fourth house: Your desire to be different and rebel against your family's expectations is strong. However, you are also attracted to paranormal things like horoscopes, fortune-telling, or other divination. There is an attraction to older people with knowledge about subjects that interest you.

Neptune in the fifth house: Your desire to be different and explore new subjects could become a problem because you may receive negative reactions from others. Your curiosity about many subjects also attracts eccentric people who have unusual practices.

Neptune in the sixth house: You're drawn to discovering secrets and mysteries, but there's also an attraction to unusual subjects like occult practices, astrology, and fortune-telling. You could be involved with the arts or even videos, movies, or dramas, dabbling in genres concerning the ethereal.

Neptune in the seventh house: You enjoy new places and explore different things, driven by your desire to be involved with occult practices from all over the map. You could also be involved in the arts or even letters, magazines, or books.

Neptune in the eighth house: Your interest in things that are outside the conventional could make you vulnerable to scams or negative energy. You may be involved in businesses related to the occult, like astrology or divination.

Neptune in the ninth house: You could become confused about who you truly are as you explore different topics because so much information and influence are coming in your direction. Keep an open mind about life and other people's feelings, beliefs, and emotions.

Neptune in the tenth house: Your mind is open to new ideas and has many original ideas. You could be involved in the arts or even more unusual subjects, like astrology or divination.

Neptune in the eleventh house: You have an attraction to unconventional people. There's also a chance you could want to live in a dreamy world where reality takes second place to your fantasies. Keep an open mind about people who are different and don't judge them for their different beliefs.

Neptune in the twelfth house: There's a higher probability of being involved with occult practices, mystical beliefs, and other superstitious practices. It's also possible that you suddenly become attracted to the supernatural or astrology.

Pluto

Pluto in the first house: You're different from other people, but there's also a higher probability of being involved with drugs or illegal substances. You could be a drug dealer or even work for someone with connections to people who deal drugs. Keep an open mind about life and people's opinions instead of being closed off to your ideas.

Pluto in the second house: You have a strong desire to be different and rebel against being forced to do things you don't want to do. Keep an open mind about life and other people's feel, beliefs, and emotions.

Pluto in the third house: There's a high probability of becoming involved with drugs, illegal substances, or even occult practices, particularly astrology or palm reading. You could also be involved with arts, like music, painting, or writing.

Pluto in the fourth house: You have a strong desire to be different and rebel against being forced to do things you don't want to do. You could also be involved with illegal activities like drugs or gambling, or even work with illegal aspects, like a drug weapons dealer.

Pluto in the fifth house: There's a high probability of becoming involved in drugs, occult practices, or other illegal activities. The difficulty is that you have to learn the hard way that these activities will hurt you more than they help.

Pluto in the sixth house: You could be the perfect candidate for any illegal activity or drug dealing, so be careful. Keep an open mind about life and people's feelings, beliefs, and emotions.

Pluto in the seventh house: You are interested in occult practices and things against conservative rules. So, keep an open mind about life and other people's feelings, beliefs, and emotions.

Pluto in the eighth house: There's a strong desire to be different and rebel against being forced to do things you don't want to do. You're also attracted to the universe's dark side, like illegal drugs and other negative influences.

Pluto in the ninth house: You are interested in occult practices and things against conservative rules. Keep an open mind about life and other people's feelings, beliefs, and emotions.

Pluto in the tenth house: You love to find out information about other people's lives and learn why they do the things they do. Your mind is open to new ideas and has many original ideas. You could also become involved in political groups or organizations with a social conscience or moral code.

Pluto in the eleventh house: You have an attraction to unconventional people. There's also a chance you could want to live in a dreamy world where reality takes second place to your fantasies.

Pluto in the twelfth house: More than anyone, you are attracted to the supernatural, particularly astrology. The difficulty is that the fantasy becomes a reality and could negatively take over your life, so watch out.

Chapter Seven: The Influence of Moon Phases

Moon phases.
https://www.pexels.com/photo/timelapse-photography-of-moon-1275413/

While the sun may take center stage, we can't ignore the moon's influence on our personalities in astrology. The moon represents the energy that prevails throughout our day, and it lets you know what you need to do to feel good enough to accomplish your life mission. It helps you with your goals, but keep in mind that you feel

---

you're embodying more of your true self because it focuses on your emotional life, which is essential to your overall well-being.

The New Moon

The new moon is the most important of all phases. There's no illumination, and during this phase, all of your dreams are realized if you are lucky. An old Spanish superstition states that catching a new moon reflection on a mirror in total darkness will bring luck. Even if the person doesn't know what they are doing or has no idea how to use it, because of its association with luck and changes in your life, that luck will happen

What does the new moon represent? The new moon represents the beginning of a journey, a fresh start, and a time when you could accomplish anything. It's an excellent time to initiate new beginnings and make big plans for the future. It could be an important part of your long-term planning, especially if you are daring and risk-taking, like starting a business or traveling to a foreign country by yourself. By doing this, you are allowing yourself to change your life around.

What does the new moon mean for your relationships? You should be in a new relationship during the new moon phase as this gives you the chance to start afresh with your partner. Be very open and tell your partner all of your emotions, as this will build trust between you. It's also worth remembering that the new moon means fresh starts and life changes. Therefore, if you have been with your partner for a while and things are wearing thin, it's best to start looking for a new relationship or putting in some effort to make it feel new.

What does the new moon mean for your relationship with yourself? The new moon offers a good time to work on yourself and make changes. Also, think about what you want from your life. You may find the new moon offers you the chance to start afresh.

Self-love Tips for the New Moon

1. Talk to yourself. Talk to your "inner self" – the one speaking at night when you feel most alone. Ask this inner voice what it has to say and listen carefully.

2. Give yourself little slices of happiness: You may focus too

much on the negative aspects of your life, so make time for a nice moment or treat yourself, take some pressure off, and it could be very uplifting. A little treat can make all the difference to feeling happy about life or setting an intention for success in the coming month.

3. Don't hold back on the compliments: It's important to compliment yourself because being critical of your self-esteem can negatively affect your mental health. Don't be afraid to take time out of the day to sit and think about what you are doing well.

Dating Tips for the New Moon

1. Take a risk: The new moon is great for taking risks in love. However, it can also encourage you to stray from good practices, so think twice before going ahead. But, if things seem right and you're sure, take that risk. You could be pleasantly surprised.

2. Let your emotions flow: There is a time during the new moon phase when your emotions are not as intense as they could be, so take this opportunity to let your emotions flow and be open about how you feel with someone you want to get close to.

3. Be open: Don't bury your emotions because the moon's light makes it easier to see what you need to see.

Relationship advice for the new moon: This is a good time to renew your vows and commitment to each other.

The Waxing Crescent Moon

When the moon creates the shape of a crescent, this is the phase when you experience a lot of transformation and loads of chances for new things in your life.

What does the waxing crescent moon represent? During this phase, you'll feel most energetic and accomplish all you desire. It symbolizes the idea of growth and being in control of your surroundings and situation. Concentrate on your goals and make plans for the long term, as it will help you.

What does the waxing crescent moon mean for your relationships? The waxing crescent moon is when things are intensifying and heating up. You start to feel more romantic or have an increased sex drive, and while this is when you are likely to be the most decisive person in your relationship, it also leaves you feeling overeager. You have a hard time saying no and will probably just say yes to any request, regardless of what it is. The waxing crescent moon also signifies the start of a new cycle when taking risks can have positive consequences and reward you. However, this moon cycle only lasts a few days to a week.

What does the waxing crescent moon mean for your relationship with yourself? The waxing crescent moon means that you give yourself permission to be fully loved and known as you open up to love and intimacy. The waxing crescent moon symbolizes the first signs of a new cycle. This cycle is about opening up and being more intimate with yourself. You may notice you have more patience with your flaws and are more forgiving of yourself when you make mistakes. This is a time when you're born again. The energy of this moon sets up new feelings and habits toward yourself and leaves old feelings and habits behind. These feelings can be mixed, but it's mainly being born again after something traumatic or painful has happened.

Self-Love Tips for the Waxing Crescent Moon

1. Treat yourself to a massage. The waxing crescent moon is a great time to pamper yourself and treat yourself to something nice. Schedule a massage or a pedicure to feel more relaxed.

2. Erase negative self-talk. One of the ways you can love yourself more easily is by giving up negative self-talk and replacing it with positive statements about who you are and how your life is going. Practicing gratitude every day is especially helpful if you're having difficulty practicing self-love on the waxing crescent moon.

3. Be forgiving with yourself if mistakes are made or if there are changes in your routine or schedule during the waxing

crescent moon cycle.

Dating Tips for the Waxing Crescent Moon

1. The waxing crescent moon is a good time to get out and meet new people. You may be more assertive and more willing to take risks during this time, so you're likely to make friends or meet potential dates at social events.

2. This phase can make you feel slightly impatient in relationships, so if you're currently dating someone, don't get too annoyed or frustrated when they aren't moving as quickly as you want.

3. This is a good time for flirting but not a great time for starting serious relationships with people who seem uninterested in you or highly negative about your feelings for them.

Relationship advice for the waxing crescent moon: If your relationship is only starting, be very mindful about nurturing it.

The First Quarter Moon

At this point, more than a crescent of the moon is illuminated. There's even more stirring in yourself for new things picking up steam.

What does the first quarter moon represent? This is a time for setting things in motion when people feel impatient, restless, and hungry for change. People experience a need to get things started and put plans into place during the first quarter moon. It also symbolizes slowing down and action that has already been taken. A new cycle begins as the moon goes from darkness into light. There's a big push and pull between what you want to do versus what you should be doing to achieve your goals. Now is the time to set things in motion, like a new job or your own business.

What does the first quarter moon mean for your relationship? The first quarter moon is when you are likely to be more intelligent and focused than usual. You feel assertive and in control of your life — but it makes you more impatient than usual with who you're involved with. People on the first quarter moon will often develop strong opinions about various issues and feel stronger about them, whether they're right or wrong. The first quarter moon is a turning point in the road. Things that were once just words or thoughts become actions and eventually come together as a solid reality.

What does the first quarter moon mean for your relationship with yourself? The first quarter moon is a time for being more objective about your feelings and thoughts about life. You notice you have more patience for other people's mistakes and shortcomings, but not for yourself. You see yourself with a harsh eye or overly critical of things you do or say. At this time, be patient with yourself as you are with those around you. Be kinder to yourself to start the new phase of the waxing crescent moon cycle on a positive note. It helps if you write down what you want to change and look at it objectively before making plans to change it.

Self-love Tips for the First Quarter Moon

1. As you feel more in charge of your life, you have more patience with yourself and others. This is when you pace yourself and ask for help when needed. Treating yourself to something special helps bring about this change.

2. Avoid being too hard on yourself every day about your weight, hair, or clothes in the first quarter moon cycle. It's okay not to feel perfect all the time during this cycle.

3. Avoid watching television or movies that show people being hurt, ridiculed, or humiliated.

4. If you find yourself in a tight spot, like not having enough money to live on and choosing between paying your rent and taking out loans, be aware that this time is about setting plans in motion for the future, so a better day is coming soon.

Dating Tips for the First Quarter Moon

1. The first quarter moon is a good time for trying out new things, so dating could be a lot of fun during this time.

2. This cycle is about setting plans into motion, so if you're thinking of asking someone out or getting more serious in general, wait until later in the cycle when you pass the half-moon phase.

3. It is a good time for flirting and not unusual to find others falling in love with you. If you're already dating or have interests besides finding love, avoid being aggressive or overly flirtatious during this moon phase.

Relationship advice for the first quarter moon: The first quarter moon is a time to be assertive, but be patient. It's natural to feel impatient and want things to happen faster than they do. But it's essential not to make this a habit so that you don't lose the love you have.

The Waxing Gibbous Moon

The only part of the moon that isn't illuminated is the crescent. It's more than half-lit but not quite fully so.

What does the waxing gibbous moon represent? The gibbous moon represents things that are still new just before a full moon when people experience a surge of optimism and enthusiasm. During the gibbous moon, people feel they are getting close to what they want to achieve in life. They get closer and closer to their goals until, eventually, it is all realized or achieved at the full moon. This cycle's phase is important because it prepares you for future achievements and changes. This aspect of life makes everything seem more worthwhile, but many people have problems staying focused on one activity or thought for too long during this cycle due to wanting so much out of life.

What does the waxing gibbous moon mean for your relationship? This is a challenging cycle for people involved in new relationships because it's not always easy to balance being positive about your relationship and wanting things to happen quickly. If you feel your relationship is not moving fast enough, it will negatively affect the person. It's essential not to shut them out if you want the relationship to work out.

What does the waxing gibbous moon mean for your relationship with yourself? You notice you get excited about your future experiences during this cycle, even if nothing has happened yet. This is when many people make plans to travel or focus on new and different things in their lives. For some people, this cycle is also when they confirm wanting to remain on their career path. They are certain there's no other way to be happy, making it difficult to adapt later in life if they change jobs or careers.

Self-Love Tips for the Waxing Gibbous Moon

1. The gibbous moon is a time to enjoy your life, so make the most of it.

2. This is a good cycle for planning out the next few weeks or months of your life.

3. You may feel like eating more than usual during this cycle and crave salty foods.

4. For people who have trouble sleeping during this time, keeping a journal on their nightstand to write down their thoughts at the end of each day will help clear their minds when they go to sleep.

Dating Tips for the Waxing Gibbous Moon

1. The gibbous moon is a good cycle to use when you want to ask someone out, but it's also a good time to settle into a relationship that has been going well.

2. This is the most romantic phase, so you should reveal more of your feelings than usual and let yourself be vulnerable.

3. If you're thinking about breaking up with someone or if they want this to happen too, don't do it during this cycle.

Relationship advice for the waxing gibbous moon: The gibbous moon is a good time for being creative and cautious about your plans. When you plan something new, it's important to think it through and not rush into anything. It's also important to be open to change and the unpredictable.

The Full Moon

When the moon is full, it shines high in the sky and is surrounded by darkness. It's fully illuminated.

What does the full moon represent? This is when people feel they have everything they want in life, although it's only a peak experience before the descent back to reality. It's important to enjoy this stage of life while it lasts because there are many steps to achieve long-term results after this period. This stage of life represents the reality of your goals and how they match up with where you are right now. For some people, reaching this stage isn't always pleasant because it shows what's missing in their lives or how far away they still are from realizing their dreams.

What does the full moon mean for your relationship? Love is strongest during this phase, so it's imperative to enjoy this time in your relationship and allow yourself to be vulnerable even if you have doubts.

What does the full moon mean for your relationship with yourself? Since the full moon is a time of balance and achievement, obtaining long-term success and happiness, it's important to not just focus on one or two areas of your life. In particular, don't become too focused on one career or subject for too long. You'll probably experience setbacks in this stage of life, so you mustn't be too attached to things that no longer serve you.

Self-love Tips for the Full Moon

1. You desire to be more creative and expressive during this cycle, so do something creative.

2. There is a powerful temptation to give up and give in to your emotions. Don't do it. This is a time when many people want things to happen very quickly. However, these cycles aren't about experiencing positive or negative events. They are about learning lessons about what's most important in your life and how you deal with challenges.

3. Some people feel they have to live up to high expectations, but it's important not to be so unrealistic about what you think you can achieve.

Dating Tips for the Full Moon

1. This is a good time to be more romantic and expressive with your partner, but don't overdo it, or you can become too needy.

2. When you're on a date, it's important to be on the same wavelength as your date.

3. It's also a good time to make plans for meeting people if this is what you want to do.

Relationship advice for the full moon: It's important not to assume that others will be ready for the effort needed to get things started in your relationship. Hold back until you're both sure these are the right steps.

The Waning Gibbous Moon

This moon is almost full, and you'll see it about three to five days after the full moon.

What does the waning gibbous moon represent? The waning gibbous moon is when people feel more alert and energized than usual. It is also a time of restlessness and boredom because the mind is not stimulated. It is a good time for people to feel like they're living in their comfort zone to take on some new challenges at work or in relationships.

What does the waning gibbous moon mean for your relationship? For people living in their comfort zone, the waning gibbous moon will be a time to relax and let go of many responsibilities. It is a great time to make changes in your life if you're looking for a break.

What does the waning gibbous moon mean for your relationship with yourself? During this moon stage, you're stuck in a rut, and there's nothing new or exciting you can do to change things for yourself. If you want to alter your life for the better somehow, it's best to wait until your dream phase starts because then you'll have more motivation for change.

Self-Love Tips for the Waning Gibbous Moon

1. This is a good time to take a break from many responsibilities, especially if you feel trapped.

2. If you have been waiting for something new to happen in your life, now is a good time to try something new and

different.

3. Don't focus on your fears or concerns for the future. Your purpose may be unclear at this point in your life, so it's important not to get too caught up in where things are going.

Dating Tips for the Waning Gibbous Moon

1. For those who are single, this is a good time to rest and relax without feelings of guilt or pressure.

2. For people in committed relationships, it's important not to use this cycle as an excuse to ignore personal responsibilities. Many couples take advantage of each other during this cycle, so spend some time alone instead during the waning gibbous moon so that you don't feel taken advantage of.

3. This is a powerful phrase for people who may be thinking about divorce.

Relationship advice for the waning gibbous moon: Refuse to let your fears control you. If you're too fearful of the future, this is not a good time to make any big changes in relationships. Instead, take some time for yourself during this cycle and recharge your batteries.

The Last Quarter Moon

This is the phase just before the waning crescent phase. It is a time for completion, moving on from something, and reorienting yourself. It's a time to wrap things up, especially whatever you began during the new moon phase.

What does the last quarter moon represent? During this moon phase, it's important not to have unrealistic expectations about what another person could be like for you. If you're going through a rough time in your life, it's best to wait until the full moon phase before trying to change things.

What does the last quarter moon represent for your relationship with yourself? If you're feeling stagnant in your life, it's important not to expect too much from yourself during this time since it's more difficult to feel the sense of connectedness needed for growth. If you feel like things are out of balance in your life, wait until the full moon phase to make changes.

What does the last quarter moon represent for relationships? This is a powerful time for decision-making about relationships because it's a highly charged phase. You should wait until the full moon phase before ending a relationship or deciding on your next step in life.

Self-Love Tips for the Last Quarter Moon

1. As this is a symbolic phase for endings and new beginnings, it's a good time for taking care of any unfinished work on your plate over the past month or two.

2. This is a good time for single people to focus less on finding someone new and more on self-improvement.

3. For those in common-law relationships, it's a good time to take some time for yourself to focus on your emotional needs instead of keeping things in the background for your partner.

Dating Tips for the Last Quarter Moon

1. During this phase of the moon, it's important to spend time alone to reflect and give attention to your needs.

2. For those in a relationship, it's best not to break up or start something new during this cycle because you will be too busy taking care of your needs.

3. For those who are single, it's best not to look for a date during this cycle because you need time for yourself right now.

Relationship advice for the last quarter moon: Your next steps in life may be unclear right now, so it's best not to make any major life decisions during this phase. This is a time for taking care of unfinished business and wrapping up loose ends in your life, especially in your relationship with yourself.

The Waning Crescent Moon

This is the final phase of the moon, where just a crescent is lit. It is a time to get to know yourself and accept who you are. It's the best time to release all the things that no longer serve you and embrace love instead.

What does the waning crescent moon represent? The waning crescent moon is a time of self-acceptance and self-love. It's a time to learn how to love yourself to better connect with others.

What does the waning crescent moon represent for your relationship with yourself? During this phase of the moon, you have the power to eliminate fears getting in the way so that you can move forward. If you feel something holding you back in your life, now is the time to figure out what it is and work through it so you no longer feel fearful when it comes up again. If you're feeling stagnant or held back from fulfilling your dreams and doing what makes you happy, this moon phase will help bring balance to your life by eliminating what's holding you back.

What does the waning crescent moon represent for your relationships? If you're in a relationship, you can see what keeps you from feeling close to them. If your marriage is on the rocks, this is a great time to resolve the problems so that you don't lose something dear to your heart. Listen carefully to what others are saying and make sure they say things aligned with how you want to live your life. If not, it may be time for some changes.

Self-Love Tips for the Waning Crescent Moon

1. For those who are single, this is a good time to take time for yourself to focus on loving yourself.
2. It will be easier to find someone new as long as you keep things light and fun and don't pressure yourself while looking for a date or mate.
3. Let go of unhealthy relationships and friends so that you can embrace more love and happiness in your life.

Dating Tips for the Waning Crescent Moon

1. If you're single, this is a great time for meeting new people.

2. It will be easier for those not currently in a relationship to attract new people during this cycle because you have more self-love and confidence in yourself than at other times of the month.

3. It may be appropriate for those currently in a relationship to look for someone new or end the relationship during this cycle because you have more love and confidence in yourself than at other times of the month.

Relationship advice for the waning crescent moon: This is a powerful time for removing things from your life so you can embrace more love and happiness. This is a symbolically charged phase, so it's important to ensure that what you do reflects your true beliefs about love and happiness in your life.

Chapter Eight: A Guide to Twin Flames

What are twin flames? The concept of twin flames has been around for thousands of years, but the term has only recently become common usage. It is a powerful and beautiful idea that has finally achieved wide recognition. If you ask anyone about twin flames these days, the chances they'll at least have heard about them in passing.

The term "twin flame" refers to two souls who have come into this world to experience togetherness and intimacy on a level most people never get to experience in their entire lives. Twin flames are two halves of the same soul that have found each other again, but this time with the awareness to love and care for one another.

Twin Flames and Spiritual Astrology

Using astrology to explore how twin flames manifest in our world is a very important but often overlooked understanding of the nature of twin flames. Astrology is used to help form an understanding of what they are and represent. The basic idea behind twin flame relationships is that your soul's journey on Earth has a purpose beyond your goals or destiny. By studying the natal charts of each person in the twin flame relationship, astrologers can distinguish the traits and tendencies shared by both of you that are expressions of your soul's mission on Earth. They also help you achieve the goal you both agreed to in this incarnation.

Signs You've Met Your Twin Flame

1. Your connection is instant, deep, and profound.

2. Your backgrounds and interests are the same or very similar.

3. You both had the same strange thoughts and dreams about one another before you met.

4. You are involved with the same people for extended periods, even if not together.

5. You feel you've known each other for much longer than this lifetime or any lifetime before it.

6. You feel you're made for one another or have known each other your entire life.

7. You finish each other's sentences and know what the other will say before they've said it.

8. You communicate on a deep intuitive level without speaking a word and can even read each other's minds.

9. Your souls recognize one another as eternal companions, past and future, in many lifetimes and dimensions.

10. You're obsessed with one another. You're drawn to one another wherever you are, constantly in touch somehow even if you don't see each other regularly (due to distance).

11. You're inseparable. You can barely function or be happy without each other, even after just a short time together.

12. You learn many things about yourself through your twin, including your strengths and weaknesses.

13. Your connection to each other feels like home, the place you belong – as if you've found your true self in your twin flame.

14. Your inner wounds feel healed when you're with each other as if they never existed.

15. You feel complete when you're with one another, finally understanding who you are and where you belong in the world.

16. You feel like you can always talk to each other about anything, have everything in common, and get to know yourself better.

17. You feel at home when you're together, even if it is only for two hours.

18. Your connection feels like a deep, lifelong friendship or family bond between souls.

19. You feel your twin is the missing piece of your puzzle, the perfect *other half,* the best friend you've ever had, or the love of your life.

20. Your connection feels bigger than just two people. It's something much larger than your two souls existing independently of one another.

The Pros of a Twin Flame Relationship

1. A twin flame relationship helps you understand and accept your sexual and spiritual identity.

2. A twin flame relationship helps you break the chains of addictive relationships with other people and substances because it shows what true intimacy feels like.

3. A twin flame relationship helps you discover who you truly are, your purpose, life's passion, higher self (the most spiritual version of yourself), and much more.

4. You have a built-in best friend for life with a twin flame who is there for you regardless of what happens or where life takes you. They never leave your side, even in their physical absence from this world or dimension (if the relationship ends due to death).

5. Twin flame relationships are a gateway to personal growth and spiritual enlightenment because they're the best chance you get to learn about your past lives, karma, and soul purpose.

6. Twin flame relationships help you break from the shackles of this life to live a full life (even if only in spirit form) in the next.

7. A twin flame relationship helps you deeply connect with your higher self (the most spiritual version of yourself), your soul.

8. A twin flame relationship greatly helps you to heal any inner wounds that have kept you from fully receiving love and intimacy in your current life.

9. A twin flame relationship brings tremendous physical healing and a better quality of life relative to your well-being before the relationship came into your life.

10. You'll never feel you've wasted time being with your twin flame, even if you have to be separated from them for extended periods or they die (if the relationship ends).

11. A twin flame relationship brings you comfort when nothing else can and reminds you there is always hope in this world when everything else is going wrong.

Cons of a Twin Flame Relationship

1. Twin flame relationships are exhausting because they pull you out of your normal consciousness level and make you live more at the moment than most people.

2. A twin flame relationship causes extreme emotional ups and downs because it splits your focus and attention among two people instead of one.

3. A twin flame relationship causes jealousy and possessiveness if you don't work to keep those emotions at bay or heal them through self-work.

4. It is hard to separate yourself from a twin flame when their problems spill over into your life. Everything becomes about them, their drama, or their issues (whether you like it or not).

5. It isn't easy to find time for yourself because everything is about your twin flame and the relationship. It is another form of codependency from that standpoint.

6. Twin flames put too much pressure on you to "figure it out" when you have no idea about what's going on or what you're doing.

7. Sometimes, it's hard to take care of yourself when you have a twin flame in your life. You have the potential to be taken advantage of, and your time and energy are sucked into something that doesn't matter, which leaves you feeling rejected.

8. A twin flame relationship keeps you from fully living in this lifetime because you're distracted by other things and neglect yourself or others around you.

9. A twin flame relationship causes unrequited love and a longer-than-usual process to get over the relationship when it ends.

10. A twin flame relationship makes you feel like you're running on an emotional rollercoaster, and no one understands what you're going through.

Challenges in a Twin Flame Relationship

1. You have to be in a place mentally and emotionally to handle the ups and downs of a twin flame relationship, meaning you have to be emotionally healthy (not codependent) and ready to handle the intensity of your twin's highs and lows.

2. You have to want this relationship in your life because it's not something everyone can handle. It takes a person who doesn't experience an adverse reaction to high emotional energy levels because they must learn to transmute them instead.

3. You have to be emotionally ready to deal with your twin's drama and issues, which might not always be appropriate or something you feel comfortable diving into. You have to be ready to separate yourself from their problems when they come into your life because they're not your own.

4. You have to handle all the attention that comes with a twin flame relationship, including the flack you may receive from other people who think you're crazy or insecure or

it's just a phase you're going through.

5. You have to handle the intense feelings you experience with your twin flame and all that goes with it when they're absent from this dimension. Once you know that they're in a better place than with you, you'll know how to release the pent-up emotions and get on with life.

6. You have to be emotionally and mentally healthy enough for a twin flame relationship because it will take over your life or drain your energy.

7. You have to be ready for your twin flame relationship to change your life more than anything else in your current life.

8. You have to be ready to learn much more about yourself and your spirituality to gain the insights, knowledge, and skills to handle a twin flame relationship.

9. You have to be emotionally and mentally prepared for your twin flame relationship to end and the pain that goes with it.

10. You have to be ready for a twin flame relationship because once it starts, it will set off a chain of events in your life that you may not be prepared for.

Advice for Being in a Twin Flame Relationship

You must first open up to your intuition and listen to it regarding your twin flame relationship. It doesn't matter how much you deny it; you're meant for each other. Your twin flame relationship will show itself in many ways, so keep an open mind, heart, and spirit. Watch for signs that your connection is not as strong as it appears and is not a soul mate bond.

Even if you think you've found your twin flame already, keep looking. You could come across others who will teach you something about life and love, even if they're not your true twin flame.

Talk to trusted friends and family members who will give you an outside perspective on what's going on in your relationship with your twin flame. They will see things you don't because they're emotionally distant from the situation. Their feedback could clear confusion or uncertainty in the relationship. Let them know how important their insights are to you, so they will be more willing to share with you without being hesitant or afraid of being wrong.

Twin flame relationships aren't for everyone, so if you're not emotionally and mentally healthy enough to handle the intensity of one, it's best to steer clear altogether. The energy exchange will pressure your mental and emotional health, causing you to burn out or break down completely if you're not ready for this type of relationship—and sometimes, even if you are.

If your twin flame is deceased and has crossed over into the afterlife or another dimension, know that they're still with you (and always will be). This causes them to appear in dreams or visions, but these are merely ways they communicate with you without burdening your physical body with their energies.

Advice for Finding Your Twin Flame

1. Re-evaluate what love means to you. If the feeling of love and happiness is all around you abundantly, ask yourself who or what is responsible.

2. List the things missing in your life from the advice of others. Your twin flame will likely be the embodiment of all that's missing. Writing the list manifests to bring them to you.

3. Look at your life and the world around you, and ask yourself who's responsible for the beautiful things already in existence.

4. Look back on your past, and ask yourself what hurt or devastated you in life to cause you to feel different about love. If love caused this deep pain, then perhaps love is responsible for the beauty in your life because it's been repressed and hidden until now.

5. Your old beliefs of love will be challenged if your soul is unprepared to learn about life. Your twin flame is likely to be someone you fear may have already experienced love that you haven't.

6. You'll know when the time is right for a twin flame relationship; your intuition will tell you.

7. If you want a twin flame relationship, consider changing your life by letting go of certain things or people holding you back. It could mean eliminating certain friends or family members, taking on a new career, moving to another place, or changing how you spend your time and money.

8. It's possible to find your twin flame, but you have to make room for them in your life. Set aside the time, energy, and resources for them, and allow yourself to feel the love you've been holding back.

9. Your twin flame didn't come into your life by accident. They are there to help you overcome your fears about love and teach you about unconditional love and relationships, meaning they'll be there when you least expect them for this teaching to happen.

10. Love is the most important thing in life, and it's the only thing that gives meaning to our existence on this planet. If you've been looking for love, you've likely been looking for your twin flame because they're one and the same. Your twin flame will teach you how to find love and give it unconditionally.

Quiz: Am I with My Twin Flame?

1. Do you often feel that time stands still with them?

2. Do you have dreams about them that come true the next day?

3. When you first met them, did they seem familiar?

4. Do you feel like you have known them from another lifetime?

5. Do you feel that you have special psychic or spiritual powers in common with them?

6. Do you think about them constantly, even when they're not physically present?

7. Does it seem like your life and everyone else's lives revolve around you?

8. Do they finish your sentences or what you're thinking?

9. Do you feel your whole world is turned upside down when you are physically separated from them?

10. Do you feel like they bring out the best in you and improve your life?

If you answered yes to six or more of these questions, congratulations!. You've got your twin flame.

Chapter Nine: A Guide to Soul Mates

What is the difference between twin flames and soul mates? What are soul mates like? What does it mean to find your soul mate? There's a lot of confusion around the concept of "soul mates," so let's clear that right up. Twin flames are two halves of a soul chosen to incarnate into a lifetime in two bodies. On the other hand, soul mates are two separate souls sharing an instant connection upon meeting, and this connection may or may not be romantic.

Soul Mates and Astrology

If you want your soul mate relationships to work, it's worth looking at the natal charts of both people involved to determine how the planets affect you both and how to dance with this person to create magic and love between you. While soul mate relationships and friendships can work without the knowledge of the planetary placements, it's worth looking at the charts to make these connections even more divine and fulfilling for everyone involved.

Signs You've Met Your Soul Mate

You sense their presence before you even see them: Other people around you notice this too, but they don't understand why. Your heart skips a beat when you first lay eyes on them. When they walk into the room and your eyes meet, you get butterflies in your stomach. You may feel nauseous and experience other physical changes in your body when they're around. This is called "love at first sight," and it's very common in soul mate relationships. The next time this happens, pay attention to what's happening right then and there because the Universe is telling you this person is your soul mate.

You feel like you've known them forever: There's no awkwardness or hesitation when you talk to each other, and you instantly feel you could tell this person anything about yourself and know they won't judge you. You feel that talking to this person is as natural as talking to an old friend or family member because, on some level, they are an old friend or family member.

You and your soul mate want the same things in life: This is where thorough astrological compatibility comes in handy. If you both have the same moon sign or have other planets in the same signs, you're bound to have similar goals and ideas about approaching your life together. It is a good thing because the more you can work together to achieve your shared goals, the more aligned you'll be in life - soul mates often feel they've known each other their entire lives.

You feel whole when you're together: When you're with your soul mate, you feel that every part of yourself has reached its full potential and purpose. Your soul mate fills a part of you that was missing or missing something, making an instant connection between you.

You have the same philosophy of life: Perhaps you feel there's one overriding theme running through your entire life as you come to understand what it means to be a soul mate. You feel that together you can bring this theme into being. With two brains working together, your goals can become even more powerful and effective than if focusing individually on your end goals in life.

You know when the other person is lying or telling the truth: On some level, you can see past their layers, read the emotions behind their eyes, sense the energies flowing between you, and see things no one else would notice. You may even share telepathy.

The Pros of a Soul Mate Relationship

Soul mate relationships are very rewarding. Soul mate relationships are some of the most fulfilling, magical, and loving relationships you can have on Earth. They're relationship goals many people choose to pursue in their lifetimes and come with the promise that once you've found your soul mate, the rest of your life will fall into place in a very beautiful way. You'll feel loved and adored like no one else can feel or give to you.

As soul mates, you have a deeper connection than most other people. When you meet your soul mate, you will feel an instant connection that is incredible, profound, and can only be described as unity and wholeness. You will feel you are one person with different bodies and minds operating simultaneously. You'll know things about each other no one else knows because you share the same consciousness or mind on some level.

Being a soul mate gives you deeper insight into people around you. The closer a soul mate relationship gets, the more you will understand the other person, and the better you can help them with their problems. You'll also feel an overwhelming sense of love and compassion for them when they need it most, and that's one of the best things you can do for a friend in need.

Your soul mate will always support your dreams. On some level, they feel they're your dreams as well. Your goals are their goals because they want you to succeed as much as you do. They'll give you all the support you need to get there.

Having a soul mate makes you feel more fulfilled and content. You may even find yourself working better in your career and life because of your deep connection with your soul mate. You'll feel you have a purpose and everything in the world makes sense to you now, and there's nothing left to do except enjoy your time with this person who is meant for you.

Your soul mate will help you heal whatever pain or past trauma weighs on your heart. Your soul mate will make you feel you're the most special and important person in the world. Whether or not your soul mate knows this is true, they will give you all of the love, attention, and care you need to heal from the pain or regrets holding you back.

The Cons of a Soul Mate Relationship

Soul mate relationships aren't always easy, and they don't come with a lifetime guarantee. Sometimes soul mates go through rough patches or differences of opinion on how to approach life. Sometimes you'll disagree on how to handle your children or deal with your extended families, etc. It doesn't mean you aren't soul mates. It only means you're going through an adjustment period and learning how to deal with each other.

Your soul mate doesn't always have the same feelings about you. If your soul mate has had a rough past, they may not have learned to love unconditionally, which is the foundation of a soul mate relationship. Due to this, they cannot truly see your strengths and all you have to offer, and also, you cannot see some of their weaknesses.

Soul mates sometimes cause each other more problems than they're worth. Probably the most common problem with soul mates, but definitely not the only one – plenty more issues can arise, jealousy or problems with family members, etc.

Soul mates can drive each other crazy. Even though you feel enormous love and joy when you're in a soul mate relationship, it can sometimes be hard on your partner. Soul mates might get jealous or depressed when they aren't getting the attention they crave from one another.

Soul mates can sometimes lead each other down the wrong path. If you've previously been in a soul mate relationship, you could use your next relationship merely as a crutch in your desire for validation and love.

Soul mates often get away with things they shouldn't. Due to your deep connection, it isn't easy to see the harm they're doing to others because personal information about both of you will now be revealed.

Challenges in a Soul Mate Relationship

Soul mates sometimes want to control each other. This happens if one soul mate feels they need to protect the other from making mistakes or causing themselves any degree of harm. If this happens, talk it out and make sure you're not becoming overly controlling with each other.

Soul mates are prone to cheating. Soul mate relationships are very passionate and exciting on the surface level, so cheating could be an issue. It can be resolved by talking about your problems and ensuring you're being 100 percent honest with one another.

Soul mates are sometimes selfish. This is another problem common in soul mate relationships because you spend much more time together and think you can get away with more. It's important always to be honest with each other and do things out of love rather than selfishness to make sure this doesn't become a chronic issue.

Soul mates sometimes only see the flaws in one another. This happens when your partner distances themselves and withdraws their love from the relationship because of past trauma or hard life experiences. It's important to work through your problems together and that you don't neglect or ignore the good things your partner does.

Soul mates are sometimes jealous of each other. Not all soul mates are created equal – some are more jealous than others, and it is a problem in many ways if not addressed. If your partner is jealous of you, make sure you're not doing or saying anything you wouldn't want your partner to do or say about you. Remember, you are both human and deserve to be loved without judgment.

Soul mates are sometimes complacent with their relationship. This is especially true when you're used to being around each other all the time and don't get enough attention or affection from your soul mate. Remind one another why you fell in love. Renew the passion by talking about your goals and dreams and how they relate to both of you.

Advice for Being in a Soul Mate Relationship

1. Always be completely honest with one another. Lies are a death sentence because nobody can have a truly authentic connection with someone who is deliberately lying.

2. Make sure that your partner is happy and sure of the relationship.

3. Don't get jealous. Jealousy is a huge turn-off and clouds judgment, so embrace your selfishness as often as possible because it's a major source of strength and could make up for shortcomings on the other end of the spectrum.

4. Make sure that you're not expecting your partner to be perfect. People are not perfect, so never expect your soul mate to be any different. If you have a problem with something they're doing, let them know immediately, rather than sitting and dwelling on it due to your fears or insecurities.

5. Never take advantage of one another. It is a major issue that will only lead to more problems and frustration in the long run.

6. It's essential never to put each other down to make yourself look better.

7. You are not the bigger person in any given situation, especially if your partner is being the bigger person and doing something for you out of love.

8. Make sure you are not constantly putting off real-life responsibilities because of your soul mate.

Advice for Finding Your Soul Mate

1. Look beyond physical appearances and ask yourself who you're truly attracted to.

2. Ask yourself what you're most attracted to about a person.

3. Admire people for their positive qualities, not only the ones you feel will be the most beneficial to your relationship.

4. Stay optimistic and avoid being too critical or judgmental of other people.

5. Pay attention to your intuition, and don't force yourself to be with someone who does not feel they're the right one for you.

6. Make sure that you're not attracted to someone purely because you share the same interests.

7. Don't be afraid of changing your mind about someone if you really think it's the right thing to do.

8. Don't be afraid of taking risks in a relationship because no soul mate will come knocking on your door or fall from the sky if you don't open yourself up to the possibility of meeting new people.

9. Be yourself and let others be themselves, too. Avoid pushing them away or distancing yourself from them because they don't perfectly match your ideals.

10. If you can't be yourself 10o percent of the time and are still in a relationship with your soul mate, perhaps that relationship isn't what you truly want.

Quiz: Am I with My Soul Mate?

1. Do you feel like you could never get tired of being with your partner?

2. Are they always willing to do whatever it takes to make sure you remain in close contact?

3. Are you able to talk about anything and everything with your partner for hours on end? Do you enjoy doing this together?

4. Does your partner love you for who you are and not what they want to make out of you due to their selfish desires?

5. Does your mate make you feel like you're the only person in the entire world for them?

6. Are your days and nights filled with so much passion you feel your life is perfect?

7. Do you feel like your partner has a purpose in your life?

8. Do they make you feel important and special?

9. Do they inspire you to be a better person?

10. Do you find their words and actions congruent with each other?

If you answered yes to 6 or more of these questions, congratulations! You've got a soul mate.

Chapter Ten: Spiritual Well-Being 101

What is spiritual well-being? It's the feeling of peace and contentment, self-acceptance, and value a person experiences when they know their worth. It happens when people fully accept themselves and take what they need. You can easily overcome sadness, anger, or anxiety by learning about your emotions and accepting what they're designed to teach you.

The Connection between Spiritual Astrology and Spiritual Well-Being

Spiritual astrology is a tool meant to help us accomplish the state of spiritual well-being, where we're embodying our true selves and accomplishing our life mission. If you want to experience true spiritual well-being, you'd be hard-pressed to find a better way than looking at your astrological chart and learning the planets and their energies that will help you rise to the level you belong in life.

Why You Should Take Your Spiritual Health Seriously

Many people today don't take their spiritual health seriously. They aren't living a purposeful life and not accomplishing what they meant to do in this lifetime. You may be one of those people, and that's okay, but don't let it get you down. Astrology will help you benefit from your birth chart and achieve the life you deserve.

Your spiritual health is important if you want to experience wholesome relationships. Why should you care? Because you'll walk through life with a greater awareness of who you are and what your life is about. Your life will be surrounded by meaningful, like-minded people making it more enjoyable and comfortable.

Your Purpose, Authentic Self, and Spiritual Well-Being

You can't live a purposeful life without knowing who you are. You'll make the most of your unique experience and feel comfortable in your skin. Your spiritual well-being is improved when you accept who you are and understand we're all connected as one being in this world. When you're willing to listen to your inner self, your life will become more meaningful, and your relationships will become more satisfying.

Practices You Can Use to Improve Your Spiritual Well-Being

Allow yourself to confront your emotions. If you're feeling angry, sad, or resentful, look at yourself and see how you feel. You're likely feeling a little uncomfortable about something, and if you can identify it, you can work through it. If you cannot understand how to improve your spiritual well-being, practice confronting the issue openly. Talk to someone to determine what's happening to you so that you can make the necessary changes in yourself.

Accept the negative emotions that arise in your life. Sometimes, it's necessary to feel anxiety or anger. Sometimes, these emotions teach us about ourselves. If you can learn to be comfortable with your emotions, they won't hold you back or get in the way of your life purpose.

Enjoy the world around you and make the most of your surroundings. The easiest way to experience spiritual well-being is to surround yourself with people you love, enjoy spending time with, and have meaningful conversations about life and its purpose. If you live your life creatively or compassionately, you'll grow stronger and stronger in yourself.

Do things that take you out of your comfort zone. When you're constantly comfortable, it's hard to feel new emotions or experiences. If you want to experience new things, make an effort to get out of your comfort zone and do something new. The more challenging the experience, the more likely you feel a deeper level of connection with yourself and the world.

Get rid of negative people from your life who don't support your spiritual health journey. If someone consistently challenges you, makes you feel bad about yourself, or otherwise brings your spirits down, it is time to let them go. Letting go of these people doesn't mean you're ungrateful for their help or aren't good friends. It means you've grown enough as a human and spiritual being to know when certain relationships no longer serve your purpose.

Develop a sense of humor about life and yourself. If you can learn to laugh at the little things in life and yourself, you'll develop more confidence as a spiritual being and an authentic self. If you can feel comfortable with yourself, you'll experience a deeper sense of well-being, making you more confident in your everyday life.

Take life seriously, but not yourself. It's okay to take your life seriously, but it's not okay to take yourself too seriously. Give yourself leeway to understand why things happen, and being more laid back will help you as an individual and spiritually.

Meditate for at least 5 to 10 minutes every day. You don't have to meditate for hours for it to be effective. Taking a few minutes out of your day can make a big difference in your life. The more frequently you meditate, the easier it is to recognize your emotions and understand where they came from and how they relate to your experiences as an authentic self and spiritual being.

Practice self-forgiveness. For many people, there's nothing easier than beating themselves up over something that happened in the past or something they did wrong along their life journey. If this is an issue in your life, you must be more forgiving of yourself. It's valuable to recognize that we all make mistakes, but it's important to learn to enjoy what you do right to preserve your authenticity and purpose.

Practice self-acceptance. You need to accept yourself for who you are to experience spiritual well-being. If you don't accept what your life has been until now, it will be difficult to accept yourself as a person capable of making the necessary changes the right way at the right time.

Signs of High Spiritual Well-Being

When you're practicing these spiritual well-being techniques, you'll notice big changes in your life. Here are a few:

Your mood improves. If you're feeling happier and more positive about yourself and the people around you, your spiritual well-being is likely improving. When you take the time to feel good about who you are and where your life path is, anxiety or depression will fade.

You develop empathy for yourself and others. When your spiritual well-being is high, you'll empathize with people going through difficult times. You recognize the emotions people are experiencing, making it easier to understand their feelings and needs and provide them assistance.

You're more open. When you feel good about yourself and the people around you, it's easier to open up to situations and new people to expand your circle of trust and friendship. If these connections help bring out more of yourself than they take away, they positively contribute to your emotional well-being.

You're more creative. Many people feel that a spiritual connection helps them be more creative, insightful, and ultimately more in touch with their intuition. When your intuition is strong and your creativity is flourishing, you feel spiritually well because you discover many ways of expressing yourself.

You see things differently. When you've grown stronger as a spiritual being, your entire perspective on life can change. You'll see beyond the limits of what life previously gave you and learn to live a much stronger and happier life as an authentic self with nothing holding them back.

Spiritual Well-Being in Your Relationship

The following are some of the ways that these techniques will develop trust, respect, and affection in your relationship:

1. You have better communication and listening skills.

2. You recognize your partner's emotions at any given moment.

3. You understand what circumstances make your partner feel good about themselves and their lives and what circumstances make them doubtful or worried.

4. When appropriate, you offer suggestions or advice on how they could make things better for themselves.

5. You become more empathetic to your partner's struggles.

Spiritual Well-Being at Home

A strong sense of spiritual well-being improves the atmosphere at home. Here are some ways it can be achieved:

1. You tolerate difficult situations with less anxiety.

2. You appreciate the small things that make your life more enjoyable, like a good cup of coffee or a massage.

3. You accept your partner or family members for who they are and where they're at in their lives.

4. You have better relationships with your partner or family members for communicating how you feel about certain situations and how to resolve them effectively.

5. You understand other people's needs and recognize that you can offer assistance during situations when necessary and appropriate.

Spiritual Well-Being at the Workplace

Here's what spiritual well-being looks like in the workplace:

1. You enjoy the benefits of a good work-life balance.
2. You embrace the creativity to express yourself at work and use it to find new opportunities for growth and development in your career.
3. You communicate with your coworkers clearly and respectfully, helping you work diligently without getting bogged down in drama or politics.
4. You're less anxious and stressed dealing with difficult situations at work or with other people in the office.
5. You know you are growing and thriving as a person, which ultimately helps you do better work every day because you're more confident about your abilities.

Spiritual Well-Being in Society

When societal well-being is high, you feel good about the world because you feel your country, state, or community is taken care of instead of being abused. Here are a few ways that spiritual well-being affects society positively:

1. You have an overall sense of peace and contentment with your surroundings.
2. You feel there is less violence and conflict in your community and country than in other areas of the world.
3. You understand people need help when they're going through a hard time – and treat them with more kindness and respect.
4. You feel more connected with other people in your community, which helps you feel safer and more secure.
5. When your spiritual well-being is high, you want to take better care of yourself and others to show gratitude for what you have in life.

These are merely a few ways spiritual well-being can improve your life when used with a healthy dose of mindfulness and gratitude.

Quiz: How High Is My Spiritual Well-Being?

Answer yes or no to the following:

1. I feel I have a purpose in life.

2. I can easily recall past events that were meaningful to me or had a positive effect on my life.

3. I attempt to make something of my life every day by working hard, learning new things, or exploring different opportunities for growth and development.

4. I understand other people's feelings or points of view, even if we disagree about a situation or about what is important in life.

5. I feel the world around me is a safe place to live in.

6. I feel I have support from other people in tough situations.

7. I'm supportive of people when they're going through a difficult time.

8. I respect other people's views, opinions, and ideas, even if they don't coincide with my beliefs.

9. I feel that the work I do is good because it's more fulfilling or meaningful to me personally than anything else.

10. I feel I can communicate with my partner or family members so they appreciate how I feel, without causing an argument, or bringing up negative feelings.

11. I tolerate difficult situations, knowing that everything will be okay regardless of what happens in life.

12. I have good relationships with my colleagues at work, even if we don't necessarily see eye-to-eye on certain things.

13. I desire to help people in the world because it makes me happy to see them get ahead and succeed.

14. I enjoy my successes without feeling arrogant or superior toward other people.

15. I am myself around people who don't necessarily agree with my way of seeing things or what I want from life.

16. I don't feel the need to always be right or correct people when they do or say something I disagree with.

17. When I see negative situations on the news, I feel compassion for other people and offer assistance if needed.

18. I feel I can make a positive difference in the world by doing what I'm good at, not necessarily because of money or success.

19. I have the ability to correct toxic problems in my life so that they don't continue to haunt me.

20. I have a strong desire to help people find their inner peace, whatever that means to them.

If you answered yes to 14 questions or more, you're doing great with your spiritual well-being.

Bonus: Guide to Refuel Your Spiritual Well-Being

Here's a 30-day guide to healing yourself spiritually.

Day 1: Go for a walk outside.

Day 2: Meditate for ten minutes in the morning.

Day 3: Write down the things that matter the most to you in a journal.

Day 4: Do something kind for someone, but make it someone who can't pay you back.

Day 5: Buy something nice for yourself.

Day 6: Look in the mirror and affirm, "You're doing great. I love you," for five minutes.

Day 7: Three times today, stop whatever you're doing and smile for one minute.

Day 8: Spend time with someone you enjoy being with. Just be there for them.

Day 9: Listen to an empowering podcast.

Day 10: Prepare yourself a healthy, sumptuous meal.

Day 11: Find a way to spend time with your favorite animal.

Day 12: For five minutes, dance to your favorite song.

Day 13: Journal for five minutes about your flaws. Do this with no judgment, only love.

Day 14: Journal for five minutes about your best qualities and bask in them.

Day 15: Donate something to a cause that matters to you.

Day 16: Ask anyone around you if there's something you can help with.

Day 17: Meditate for ten minutes before bed.

Day 18: Write down ten things that you're thankful for.

Day 19: Write down five things you love about the person dearest to you.

Day 20: Dress up sharp and beautifully.

Day 21: Spend five minutes journaling about your progress in life.

Day 22: Have fun at the park or in your yard without your phone for an hour.

Day 23: Meditate for fifteen minutes in the morning.

Day 24: Write down five things you know you need to stop doing. Pick one and end it.

Day 25: Make a list of the toxic people in your life. Pick one and cut them out of your life.

Day 26: Work out for five to ten minutes and be present and feel your body.

Day 27: Stay off social media.

Day 28: Pay attention to your water intake, and stay hydrated.

Day 29: Meditate on all the good things in your life, and feel deep appreciation for them. Do this for ten minutes.

Day 30: when you eat, be more mindful and present. Pay attention to the colors, smells, and textures as you eat.

Here's another book by Mari Silva that you might like

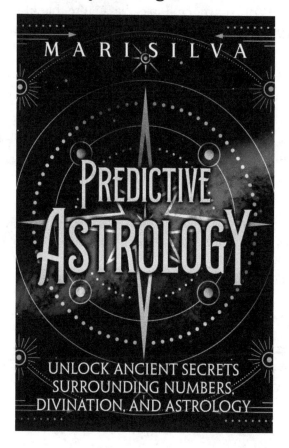

Your Free Gift (only available for a limited time)

Thanks for getting this book! If you want to learn more about various spirituality topics, then join Mari Silva's community and get a free guided meditation MP3 for awakening your third eye. This guided meditation mp3 is designed to open and strengthen ones third eye so you can experience a higher state of consciousness. Simply visit the link below the image to get started.

https://spiritualityspot.com/meditation

References

Bailey, A. A., & Khul, D. (1997). Esoteric astrology (Vol. 3). Lucis Publishing Companies.

Barton, T. (2002). Ancient astrology. Routledge.

Campion, Nicholas (1982). An Introduction to the History of Astrology. ISCWA.

Campion, Nicholas (2008). A History of Western Astrology. The Ancient World (vol. 1). London Continuum.

Holden, James Herschel (2006). A History of Horoscopic Astrology (2nd ed.). AFA.

Kay, Richard (1994). Dante's Christian Astrology. Middle Ages Series. University of Pennsylvania Press.

Newman, W. R., Grafton, A., & Viano, C. (2006). Secrets of nature: astrology and alchemy in early modern Europe. Aestimatio: Critical Reviews in the History of Science.

Parker, Derek; Parker, Julia (1983). A history of astrology. Deutsch.

Robbins, Frank E., ed. (1940). Ptolemy Tetrabiblos. Harvard University Press (Loeb Classical Library).

Tester, S. J. (1987). A history of western astrology. Boydell & Brewer.

Veenstra, J.R. (1997). Magic and Divination at the Courts of Burgundy and France: Text and Context of Laurens Pignon's "Contre les Devineurs" (1411). Brill.

Wedel, Theodore Otto (1920). The Medieval Attitude Toward Astrology: Particularly in England. Yale University Press.

Wood, Chauncey (1970). Chaucer and the Country of the Stars: Poetical Uses of Astrological Imagery. Princeton University Press